NUEVA YORK
1613–1945

Nueva York
1613–1945

Edited by

Edward J. Sullivan

The New-York Historical Society

in association with

Scala Publishers

CONTENTS

FOREWORD

In 1613, when our great city was no more than a trading post on the Hudson River, a man from Hispaniola/Santo Domingo named Jan Rodrigues (or Juan Rodríguez) stepped off a Dutch ship and became the first non–Native American "New Yorker." His story, and those of successive generations of Spanish speakers in "Nueva York"—a name by which the city has been known for nearly four centuries—is not often studied, learned, or told. And yet from Jan Rodrigues to the twenty-three Sephardic Jews from Recife who settled in New Amsterdam in 1654; to Spain's first minister to the United States, Don Diego María de Gardoqui, who laid the cornerstone of our city's first Catholic Church in 1785; to the Rionda-Fanjul family from Cuba, whose sugar business was already well established in Manhattan by the 1870s; to the Puerto Rican–born educator and revolutionary Eugenio María de Hostos, who came to New York in 1869; to the early twentieth-century Mexican artists like Diego Rivera and José Clemente Orozco whose great murals define some of our city's best-known landmarks; to our own moment in time, the city's commerce, culture, and people have reflected the influence of the Spanish-speaking world.

Why is it that the roots of our Latino history, much of it conveyed in this volume and in the exhibition *Nueva York: 1613–1945*, are so unknown, unexamined, and unappreciated? As Mike Wallace points out in his authoritative essay, it is largely because the history of our city—indeed of our nation—has most typically been examined on an east-west axis. Realigning our history north-south challenges received wisdom about our city's past and reorients our sense of who we are and have been as a people. With the population of New York today approaching the milestone of being one-third Latino, now is a good time to recognize that the roots of Nueva York run deep.

Since this project was first conceived as a collaboration between the New-York Historical Society, New York's oldest museum, and El Museo del Barrio, its most important center for Latino art and culture, it has been our purpose to bring together the best scholars of history and art history to tell this story. Along the way we have had the good fortune to be able to count on the knowledge and advice of historians, art historians, and many others. Mike Wallace authored the original concept paper for the project, and he, Carmen Boullosa, Juan Flores, Gabriel Haslip-Viera, Miriam Jiménez-Román, Claudio Remeseira, Virginia Sánchez-Korrol, Robert Smith, and Silvio Torres-Saillant generously offered their time for a major "brainstorming" session in the fall of 2007; Marci Reaven of City Lore skillfully curated the exhibition; Edward Sullivan agreed to advise on selecting and helping to secure the exhibition's spectacular works of art, and also to edit this volume; and Valerie Paley worked tirelessly as its project editor and coordinator. From the New-York Historical Society, a hard-working team of colleagues was headed by Stephen Edidin and Kathleen Hulser, and at El Museo, Elvis Fuentes played a key role in virtually everything. I am personally grateful for the colleagueship of Dr. Julián Zugazagoitia, who as director of El Museo del Barrio so enthusiastically agreed to pursue this collaboration, and who helped to see it through even after leaving our city to take over as director of the Nelson Atkins Museum in Kansas City. I give thanks to the benefactors of *Nueva York: 1613–1945*, who in this most difficult of economic environments recognized the importance of this project and financed it. Lead sponsorship was provided by Cablevision's Optimum family of products. Generous support from American Express made possible a robust series of exhibition-related public programs, and a grant from the Ford Foundation helped support the exhibition and education programs. *Nueva York* was organized with a grant from The Rockefeller Foundation New York City Cultural Innovation Fund and was supported, in part, by public funds from the New York City Department of Cultural Affairs. Additional assistance was provided by Goldman Sachs, Con Edison, and the Fanjul family in memory of their ancestor, Manuel Rionda. This volume is supported by a grant from Furthermore: a program of the J. M. Kaplan Fund. Above all, I want to recognize the Board of Trustees of the New-York Historical Society and its chairman, Roger Hertog, for their extraordinary support of history—and of telling those stories that the textbooks so frequently leave out.

Dr. Louise Mirrer
President and CEO, New-York Historical Society

PREFACE

The exhibition *Nueva York: 1613–1945*, presented at New York's El Museo del Barrio, organized with the New-York Historical Society, and curated by City Lore, explores the history of New York City and its relations with the Spanish-speaking world, including Spain and those parts of the Americas and the Caribbean that Spain once ruled as colonies. Over the course of five galleries and 4,000 square feet, the visitor is able to follow New York's transformation from a tiny seventeenth-century trading port on the periphery of the great European empires to a great mid-twentieth-century city at the commercial and cultural center of an American empire. This account is unusual in that it links the city's transformation to its deep connections to the Spanish-speaking world.

These relations were crucial to New York's prosperity. The exhibition reveals an extensive and vibrant presence of people of Spanish and Latin American heritage in the city beginning in the 1800s. And it proposes that social and cultural encounters during these early years were connected to political changes sweeping the Western Hemisphere as Spain's hold diminished and that of the United States expanded. Scholars and activists have labored for years to recover this forgotten history, and the partnership of the exhibit's two organizers is part of this ongoing effort. The New-York Historical Society, founded in 1804 as an expression of establishment "Anglo-Dutch" New York, joins hands here with El Museo del Barrio, founded in 1969 as a project of activist Puerto Rican Nueva York. Both institutions have evolved over the years, but together they represent the different parts of the city's past that this exhibit brings together.

For most New Yorkers, the surprise of the exhibition will be that our account of Nueva York does not begin after the Second World War, the period of massive Hispanic migration to the city, but three hundred years earlier, in the early 1600s. The Dutch founded their tiny base on the Hudson to get close to the Spanish, and to take from them the silver they were extracting from the mines of Mexico and Peru. Plundering Spanish ships loaded with bars of gold and silver and chests of silver coins promised riches beyond belief. Years later, Revolutionary-era New York City was still using Spanish silver coins as currency. But by then trade, more than piracy, generated the cash.

Immigration plays a large role in our story, with the first arrivals from Spanish-speaking lands coming from Cuba. New Yorkers were fascinated with Cuba as early as the 1700s. Imperial rules impeded but hardly prevented trade between New York and Havana, and by the early 1800s commerce was flourishing. New York's development into the world's leading center of sugar refining evolved from this commercial connection.

Ferocious revolutionary wars brought independence to Latin America in the 1820s, but they did not free Spain's island colonies in the Caribbean and the Pacific. For the rest of the nineteenth century, Cubans and Puerto Ricans hoping to liberate their homelands used New York City as a staging ground for rebellions. Some of these ventures involved alliances with North Americans eager to gain access to Spain's valuable colonies. In 1898, the Spanish-Cuban-American War brought an end to this period when the United States stepped into Spain's imperial shoes.

Commerce, politics, and the growing ease of international travel for people of means heightened the likelihood of cultural encounters in the 1800s. Washington Irving journeyed to Madrid from New York; José María Heredia traveled to New York from Havana; and many other North Americans, South Americans, and Spaniards began to observe and depict one another. They frequently did so from New York— the base of most shipping lines, and the headquarters for art galleries, newspapers, telegraph lines, and publishing and printing houses through which they could get their opinions out to the rest of the world.

New York in the 1800s also became a destination for settlement, especially for Spanish Americans escaping Spain's rule or seeking educational and economic opportunities. The well-off came first. But after 1898, when the United States took control in the Caribbean, those arriving in New York reflected a broader range of backgrounds. During the first half of the twentieth century, especially after Puerto Ricans were made U.S. citizens in 1917, the presence of Spanish-speaking residents in the city escalated dramatically. Communities formed, newcomers organized to improve their lot, and in fields such as music, interactions between Latino and non-Latino New Yorkers created new forms of art and culture. Entrepreneurs and professionals entered the city's mainstream. Institutions like the Hispanic Society and the Museum of Modern Art showcased the fine arts of Spain and Latin America. A new social landscape evolved in the city.

Multimedia experiences conclude the exhibition by extending its story line into the second half of the twentieth century. Here we show the great migration of Puerto Ricans to New York City and the waves of immigration that followed.

City Lore was very pleased to be invited to curate this exhibition. For over twenty years, we have been creating programs in schools and community settings that celebrate how New Yorkers recall and use the past as an asset in their everyday lives. We hope that our work on this exhibition will help to make available an additional set of historical memories that together we can use to build a better city.

Marci Reaven, Ph.D.
Exhibition Curator

INTRODUCTION

EDWARD J. SULLIVAN

Nueva York, like the exhibition organized by the New-York Historical Society in association with El Museo del Barrio and curated by Marci Reaven, presents a panorama of the commercial, cultural, and artistic stamp that has been indelibly placed on the spirit and character of the City of New York by the citizens, émigrés, visitors, tourists, and traders of Spanish and Latin American heritage from the later years of the seventeenth century until the end of the Second World War. New Yorkers of today probably do not think twice about the deeply ingrained "Hispanic" aspects of the city, as they are ubiquitous. "Spanish" foods, music, and language are integral parts of the fabric of our lives. Yet their history and meanings within the larger political and aesthetic picture of the city's development are as little known as they are compelling. How Nueva York came to be is as fascinating a story as any to be told about our vibrant metropolis. This volume relies on the expertise of many scholars who present vivid descriptions of both the macro and micro elements of the many interwoven tales of this long chapter in New York City history. From Caribbean pirates to the pioneers of the Puerto Rican communities of the 1920s and '30s, and from Upper East Side connoisseurs of Spanish art to the founders of El Barrio's first record stores, the individuals who inhabit these tales are as intriguing as the stories themselves. The essays in this book are designed to remind scholars of the essential facts of these histories and to appeal to the general public's curiosity about an essential chapter in the historical evolution of the five boroughs of New York and beyond.

The eleven essays in this book cannot hope to tell every detail of each episode in the chronicle of Nueva York, yet we have attempted to come as close as possible to that goal. While most of the articles here are of moderate length, the stage-setting overview by Mike Wallace, doyen of historians of Gotham (to use the title of his best-known book), is a complex yet lucidly written narrative of the principal dramatis personae and the events they helped shape from around 1625 to 1945. Indeed, it is to Wallace that we must first turn in our long list of acknowledgments of those whose stimulus and encouragement of the *Nueva York* project began the chain of events that led to this volume and the fall 2010 exhibition at El Museo del Barrio. Among the essays in this book, a number of convergent and related ideas, as well as several recurrent names, emerge. A subject suggested in one essay is taken up more fully in another; a personality hinted at in a text in the first part of the book reappears in more detail in one at the end. There is a felicitous cohesiveness to this volume.

Mike Wallace begins his narrative by presenting us with a paradox. In the beginning—that is, in the mid-seventeenth century—New York, or Nieuw Amsterdam, was a tiny town far from the world of imperial Spain, the virtual master of most of the mainland and island territories of the hemisphere. Yet, as Wallace explains, the Dutch were very strategic about their North American outpost and hoped that eventually it would allow them greater access, by trade or plunder, to the riches of the Spanish New World. Unfortunately for them, the English gained control of the city, renaming it New York in 1664. Under the English, Spaniards were not initially welcome, except for a small band of twenty-three Sephardic Jews, whose ancestors were Spanish exiles and who had made their way from Brazil to Curaçao to Gotham. By 1762–63, trade with the Spanish colonies, especially with Cuba, began in earnest. Shortly after the British colonies became the United States, the presence of an official Spanish representative to the country, Diego de Gardoqui, served to facilitate trade relations with the Iberian colonies to the south. The tolerance of Spaniards— and Catholics—had certainly eased, and by 1785 the first Catholic Church, St. Peter's, was opened on Barclay Street, a haven for worshippers whose language was Spanish. In the late eighteenth and especially by the early nineteenth century and even later, New York also became a refuge for revolutionaries who sought temporary or even lifelong asylum outside the many nations that were seeking their freedom from Spain. Such political luminaries as Francisco de Miranda and Antonio Páez from Venezuela came to Manhattan, as did, in 1880, the brilliant writer, literary and art critic, and Cuban patriot José Martí. Wallace carefully outlines their respective roles in New York political and cultural life. Nonetheless, he also points out that so much of the contact between Anglo New Yorkers and the Spanish-speaking world was driven by the possibility of financial gain. We are reminded here of the description of a famous nineteenth-century *French* visitor to New York, Alexis de Tocqueville, when he wrote to his brother Édouard in May 1831 that "[here] [t]he one passion that runs deep, the only one that stirs the human heart day in and day out, is the acquisition of wealth."[1]

By the 1820s there was a very lively trade, and by the time of the American Civil War, sugar, tobacco, coffee, and many other products were flooding into the city from Cuba, Puerto Rico, and other places in the Caribbean. The importance of these crops is attested to by the fact that their cultivation became the principal subject for many works of both visual and literary art by the painters and writers of the time. One splendid example is the 1885 painting *Hacienda la Fortuna* (featured in the exhibition) by Francisco Oller, the most important Puerto Rican painter of the nineteenth century. Like other depictions of the Caribbean countryside, this work offers a clear picture of rural labor and serves, at the same time, as an outstanding example of an Impressionist-era landscape.

The nineteenth century also witnessed a growth in the publishing industry; Spanish-language books were printed by the thousands for export to Latin America. In addition, the bank notes for many nations south of the U.S. border were printed by the American Bank Note company in Manhattan. A number of prominent New York families made fortunes in trade with the Spanish-speaking Americas; an outstanding example is that of the Havemeyers, whose wealth came mostly from the sugar industry. Shipping and, by the early twentieth century, air travel to Havana, San Juan, and beyond earned vast amounts of money for families such as the Graces and the Trippes.

Substantial colonies of Latin Americans and peninsular Spaniards established themselves beginning in the 1820s, an immigration that has continued in successive waves up to the present. This large Hispanic presence was felt in many ways by non-Hispanic populations of the city. By the 1920s, the interest in Spanish language and culture was immense, judging by the substantial upturn in enrollments in Spanish classes at institutions like Columbia and New York University. Also by this time there was a full-blown Hispanic cultural life in Manhattan, with Spanish-language newspapers as well as theaters showing Spanish and Latin American films, plays, and musical entertainments (e.g., Spanish comic operas, or *zarzuelas*). Numerous Hispanic restaurants, cafés, nightclubs, and hotels catering to Spanish and non-Spanish patrons alike opened throughout Manhattan, Queens, the Bronx, and Brooklyn. This intense activity led to a symbolic moment, Wallace explains, when in 1945 the name of one of Manhattan's principal arteries, Sixth Avenue, was officially changed to Avenue of the Americas.

Cathy Matson skillfully fleshes out the earliest chapters of this story. Her essay describes the commercial exchanges with Spain's possessions before 1800. She charts the course of imperial control of the Americas by analyzing the rivalries, tensions, and warfare between the Spanish, Dutch, and English on the high seas, in the ports, and through the inland regions of the Caribbean and mainland Central and South America. She points out that by 1650 New Amsterdam had become, in fact, a crossroads for people throughout the Atlantic world, including the Spanish colonies. Matson details how the English had circumvented trade restrictions with Spanish ports in the Americas by the 1720s through piracy and smuggling as well as legitimate commercial operations in ports such as Havana and Monte Cristi on the island of Hispaniola.

Driving much of the intense interest in trade was the immense appetite New Yorkers had developed for sugar and all possible products, sweet and savory, solid and liquid, made from it. Sugar was processed in the Americas until as late as the last decades of the nineteenth century by slaves imported from Africa, and Matson describes the role of New Yorkers in this nefarious enterprise. Her essay is an object lesson in explicating how, after the American Revolution, New York merchants served as a fulcrum around which turned an enormous commercial machine of global proportions—much of it centered on the Hispanic world.

In his discussion of Cubans in nineteenth-century New York, Lisandro Pérez offers us a view through the lens of individual stories. His is a fascinating analysis of specific people and why they came to New York. Beginning with the story of a well-to-do member of the sugarocracy, Cristobal Madan y Madan (of Irish extraction; his surname was probably originally spelled Madden), and continuing with that of the educator, philosopher, and advocate of Cuban sovereignty Father Félix Varela, Pérez analyzes the combination of commercial and political motives that drove the first businessmen, their families, and others to visit (and in many cases stay in) Manhattan and the other boroughs. We also read about the complex story of what happened to those peninsular Spaniards living in Cuba and loyal to Iberia (as well as those Cubans who were themselves loyal to the colonial power) who immigrated to New York during the Ten Years' War, the first in a long series of battles for independence that culminated in the Spanish-American War in 1898. And finally, we are again introduced to the charismatic personality of José Martí, who revived the spirit of revolution through the political texts he wrote during his stay in New York. His sojourn lasted until 1895, when he returned to Cuba to take part in its liberation, dying in an ambush of Spanish soldiers only months after his arrival.

Virginia Sánchez Korrol tells the story of the first Puerto Rican communities in New York in a manner that dovetails with the methodology of Lisandro Pérez. She also underscores the significance of the early liberation movements in the Caribbean as catalysts for the arrival in Manhattan of many families and individuals, not only Cuban but Puerto Rican as well. The Grito de Lares or the Lares Revolution, so-named for the town in Puerto Rico where it began, had similar goals to the Ten Years' War on the neighboring island of Cuba. Its failure compelled many freedom-seeking intellectuals and political activists to leave for New York, where there was soon a network of Puerto Rican political organizations, mutual-aid societies, and women's clubs. Sánchez Korrol also writes of the rapid rise of the tobacco industry in nineteenth-century New York and the key role that Puerto Rican émigrés played in it, and describes the number of important individuals, many of them women, in the early and more recent history of Nuyorican life. Among them is Amelia Agostini del Río, who became a professor of Spanish literature at Barnard College and authored over forty-five books, at least one of which became a standard text for college students. We are introduced to Pura Belpré, the city's first Puerto Rican librarian, and Victoria Hernández, a former factory worker who opened the first Puerto Rican music store in 1927 at 1735 Madison Avenue. Appropriately enough, the author suggests the impressive achievements of contemporary women of Puerto Rican heritage by ending her study (or suggesting the next phase of it) with Sonia Sotomayor's confirmation to the U.S. Supreme Court in 2009.

Who wrote the first novel in Spanish or the first poems in that language in New York City? This question forms the basis of Carmen Boullosa's contribution, in which she conjectures that the great wave of creative writing in Spanish that began in earnest in the nineteenth century may have been anticipated several centuries earlier. She traces the known history of the arts of prose and poetry in Spanish to authors who were included in the first wave of Cuban immigration to New York in the 1820s, and singles out Félix Varela's 1826 novel *Xicoténcatl* (set in Mexico) as the first novel in Spanish by a writer living in New York City. Although Varela's prose may not be often read today, Cirilio Villaverde's *Cecilia Valdés*, published in New York in 1882, is still examined by every serious student of Cuban (and Latin American) literature.

Boullosa also reminds us that the Nicaraguan poet Rubén Darío, the towering figure of literary *modernismo*, visited New York three times, and met the great Cuban writer Martí there. While impressed with New York, Darío also saw it as the embodiment of an imperial nation that he felt was threatening Hispanic America. This sentiment is most strongly expressed in his 1905 poem "To Theodore Roosevelt." Boullosa also looks at Mexican writers from late nineteenth- and early twentieth-century New York such as José Juan Tablada, who not only wrote, but opened a Spanish-language bookshop there. The Spaniards José Moreno-Villa, Juan Ramón Jiménez, and Federico García Lorca are also invoked as towering figures in Spanish-language writing in Manhattan. Boullosa ends her piece with a touching evocation of the Puerto Rican poet Julia de Burgos, who died penniless and miserable on the streets of El Barrio, and whose body went unrecognized for weeks, until it was claimed and returned to Puerto Rico for a proper burial.

Katherine Manthorne turns her attention to art, commerce, and high society in nineteenth-century New York, discussing a number of the city's residents who were smitten by the lure of Latin America as early as the 1860s, including the Hudson River School painter Frederic Edwin Church. She reminds us of the enormous impact of his painting *Heart of the Andes* on an American public immersed in the philosophy of the Monroe Doctrine; it was exhibited in the city and throughout the country as a panoramic overview of the grandeur of Latin American scenery. Manthorne also mentions, as do other authors, that much of the nineteenth-century interest in the Americas was fueled by the sugar craze, and she engagingly discusses the ramifications of this phenomenon for the visual arts.

Latin American politicians, artists, and society figures also flocked to Manhattan in the later nineteenth century. Manthorne's discussion of General Antonio Páez and his son, the painter Ramón Páez, sheds light on the lively interactions between the Hispanic and Anglo portions of New York's fashionable public of the time. Many wealthy Mexican families moved to the city, including former president Antonio López de Santa Anna, who sought asylum in New York in 1866. Throughout the Reconstruction era and into the Gilded Age, Latin American and Caribbean luminaries continued to come to the city and formed an integral part of Manhattan's high society.

High society and the taste for Spanish art and architecture in the drawing rooms of Fifth and Park Avenues is the subject of Richard Kagan's lively account of how New York's most fashionable residents became enamored of the Iberian aura as early as the 1830s and '40s. He traces the roots of this affinity to the popular writings of Washington Irving, the U.S. Minister to Spain in 1842–46. When Irving assumed this role, he was no stranger to Spain, having been there in the 1820s and '30s, living for a time in the great Moorish palace in Granada known as the Alhambra. In 1832 he published his famous *Tales of the Alhambra*, which, according to Kagan, started the ball rolling and encouraged people to visit Spain, purchase Spanish art (which by mid-century was flooding out of Spain and into the sale rooms of Paris and London), or erect buildings in the "Spanish" style, such as McKim, Mead and White's second Madison Square Garden, whose tower imitated the Giralda in Seville.

After the Civil War, U.S. artists flocked to Spain; William Merritt Chase, John Singer Sargent, Hudson River School painter Samuel Colman, and many others made the pilgrimage. Their paintings were purchased by some of the sugar baron families in Manhattan who also became great collectors of Spanish Old Master paintings. The most prominent family was the Havemeyers, whose well-known collections of El Greco, Velázquez, Goya, and other Spanish artists were later acquired by museums such as the Metropolitan Museum of Art and the Art Institute of Chicago.

My own essay deals exclusively with the visual arts and charts many of the personalities from both Spain and Latin America who came to New York or whose work was collected by New York aficionados or institutions. Among the Spaniards, I examine the great popularity of the work of the Catalan painter Mariano Fortuny in the later decades of the nineteenth century, and of Joaquín Sorolla and Ignacio Zuloaga in the early twentieth. New York has served as a magnet for Latin American artists, who started coming regularly after 1900, in some cases to study at the Art Students League, or to fulfill commissions for large-scale mural paintings, as did the Mexicans Diego Rivera and José Clemente Orozco. I also suggest the importance of a number of institutions and galleries that collected and exhibited the work of Latin Americans, both famous and obscure. The greatest of all such collections is at the Museum of Modern Art. Soon after MoMA's founding in 1929, its director, Alfred H. Barr Jr., turned his attention to Latin American painting and sculpture, an interest encouraged by members of the Rockefeller family (especially Nelson), who had strong links with the museum and with Latin American land and oil holdings. Other lesser-known venues like the Riverside Museum also provided a platform for important shows of Latin American artists, especially in the 1930s and '40s.

James Fernández continues the discourse on personalities established earlier in the book by Pérez and Sánchez Korrol to consider the rising importance of Spanish commercial establishments and intellectual institutions in the first half of twentieth-century New York. He offers us a lively description of the many neighborhoods in Manhattan, especially sections of the West Village and Chelsea, where groups of Castilians, Basques, Catalans, Valencians, and many other groups from virtually all of Spain's regions settled and flourished during a great wave of Spanish immigration from the late nineteenth century through the 1930s (culminating with the generation of émigrés to the city during and after the Spanish Civil War). In addition, Fernández charts the rise of the "Spanish craze" among non-Hispanic New Yorkers in their dress (e.g., Andalusian *mantillas* and shawls), music, and food. He devotes considerable attention to the captivating figure of Andalusian poet and playwright Federico García Lorca, who came to Manhattan to learn English at Columbia University and immediately entered a world of highly regarded Spanish intellectuals who had settled in New York before his arrival (such as Federico de Onís, founder of Columbia's Department of Hispanic Studies).

The works of art commissioned by the New School for Social Research (also called The New School) and the artists who taught there are the subjects of the careful and enlightening scrutiny of Anna Indych-López. The New School, an important New York educational institution founded in 1918, showed an intense support of the art and artists of Latin America for several decades. Many art lovers are aware of Orozco's 1930–31 fresco series extolling the virtues of universal brotherhood for the university's main building on West Twelfth Street, designed in 1930 by Austrian architect Joseph Urban. However, the important contributions of Ecuadorian painter

Camilo Egas, who also executed murals and taught at The New School for decades, were all but neglected until recent scholarship gave new life to his fascinating career. Indych-López explores Egas's work and his teaching in depth. She also focuses on the institution itself and the liberal outlook it fostered as a place highly receptive to original experimentation in the arts. We are presented with a cast of many characters from both Spain and Latin America whose interventions in the city's creative life in the 1930s and '40s contributed a great deal to making Nueva York the epicenter for artists from the Americas and Iberia. Indych-López examines, among others, the work of the Spanish sculptor José de Creeft, the Cuban Mario Carreño, the Mexican photographer Emilio Amero, the Argentine graphic artist Antonio Frasconi, and the Puerto Rican printmaker and painter Julio Rosado del Valle—all of whom contributed to the liveliness of the visual arts panorama of The New School.

The book's final essay concerns what is perhaps the most widely known manifestation of Hispanic artistic creativity: Latino music. Juan Flores analyzes some of the most popular Latino songs of the 1920s and '30s, as well as the principal musical genres from the Caribbean, showing how they were adapted to the special circumstances of Nueva York. He presents a powerful description of how race and class played crucial roles in the music's development and reception (by Hispanic and non-Latino audiences alike). Flores also documents the ways and the venues in which this music was recorded and marketed in New York, giving us the "feel" for the look and sounds of a number of the studios, clubs, and record shops that increasingly cropped up in uptown Manhattan, the Bronx, and other boroughs from the 1920s onward. Specific dance crazes—the mambo, cha-cha, rumba, and others—are discussed with relish by Flores, who takes us on a tour of some of the hottest Latino entertainment spots of the period, from the Havana Madrid Night Club on Broadway and Fifty-first Street to the wildly popular Latino performances at Carnegie Hall.

Although the title of *Nueva York*, the book, does not carry an exclamation point, it could easily have been given one (*Nueva York!*). By the end of the texts the reader will have absorbed not only a vast historical panorama, but one that is immensely vibrant as well. But perhaps the most intriguing thing about the process described here—the making of Nueva York—is that it is a living, continually expanding, and developing phenomenon. Perhaps we ought to have titled the book *Nueva York: Part One*. In any event, we will await the future appearance of *Nueva York . . . The Tradition Continues!*

NOTE

1. Alexis de Tocqueville, letter to Édouard de Tocqueville, New York, May 28, 1831, in Tocqueville, "Letters from America," trans. Frederick Brown, *The Hudson Review* 62, no. 3 (autumn 2009): 372.

NUEVA YORK: THE BACK STORY

New York City and the Spanish-Speaking World from Dutch Days to the Second World War

MIKE WALLACE

INTRODUCTION[1]

For approximately the first third of its existence, New York was an anti-Spanish city, its front door signposted, figuratively speaking, "No Spaniards—or Catholics—Need Apply." Whereas now, demographers tell us, New York is coming up on being one-third Hispanic, and may well emerge as one of the great Spanish-inflected cities of the twenty-first century. How did this transformation come about?

Today's "Nueva York"—Gotham's massive and tremendously diverse constellation of Hispanic residents—is a relatively recent phenomenon. It began with the surge of new arrivals from Puerto Rico after the Second World War, and expanded dramatically in size and composition over roughly the last quarter century. But long before that, around the time of the American Revolution, a stream of Spanish and Cuban immigrants began trickling into the city. Over the nineteenth and twentieth centuries, that stream evolved into an ever more ample river, fed by a growing network of Latin American and Spanish tributaries. And then, after World War II, it widened out into a mighty delta.

Contemporary Nueva York thus has a lengthy back story—a centuries-long prequel—of which this essay, like the *Nueva York* exhibition it complements, offers a satellite's-eye overview. It will recall the seventeenth- and eighteenth-century town's obdurate antipathy to Spaniards; recount the establishment of extensive relations with Spain and its empire (and then its ex-empire) during the nineteenth and early twentieth centuries; and relate the concomitant formation and expansion *inside* the city of Spanish and Latin American communities. It was upon the resulting foundation, the product of three hundred years of history, that postwar generations would build Nueva York.

But the past is never merely prologue. By 1945 those centuries of interaction had already been crucial to New York City's development—in commerce, culture,

Map of Ward Line Routes between New York and Havana, Cuba and Progreso, Vera Cruz and Tampico, Mexico, 1930. Courtesy of Michael Alderson, www.wardline.com.

In 1881 the Ward Line, established in New York in 1856 as a sailing fleet, was officially renamed (after its shift to steam) the New York and Cuba Mail Steamship Company, but it remained popularly known as the Ward Line. Its vessels docked at East River Pier 13, south of Pine Street, or at nearby piers.

communication, manufacturing, and finance—and many of Gotham's greatest fortunes, political as well as economic, had been amassed in the process. (The reverse was true as well: New York–based initiatives had a tremendous impact on the Spanish-speaking world, for good and ill, a story that can only be touched upon here.)

Gotham's intimate engagement since its earliest days with Spain and Latin America is often lost sight of, partly out of Anglo-provincialism, partly because the history of the city is usually conceived as an East-West affair. The conventional focus is Eurocentric (with relatively little attention paid to Spain), though the lens has widened recently to embrace Africa as well. Scholars have always been aware of New York's relations with Latin America, but have seen them out of the corner of their collective eye, as such linkages did not fit comfortably into the predominant narrative. Turning the optic ninety degrees, and adopting a North-South perspective that privileges things Spanish, reveals formerly peripheralized actors to be major characters in a different drama. Adding this longitudinal story line to existing latitudinal ones affords a richer, more complex way of seeing the city, and helps us recognize how contemporary Nueva Yorkers fit into the lengthy slipstream of its history.

COLONIES, EMPIRES, REBELLIONS (1500s–1825)[2]

In its 1620s beginnings, New York—then New Amsterdam—was a Dutch town. The Dutch hated the Spanish, to whose monarch they were subject. Enraged by Spain's abrogation of Dutch political liberties and its attempts to impose Catholicism upon Protestant "heretics," the Netherlands had been in revolt against its Iberian overlord since the 1560s. In the six subsequent decades of struggle, the Dutch had suffered grievously at Spanish hands—the sack of Antwerp, the depredations of the Duke of Alba—and Hispanophobia had become central to their identity. This animosity had been further stoked by indictments of Spain's cruel conquest of the Americas, such as Bartolomé de Las Casas' *Brief Account of the Destruction of the Indies* (1552), translated into Dutch, in 1579, as *Mirror of Spanish Tyranny, in Which Are Told the Murderous, Scandalous, and Horrible Deeds Which the Spaniards Have Perpetrated in the Indies.*

New Amsterdam, Holland's offspring, was also at odds with Spain, by way of cultural inheritance and its own raison d'être. The tiny village was operated by the Dutch West India Company (DWIC), a private militarized corporation, which had been set up in 1621 to wage war on Spain's empire in the Western Hemisphere, and to make money doing so.

At first the minuscule outpost—far removed from the centers of Spanish power— languished along on its own, relegated to the beaver trade, while the company concentrated on more rewarding initiatives farther south. The DWIC was not strong enough to directly assault Spanish strongholds like Mexico and Peru, where silver and gold

Franz Hogenberg. *The Spanish Fury at Antwerp* [1576], from *Le Miroir de la cruelle, & horrible tyrannie espagnole perpetrée au Pays Bas...*, by Jan Evertszoon Cloppenburch, 1620. Hyde Collection, Houghton Library, Harvard University.

The Council of Blood, from *Waarachtighe Beschrijvinge ende levendighe . . . vande Meer dan Onmenschelijke ende Barbarische Tyrannije.* Amsterdam, 1621. Houghton Library, Harvard University.

These engravings recounting Spanish outrages committed in trying to suppress the Dutch revolt— the depredations of the "Council of Blood" set up by the Duke of Alba in 1567, the sack of Antwerp in 1576—helped make antipathy toward Spaniards integral to the emerging national identity of the Netherlands. When coupled with a conviction that Spain was *uniquely* prone to such atrocities, it helped create the Black Legend, which would dominate attitudes toward Spain for centuries.

Map of the Spanish Main. © BlindKat Publishers.

The term "Spanish Main" initially referred to the mainland—dotted with Spanish ports and forts—that stretched from Veracruz down the eastern coast of Central America and on across the northern coast of South America to the Orinoco delta. In time it came to include the body of water of which it formed the southern and western border—what the English called the Caribbean Sea—whose northern and eastern borders were the Greater and Lesser Antilles islands. It thus became possible to sail *on* as well as *to* the Spanish Main.

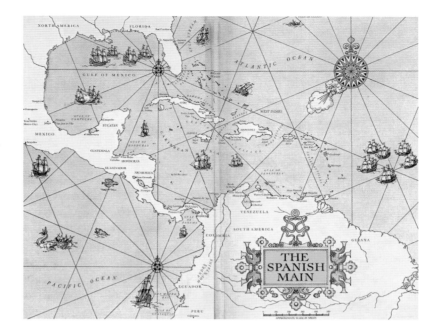

Dutch admiral Piet Hein bottles up the Spanish Silver Fleet in Matanzas Bay, ca. 1628. Engraving. Library, Rijksmuseum.

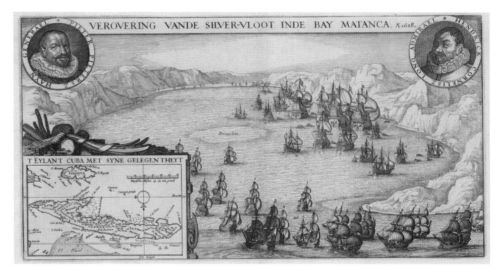

were mined by Indian and African labor. Nor was it able to seize the seaports from which that bounty was dispatched back to Spain—the fortified towns studded along the Spanish Main like Cartagena de Indias (in today's Colombia) and Porto Bello (in today's Panama)—or Caribbean island bases like Cuba's Havana, where transatlantic convoys formed up. Indeed, in 1625 the company even failed to capture Puerto Rico, a secondary outpost, though the invaders did manage to sack San Juan before withdrawing—taking with them church bells that were later rehung in New Amsterdam's Dutch Reformed Church.

The company did far better at raiding Spanish shipping. In 1628, under Admiral Piet Hein, its naval forces seized (in the Bay of Matanzas on the north coast of Cuba)

Hendrick Couturier (active 1648, died ca. 1684). *Peter Stuyvesant (1592–1672)*, ca. 1660. Oil on wood. 22½ x 17½ in. (57.2 x 44.4 cm.) New-York Historical Society, Gift of Robert Van Rensselaer Stuyvesant (1909.2).

*And even earlier: Esteban Gómez, a Portuguese sailor in the service of Spain, had poked around the harbor in 1525 just after Giovanni da Verrazzano had done the same (in 1524) for France. But as Gómez had discerned neither a passage to China nor a source of immediate wealth—"no gold is found," he noted—Spain laid no claim, though Spanish maps would continue for a while to label the area "Tierra de Estevan Gómez." Henry Hudson's arrival on a similar passage-seeking quest in 1609 was made possible by the establishment that year of a temporary truce in the eighty-year Dutch war of liberation from Spain. And in 1613, with various Dutch traders still exploring the area, the first non-ship-supported residency was embarked upon by Jan Rodrigues, a free mulatto from Santo Domingo. He was left ashore by a Dutch merchant vessel and given a musket, a sword, some knives, and eighty hatchets, probably to use for trading with the Indians until the ship returned. Rodrigues was indeed encountered by several Dutch merchants the following year, but vanished from recorded history before the 1624 drop-off of thirty families by the DWIC on Governors Island that is usually taken as the beginning of continuous European settlement in New York. (Scholars from CUNY's Dominican Studies Institute, combing through seventeenth-century archives, have located three residents of Hispaniola named Juan Rodríguez who are known to have had dealings with Dutch merchants; one of them might be the man the Dutch called Jan Rodrigues.)

a Spanish treasure fleet laden with silver from the mines of Mexico. The haul netted them twelve million guilders, a colossal sum; they had just paid a trifling sixty guilders for Manhattan Island in 1626. Hein's windfall bankrolled an assault on Brazil, where the Portuguese (then under Spanish dominion) had established sugar plantations, worked by slaves the Portuguese brought over from West Africa. After conquering parts of northeast Brazil in 1630, the Dutch West India Company, in 1634, took over the small island of Curaçao, just off the coast of Venezuela.

In 1642 Curaçao, with two other islands, was placed under Peter Stuyvesant, a DWIC official. As military commander, he attacked the Spanish settlement of Puerto Cabello on the coast of Venezuela, and in 1644 tried to snatch their island of St. Martin, losing his leg in the process. The company—its New Amsterdam property having sunk to near ruinous condition—considered Stuyvesant the best man to whip it into profitable shape, and DWIC management added their North American holdings to his portfolio. In 1647, when the now peg-legged Stuyvesant arrived in New Amsterdam to take charge, his formal title was "Director-General of New Netherland, Curaçao, Bonaire and Aruba." Manhattan island, politically speaking, had been linked to a Caribbean archipelago.

Economically, too, New Amsterdam grew more involved with Spain's domain. In 1640 the Portuguese in Brazil had begun a revolt against Dutch dominion that finally drove out the company in 1654. Deprived of its sugar plantations, the DWIC, which had taken over Portugal's slaving bases in West Africa, refocused on importing and selling human cargoes. Under Stuyvesant's oversight, Curaçao became a transshipment depot, distributing slaves to various Spanish colonies. The director general gave New Amsterdam an important supporting role in the new enterprise. It exported foodstuffs (flour, corn, salted meat) to its sibling island, and received in return slaves, sometimes 300 per consignment, whom the company set to work building the town's streets and docks, its road to Harlem, and its wall on Wall Street. From its earliest days,* therefore, New Amsterdam was interlaced with the Spanish (and Portuguese) world—both antagonistically, as a cog in the Dutch campaign to hammer Spanish interests, and complementarily, as an (indirect) trading partner.

Culturally, however, New Amsterdam—and particularly Stuyvesant, a Protestant zealot—remained unambiguously disaffected from "despotic" Spain and the Catholic faith of which Spain was the preeminent defender. The anti-Spanish bastion was as disinclined to lay out a welcome mat for Spanish settlers as the latter were disinclined to come. One exception was a group of twenty-three Sephardic Jews, a small portion of the many who, fearing reactivation of the Inquisition, had fled Brazil after it was reclaimed by the Portuguese (most had gone to Curaçao, or to *old* Amsterdam). Stuyvesant sought to bar them entry. Jewish investors in the Dutch West India Company persuaded management to overrule him, on grounds that a lib-

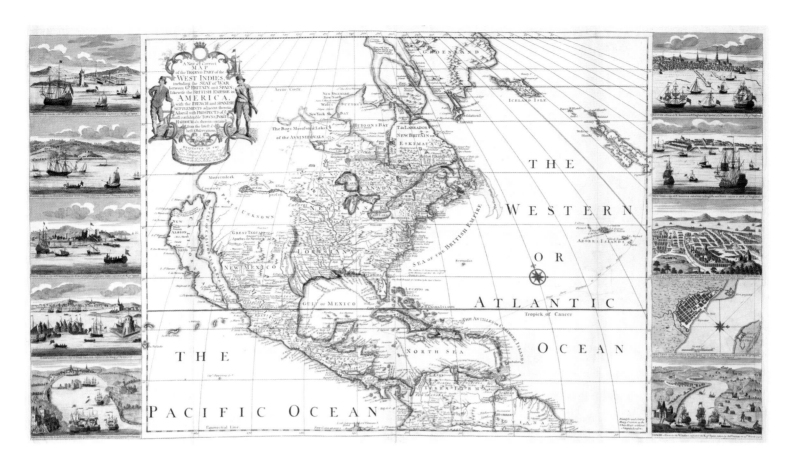

A New & Correct Map of the Trading Part of the West Indies, including the Seat of War between Gr. Britain and Spain; Likewise the British Empire in America, with the French and Spanish settlements adjacent thereto; Adorn'd with prospects of ye most considerable Towns, Ports, Harbours &c. therein contained from the latest & best Observations. London: Printed for and sold by Henry Overton, at the White Horse without Newgate London, 1741.

The war referred to in the map's title was the War of Jenkins' Ear (1739–48), named for the putative casus belli, an English ear severed by cruel Spaniards, in the Anglo version of events. It was one of many battles fought between the expanding British empire and its still powerful Spanish rival, and was marked by major English assaults on cities around the Spanish Main. By draining New York of troops to fight in the Caribbean, it also set the stage for the so-called New York Slave Conspiracy of 1741.

eral immigration policy was good for business (Portuguese- and Spanish-speaking Sephardim had been useful in maintaining commercial links with Spain's empire). But this much-touted instance of "toleration" was more situational than principled, and the openness was not extended to Catholics.

In 1664, after Stuyvesant had gotten New Amsterdam all spiffed up, the English sailed in, took it over at cannon point, and renamed it New York. For much of England's 119-year run of controlling the city, its dealings with Spain's empire were as combative as those of the Dutch had been. English privateers (licensed pirates) had been raiding Spanish treasure fleets since the 1560s. And beginning with the Anglo-Spanish wars of 1585–1604 and 1654–60 (when the English seized Jamaica), the British engaged in a series of assaults on Spain's holdings. These carried on throughout the eighteenth century—with conflicts in 1701–14, 1718–20, 1726–29, 1739–48, and 1761–63 (when the English briefly captured Havana).

New Yorkers participated in these wars. Privateers seized and sold Spanish merchantmen and their cargoes. Merchants and farmers provisioned the English fleets sent to assault Spanish possessions (and often provisioned the possessions as well, given that end-running British naval blockades garnered high profits). Peace, too, could be good for business. New Yorkers supplied foodstuffs to the sugar-producing

23 Nueva York: The Back Story

islands England wrested from Spain. At times they supplied the islands Spain still held, as during severe hurricane seasons, when Spain temporarily relaxed its ban on non-Spaniards trading with its colonies. In 1762–63, when the British captured Havana and held it for eleven months, a brisk trade sprang up between the Spanish city and England's North American colonies, providing a mouthwatering demonstration for Cubans and Anglo-Americans alike of the island's profit potential.

These occasional interactions did not mute the city's cultural and political antagonism to things Spanish, which colonial New York had imbibed from its parent country, as colonial New Amsterdam had from the Netherlands. Las Casas had been translated into English, too, and his text helped foster the Anglo-Dutch conviction that Spain's depredations were *uniquely* vicious, embedded in its national character. By missing the motes in their own eyes—eliding the horrors of the slave trades over which they presided—they constructed a comforting narrative, which came to be known as the Black Legend, that afforded them an unwarranted moral complacency.

New York's culture was also deeply anti-Catholic, apart from a parenthetical period (1683–88) when the colony's Catholic proprietor, the Duke of York, installed a Catholic governor, Thomas Dongan, who proclaimed religious liberty for Christians and even had mass celebrated in the Fort. But this springtime for toleration was quickly frosted over when the duke, having become King James II in 1685, was overthrown three years later by the anti-Catholic Glorious Revolution, and his representatives in New York were similarly removed by local rebellion. For the subsequent century of Britain's reign over Gotham, priests were banned from the colony on pain of life imprisonment or death, "papists" barred from voting, and Protestant rule enforced by periodic "no-popery" riots. Some Catholics did filter in during the 1750s and 1760s, recruited as soldiers or servants, but they were overwhelmingly Irish; Spaniards remained personae non gratae.

There were two exceptions. Spanish Jews were more welcome under the English than they had been under the Dutch, appreciated as commercial links to Sephardic merchants in Barbados, Curaçao, and Jamaica. New refugees from Spain and Portugal replenished their depleted ranks and—allowed public worship as Catholics were not—formed the Shearith Israel congregation, which opened its first purpose-built structure on Mill Street in 1730. Known as the Spanish and Portuguese Synagogue, it started a school that would include Spanish in the curriculum.

The second exception—the so-called "Spanish Negroes"—forcefully proved the rule. In 1739, as another Anglo-Spanish war got under way, most of the English garrison in New York left town for service in the Caribbean and Spanish Main. In 1740 an English privateer captured a Spanish vessel and, back in New York, sold off its dark-complected crewmen as slaves, ignoring their claim that they were free subjects of Spain. In 1741 a series of suspicious fires broke out. The terrified white townsfolk,

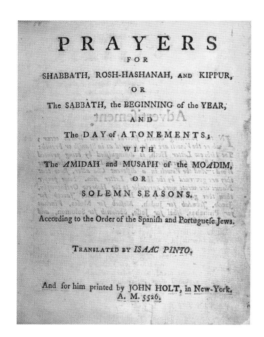

Title page from *Prayers for Shabbath, Rosh-Hashanah, and Kippur, or The Sabbath, the Beginning of the Year, and the Day of Atonements; with the Amidah and Musaph of the Moadim, or Solemn Seasons. According to the Order of the Spanish and Portuguese Jews.* Isaac Pinto, translator. New York: John Holt, 1766. New-York Historical Society Library, Y1766.Sid Pra.

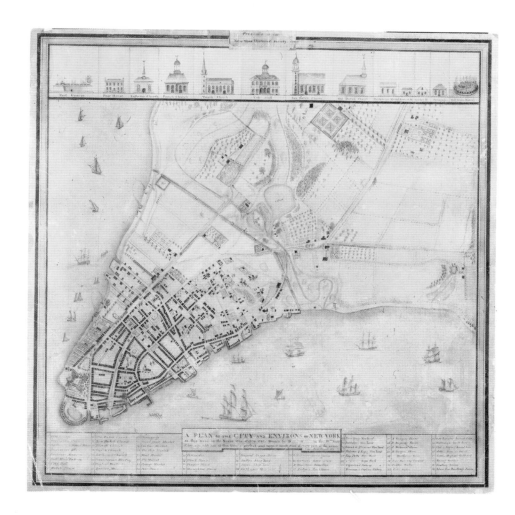

David Grim. *A plan of the City and Environs of New York as they were in the Years 1742–1743 and 1744.* New-York Historical Society (NS13.M2.1.1).

Page 28 from Daniel Horsmanden, *The New-York Conspiracy, or a History of the Negro Plot, with the Journal of the Proceedings Against the Conspirators at New-York in the Years 1741–2.* New York: Southwick & Pelsue, 1810.

In 1741, with British troops off fighting the Spanish, a panic broke out in New York. Rumors flew that the slaves were rising in revolt, with "Spanish Negroes" and a supposed Catholic priest as the key players who planned to turn the city over to Spain. The "insurrection" was suppressed, suspects rounded up and "tried," and vicious punishments meted out. On the map above, David Grim drew in gruesome little numbered icons (#55: "Plot Negro's [sic] burnt here"; #56: "Plot Negro Gibbeted"), just below the Collect Pond. The page from Horsmanden's account describes a "cry among the people" to "*take up the Spanish negroes.*"

Towards noon a fire broke out in the roof of Mrs. Hilton's house, at the corner of the buildings next the Fly-Market, adjoining on the East side of captain Sarly's house: it first broke out on that side next Sarly's, but being timely discovered, was soon prevented doing much mischief, more than burning part of the shingles of the roof. Upon view, it was plain that the fire must have been purposely laid on the wall-plate adjoining to the shingle roof; for a hole had been burnt deep in it, next that part of the roof where the fire had taken hold of the shingles; and it was suspected that the fire had been wrapped up in a bundle of tow, for some was found near the place: thus the fact was plain, but who did it, was a question remained to be determined: But there was a cry among the people, *the Spanish negroes; the Spanish negroes; take up the Spanish negroes.* The occasion of this was the two fires (Thomas's and Hilton's) happening so closely together, only one day intervening, on each side of captain Sarly's house; and it being known that Sarly had purchased a Spanish negro, some time before brought into this port, among several others, in a prize taken by captain Lush; all which negroes were condemned as slaves, in the court of Admiralty, and sold accordingly at vendue; and that they afterwards pretending to have been free men in their own country, began to grumble at their hard usage, of being sold as slaves. This probably gave rise to the suspicion, that this negro, out of revenge, had been the instrument of these two fires; and he behaving himself insolently upon some people's asking him questions concerning them, which signified their distrust: it was told to a magistrate who was near, and he ordered him to gaol, and also gave direction to the constables to commit all the rest of that cargo, in order for their safe custody and examination.

feeling vulnerable to foreign fleets, decided the blazes were the work of slaves (notably the Spanish Negroes), egged on by a supposed Catholic priest (in fact an Anglican schoolmaster visiting from Philadelphia), who aimed to turn the town over to the Spanish crown. After a "trial"—at which Sephardi Mordecai Gomez served as interpreter—those convicted were deported, hung, or burned at the stake. Juan de la Silva went to his doom praying in Spanish.

Only with the outbreak of the American Revolution did relations with the Spanish-speaking world begin to change significantly. Imperial Spain, though hardly approving of colonial rebellions or the rebels' anti-Catholicism, nevertheless decided to aid the North Americans against their great rival, England. The Spanish provided arms, soldiers, and ships. They also allowed rebel merchants to trade with Havana, their chief garrison—a profitable commerce whose pecuniary benefits, however, flowed to Philadelphia and Baltimore, not New York, which was occupied by the British for the duration.

After victory, a small contingent of Spanish diplomats, soldiers, and merchants arrived in town, among them Don Diego de Gardoqui, a Basque banker who had helped funnel funds to the rebels, and been appointed Spain's first minister to the United States in 1784. This small but rapidly growing Catholic community began to cautiously celebrate mass in Gardoqui's house and then, New York's revolutionary constitution of 1777 having eliminated restrictions on public Catholic worship, set about building the city's first Catholic Church. The effort was led by lay figures like Thomas Stoughton, a Catholic merchant in the Spanish trade who had moved from Bruges to New York in 1783 to start up a mercantile business, and his partner, Dominick Lynch, son of a rich Galway merchant. In 1785 they obtained authorization to construct St. Peter's on Barclay Street. The necessary funds were provided by Spain's King Carlos III, whose donation of 1000 *pesos fuertes* was a substantial sum for the time, and by Mexican silver barons, the Bishop of Puebla, and the Archbishop of Mexico City, who also contributed an oil painting of the crucifixion, by Mexican artist José Maria Vallejo, that hangs above the high altar to this day. At the cornerstone and consecration celebrations, a Spanish ship in the harbor fired salutes in honor of the king, and Gardoqui threw a party for "the first personages of this City," including the governor, and these civic worthies toasted "a lasting and close friendship between His Catholic Majesty and the United States of America."

At the very moment Spain was establishing a New York presence, Francisco de Miranda—the St. John of the Latin American independentista movement—arrived in town (in 1784) to seek backing from prominent Gothamites for freeing South America from Spanish "tyranny." Miranda, raised in Caracas, Venezuela, had joined the imperial Spanish forces and served in various colonial garrisons around Europe, Africa, and the Americas before becoming a passionate convert to Enlightenment ideals of liberty. It was "in the city of New York," he would write, where "I formed a project for the liberty and independence of the entire Spanish-American Continent"—a project that garnered the support of (among others) Alexander Hamilton, who was an enthusiast for extending republicanism southward. Thus encouraged, Miranda went off to seek British backing as well. Receiving a lukewarm response, he crossed the Channel to lobby the French, got ensnarled in revolutionary crosscurrents that nearly cost him his life, and in 1798 refocused on getting England and the United States to detach South America from Spain. Hamilton, still interested, proposed creating a joint strike force that would combine the British navy with an American army (commanded by himself), but the enterprise was nixed by President John Adams.

Most of the New York mercantile elite, though not as bellicose as Hamilton, were intrigued by southern possibilities for more commercial reasons. Independence had interrupted the city's longstanding trade links with Britain's West Indian sugar islands. France's St. Domingue had become the major alternative to Jamaica and Barbados, but after the slave revolution there (1791-1804) annihilated its sugar industry, attention shifted from the new Republic of Haiti to Cuba and Puerto Rico.

The EXECUTION of ten of MIRANDA'S Officers.

Spain had long used its Havana entrepôt as a hub for trans-shipping mainland metals. But Cuban *criollos* had segued into sugar production, and Spain had gone along with the transformation by opening up the empire (in 1789) to British slave traders, who supplied a massive influx of African labor power. Sugar monoculture also created a demand for foodstuffs that Spain proved unable to fulfill from afar, especially amid the turmoil of European warfare. So in 1797 Madrid reluctantly opened ports to neutral shippers. New York merchants could now legally trade with Havana. Still, commerce remained volatile and risky—given wars, embargoes, and the intermittent reimposition of constraints by Spain, alarmed at the erosion of its trading monopoly. This set many Gothamites to dreaming of the potential fortunes that might be made were Spanish controls removed altogether.

THE BOLIVARIAN MOMENT (1806-25)[3]

The opening move of the liberation struggle that would eventually accomplish the ouster of Spain from the hemisphere was made in New York City. In 1806 the dogged Miranda chartered a ship, loaded it with munitions and roughly 180 New York volunteers, and sailed off to liberate Venezuela. (At just this moment, New Yorker Aaron Burr, who had killed Hamilton in a duel two years earlier but shared his victim's imperial dreams, was trying to mount an invasion of Mexico; Burr kept his distance from Miranda, whom he considered a rival.) Imperial Spanish authorities, having been informed of Miranda's movements by Thomas Stoughton (who in 1794 had been appointed Spain's consul general in New York), intercepted the expedition off Puerto Cabello. Miranda escaped, but sixty of his men were captured, ten of them hung, the remainder dispatched to Spanish dungeons. His backers in New York were tried for violating federal neutrality laws, but acquitted by a sympathetic local jury. Though the expedition was a failure, and Miranda generally adjudged a tilter-at-windmills, the attempt inspired younger revolutionaries, among them Simón Bolívar, who himself visited New York City the following year (1807).

In 1808 Napoleon invaded Spain and forced its king to abdicate. In 1810 rebellions against the empire broke out across the hemisphere. During the ensuing wars of liberation, the U.S. administration maintained a neutral stance, aiming to stay in Spain's good graces so it could buy Florida (as it did in 1819) and because it feared a counterintervention by European monarchies. Popular support for the Latin American rebels remained substantial (particularly in Gotham) for ideological and commercial reasons, and some New Yorkers intervened in the fighting, notably on the remote western coast of South America.

In 1811 the revolutionary government of Chile had thrown open its port of Valparaíso to foreign commerce. The New York merchant firm of Leroy, Bayard jack-rabbited to the scene, where its *Colt* picked up a cargo of copper and headed on to Canton. But in 1813 the Chilean rebels came under successful counterattack from neighboring Peru, a royalist stronghold, and the imperial trade monopoly was reimposed. Seeking naval capability to regain the initiative, Chilean rebels sent agents to Gotham with funds from the silver mines, and in 1817 enlisted the services of Captain Charles W. Wooster, who had been a successful privateer during the War of 1812. Wooster signed up a crew of New York officers and seamen, procured a ship (the *Columbus*, renamed the *Araucana*), sailed it around the Horn with a clandestine load of munitions, and accepted a commission in the fledgling Chilean navy. The Chileans also contracted with two leading East River shipyards for the construction of warships; one of them, the *Independencia*, arrived in Valparaíso in 1819 and was set to blockading Callao, the port of Lima, Peru's capital. In New York, business being business, some Gothamites turned to helping the Spanish evade that blockade. John Jacob Astor, on his way to becoming the richest man in New York, sent his ship *Beaver* to the area, carrying weapons probably intended for the rebels, but when the cargo was confiscated by pro-Spanish forces, the *Beaver*'s captain, following the path of profitability, spent the next two years running goods into Callao under royalist aegis. Stephen Whitney shipped flour, purchased in New York at $5 a barrel, down to blockaded Lima, where it fetched $24; like Astor, Whitney would die one of Gotham's richest men, the founder of a local dynasty.

Despite such windfall possibilities, given the number of navies, privateers, and pirates afloat, commerce remained marginal until, with mounting rebel victories and the attendant passage of free trade laws, the volume began to swell. During 1816 a scant nine ships had returned to Manhattan from South America and the Spanish Main. In 1822 the number rose to 52, and in 1825 climbed to 111. By then, with inde-

Hammatt Billings, engraver. *Lading and Unlading Ship Beaver, Roadstead Guanchaca* [Huanchaca, Peru]. From Richard J[effry] Cleveland, *A Narrative of Voyages and Commercial Enterprises*. Boston: C. H. Peirce, 1850.

In 1819 Astor's ship, the *Beaver*, captained by Richard Cleveland, was working under Spanish license, though the crew wanted to desert and join the Chilean rebels. The vessel is seen here picking up a cargo of wheat at a Peruvian harbor.

pendence achieved for all of Latin America—except Cuba and Puerto Rico—the coasts were clear. And even those two islands were effectively opened up to free trade by Spanish authorities, lest they join the others in revolt. With both New York and (most of) Latin America now freed from their respective empires, the stage was set for a flowering of commerce and an intermingling of peoples.

VENTURING SOUTH (1825–65)[4]

In Cuba and Puerto Rico the sugar boom shifted into overdrive. As Creole planters applied the new technology of steam power to grinding slave-grown cane, the resulting outflow of product reached flood proportions, and the great bulk of it went to New York. In 1860 the port received 211,000 tons (of which 171,000 were from Cuba, 22,000 from Puerto Rico)—constituting nearly two-thirds of all U.S. sugar imports that year. (Cuba's soaring cigar output also headed up to Gotham, which imported 243 million cigars in 1860, over half the national supply.)

Cuban cargoes traveled predominantly in New York bottoms. In 1816 Gardiner Greene and Samuel Shaw Howland formed G.G. and S.S. Howland and sent their first schooner to Matanzas; by 1830 the Howlands ruled the Latin American waves and had spawned a new generation of traders. Moses Taylor began as a clerk with the Howlands, and after diligent wharf and countinghouse service, was allowed to trade on his own account. In 1832, with his accumulated profits, Taylor set up as a commission merchant specializing in the sale and transport of sugar from Havana to New York. By 1865 his firm, run out of 44 South Street, had captured roughly one-fifth of the entire sugar trade between Cuba and the United States.

Gotham vessels fanned out as well to new republics throughout the hemisphere. Howland boats visited the Venezuelan ports of La Guaira, Puerto Cabello, and Maracaibo, exchanging coffee for New York flour, and New York schooners worked their way up the Orinoco River to take on cargoes at Angostura (after 1846, Ciudad Bolívar). Coffee was the big attraction in Brazil, too, and of the 72 million pounds of coffee that arrived in New York in 1860, 46 million came from Rio. In Argentina, pampas-fed cattle were turned into hides and shipped out from the two Río de la Plata ports, Buenos Aires and Montevideo; as early as 1817 Buenos Aires alone shipped out a million skins, a traffic dominated by the DeForest family (another powerful New York clan). The Peruvian trade was based on sea bird droppings (a.k.a. guano)—the demand for droppings having ballooned in the 1840s with the expansion of U.S. commercial agriculture and the attendant need for fertilizer. The point man in Peru was Irish-born William Russell Grace, who went to sea, roved the world, and settled in Callao; there he worked for a shipchandler's firm that he and his brother eventually took over, then prospered further by exporting guano from the Chincha Islands to New York. In Mexico, Edward K. Collins, later a giant of transatlantic commerce, helped his father Israel Collins start up (in 1827) the first regularly scheduled service to Veracruz, Mexico's chief Gulf Coast port. There the boats (armed, to ward off pirates) picked up cochineal, a dye, and silver—the casks of coined "dollars Mex" that were indispensable for the trade with Canton.

There were several reasons so much of this trade was drawn to New York rather than contending cities from New Orleans to Boston. One of the North American products most in demand was flour. In 1825 the Erie Canal opened, connecting New York directly with the Midwest. Soon canal barges were deluging the city with amber waves of grain. This sparked a massive expansion of port facilities, especially in Brooklyn, where grain elevators went up at the new Atlantic Docks and Erie Basin, giving New York an unmatched capability to meet demand. Another advantage was Gotham's establishment in 1817 of regularly scheduled service to Liverpool. This made New York the critical link between the United States and Europe, and the favored entrepôt for transatlantic shippers of manufactured goods. Substantial amounts of such items were reexported south, helping make New York a critical link between the U.S. and Latin America as well.

METROPOLITAN SPINOFFS (1825–65)[5]

One consequence of the explosion of maritime traffic was the rapid development of New York's own manufacturing and financial capabilities.

Among the city's biggest appeals for Caribbean sugar producers was Gotham's unmatched capacity for processing their molasses and muscovado. New York fortunes had been invested in sugar refining since the 1720s, when the Bayards, Livingstons,

and Roosevelts had transformed British West Indian product into processed sugar
or rum. In 1807 latecomers Frederick C. and William Havemeyer opened their first
sugar house on Vandam Street in Manhattan, with five employees. As Moses Taylor
and other merchants funneled vast amounts of sugar into the city, and as refinery
technology improved, the Havemeyers (in the 1850s) bought up waterfront tracts in
Williamsburgh and erected a million-dollar plant complete with its own docks and
warehouses. By 1860 the Havemeyers and their thirteen competitor firms were producing half the nation's supply, and Brooklyn had become the greatest sugar-refining
center in the world. William Havemeyer, moreover, became one of the first to trans-
mute economic power gleaned in the Latin American sphere into political power in
Gotham, serving three terms as mayor of New York.

The existence of multiplying commercial connections underwrote the city's
wider manufacturing sector. Local industrialists, faced with a burgeoning and accessible Latin American market, began producing items tailored to its needs. The Novelty
Iron Works built sugar-mill machinery for plantations and steam engines for ocean-
going vessels (clients included the Mexican, Peruvian, and Spanish governments).
Carriage maker James Brewster's Broad Street establishment advertised (in 1828)
fine carriages "calculated for Spanish and other markets" and established agencies
in Cuban ports. In 1844 C. & A. Beatty built "splendid omnibuses for service from
Havana to a few miles in the country," and in 1858, whole locomotives were being

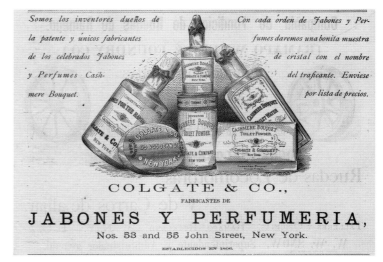

**Advertisements from *La America*, ca. 1880.
Courtesy of Instituto de Literatura y Lingüística,
Havana, Cuba.**

produced to run between Matanzas and nearby plantations. West Side furniture makers churned out Windsor chairs; William Colgate's factory shipped bars of soap and other toiletries south; and Samuel G. Redmond proclaimed its elegant umbrellas were "well adapted to the Spanish and South American markets."

As New York became the country's printing and publishing capital, it turned its attention to Latin American readers. In the 1840s the publisher D. Appleton translated a series of successful English readers into Spanish, loaded several cases aboard a vessel bound for Argentina, and consigned them to an unknown commission merchant. The titles sold like hotcakes, creating a new market, and soon children's books, textbooks, and scientific and technical works were streaming south too. New York printed money as well as books: the American Bank Note Company (1858) set its engravers and presses to printing tons of paper pesos, mil-reis, sucres, colons, and gourdes—for Mexico, Brazil, Costa Rica, Ecuador, and Haiti.

Nevertheless, Great Britain continued to be the dominant player in Latin America, in part because British merchants hawking British manufactures were

William Momberger, *Beldad y la Bestia* (Beauty and the Beast). New York: D. Appleton, ca. 1856. New-York Historical Society (YC1864.Beau).

backed by British diplomacy, British finance, and the British Navy, while the U.S. versions of such collateral supports remained rudimentary. Marine insurance companies did mitigate risks—Astor had even taken out a policy covering shipment of illegal goods to cover his gun-running—and merchant countinghouses, like that of Moses Taylor, did advance credit to Cuban planters against their next crop, enabling them to invest in slaves and buy New York–made machinery or luxury goods. Some commission merchants went farther and made actual loans, but Gotham merchant capitalists tended to prefer infrastructure development, especially transportation.

Once the discovery of gold in California—just after the territory had been forcibly subtracted from Mexico—heightened demand for speedy service to the West Coast, local entrepreneurs moved aggressively into Central America. New York merchant William Aspinwall and steamboat operator George Law ran goods on boats down to Panama City, across the isthmus on Aspinwall's Panama Railroad, then up to San Francisco on ships of Aspinwall's Pacific Mail Steamship Company. Their fabulous profits whetted the cupidity of transport magnate Cornelius Vanderbilt,

Advertisement for Pacific Mail Steam Ship Line, ca. 1870. Courtesy of Central Pacific Railroad Photographic History Museum.

who wangled a franchise from the Nicaraguan government to establish a faster route, soon earning Vanderbilt a million dollars a year.

Merchants also turned Latin American profits into bank capital, which was then invested in New York or U.S. projects. When Gardiner Greene Howland retired from the sugar trade in the 1830s, he became a director of the Bank of New York and a chief promoter of the Hudson River Railroad. Moses Taylor bought shares in City Bank (from which today's Citibank descends), becoming a director in 1837 and its president in 1856, a position he held until his death in 1882. Backed by the bank's financial clout, Taylor helped underwrite the Atlantic Cable (which connected New York to Europe) and the Manhattan Gas Light Company (which illuminated the city), then segued into coal mines and iron (then steel) production. Taylor became one of the richest men in Gotham, in the process founding a dynasty of New York bankers when his assistant and son-in-law, Percy Pyne, succeeded him as head of City Bank.

COLONIAS (1825–65) [6]

Nurtured by the thickening trade connections with Spain's colonies and former colonies, a small but flourishing Spanish-speaking community grew up in Gotham—more precisely, two communities, one Latin American (overwhelmingly Cuban plus a sprinkling of Puerto Ricans and others), the other peninsular Spanish.

That Cubans were the first body of Latin Americans to settle in New York followed from the tremendous scale of U.S.-Cuban commerce—by 1835 the island was the country's third-ranked trading partner, just behind England and Canada. The first arrivals were chiefly merchants, come to engage in commercial dealings with their Anglo-American counterparts. Initially the numbers were tiny, though sufficient to precipitate the city's first Hispanic institutions. In 1828 the newcomers established Gotham's earliest Spanish language paper, *Mercurio de Nueva York*—primarily a commercial/advertising publication, it also carried news from Latin America and Spain—and by 1830 they had organized the Sociedad Benéfica Cubana y Puertorriqueña, also to promote commerce with their part of the Caribbean.

Two decades later, in 1850, there were 207 Cuban-born persons living in Manhattan, and the still-predominant merchants had been joined by some skilled craftsmen and a handful of retailers, professionals, and students (sons of merchant and planter families enrolled in boarding schools, or the Jesuit-run St. John's College, as Fordham was then called). A decade later the Cuban-born population had tripled to more than six hundred, and occupational diversity had been enhanced by the addition of clerks, artists, teachers, cigar workers, small businessmen, laborers, and servants. And while in the 1820s Hispanics had been too few and too scattered to constitute a distinct geographical community, by 1850 the Cubans, mostly of affluent or middling status, tended to cluster in elite residential neighborhoods—in lower

COLEGIO DE SAN JUAN,

EN FORDHAM, CIUDAD DE NUEVA YORK.

Bajo la direccion de los Padres de la Compañia de Jesus

Este establecimiento con privilegios de Universidad, tiene fácil acceso por las anchas avenidas, sea en coches particulares, ó en los públicos del ferro-carril urbano, que llegan hasta el mismo colegio y más fácil aún en los trenes de vapor.

El año escolar principia el primer miércoles de Setiembre y termina el último de Junio.

Cuatro carreras pueden hacerse en Fordham : la comercial y la de estudios clásicos, Filosofía, Mineros é Ingeniatura Civil.

Aunque el idioma oficial para Profesores y alumnos es el Inglés todos aprenden además, el Francés que se enseña en todas las clases del Colegio.

Hay tambien clases de Español y Aleman.

Las clases comenzarán el Miércoles 6 de Setiembre.

Rev. P. F. DEALY, S. J.,
Presidente.

El año Colegial e divide en dos secciones.
El primero empieza el primer viérnes de Setiembre.
El segundo con el primero de Febrero.
Se admiten alumnos en toda época.

Advertisement for St. John's College (Fordham), *La America*, ca. 1880. Courtesy of Instituto de Literatura y Lingüística, Havana, Cuba.

Portrait of Don Félix Varela, frontispiece from José Ignacio Rodríguez, *Vida del presbítero Don Félix Varela*. New York: Imprenta de O Novo Mundo, 1878. New-York Historical Society (CT. V2934 R6).

Manhattan, Greenwich Village, or the area between Union and Madison Squares— and a sixty-strong offshoot took root in Brooklyn.

If most Cubans were pulled to New York by commerce, some were pushed there by politics. Rebels who tried to throw off Spanish rule, as had the rest of Latin America, were often forced into exile. One of the first such was Félix Varela y Morales. Born in Havana to Spanish parents, Varela had prepared for the priesthood, become a professor of philosophy, and in 1821 been sent as a representative to the Spanish Cortes, where he called for Cuban independence and an end to the slave trade. In 1823, however, the restored King Fernando VII abolished the constitution and went after liberal deputies, forcing Varela to flee Madrid. He caught a ride on a freighter carrying almonds to New York, expecting to travel on to Havana, but never did, having been sentenced to death in absentia. In New York Varela continued to advocate Cuban self-government and the abolition of slavery, sentiments he promoted in a bristling political magazine, *El Habanero*, which he smuggled down to Havana. In 1824 Bishop John Connolly appointed him to a post at St. Peter's and he began a pastoral ministry among the Irish, battling Protestant nativists and immigration restrictionists. Varela became vicar-general of the New York Diocese and was even considered for the position of bishop, a possibility precluded by Spain's intervention against him in Rome, and by the fact that the New York church quickly

Portion of La Casa de Las Monjas, Uxmal. Plate 15 from Frederick Catherwood, *Views of Ancient Monuments in Central America, Chiapas and Yucatan*. Andrew Picken, lithographer. London, 1844. Mortimer Rare Book Room, Smith College.

In the early 1840s John Lloyd Stephens, an archaeologically inclined travel writer, published two accounts of his exploration of Mayan ruins in Central America and Mexico, illustrated by Frederick Catherwood's phenomenally accurate engravings. Stephens also carted off hundreds of Mayan artifacts from Uxmal, in Mexico's Yucatán peninsula, to New York City for a proposed Museum of American Antiquities. In 1842 he decided to exhibit them in The Rotunda, a building Catherwood had constructed in lower Manhattan at Broadway and Prince Street, but the building caught fire and all its contents were destroyed.

became dominated by the Irish, with Hispanic immigration being but a trickle in comparison.

Another rebel arrived in 1823, the twenty-year-old Cuban poet José María Heredia, who took refuge in New York after Spanish authorities had ordered his arrest. Heredia earned his living teaching Spanish in a private academy and wrote some of his most famous poems in Gotham, notably "Ode to Niagara," which was included in a collection he published there in 1825.

Heredia's verses sparked one of the first significant cultural connections between Gotham and Latin America when they came to the attention of another young poet, William Cullen Bryant. He had moved to New York from Massachusetts to work as a magazine editor in 1825, just as Heredia left for Mexico, and the two never met in person. But Bryant was boarding in the home of the Salazars, a Spanish family with business connections in Cuba, and it was probably someone in their circle who called his attention to Heredia's work. In 1827 Bryant collaborated in translating

Statue of Benito Juárez, Bryant Park, New York. Photograph by Wally Gobetz.

In 2004 the Mexican State of Oaxaca presented the City of New York with a statue of Juarez—the first ever bronzed Mexican here—and it was installed in . . . Bryant Park.

"Niágara," beginning a lifelong sub-career—by the 1830s he was widely considered the country's premier poet—as a translator, publisher, and reviewer of Spanish-American literature. Bryant's enthusiasm was reciprocated by Latin American writers, who translated his poems into Spanish, and he gained further acclaim for his vigorous support of Latin American liberation movements (he hailed Bolívar) and his travel writing (*Cuba and the Cubans*, a report on his first trip there in 1849, was one of the earliest U.S. narratives about the island). When he visited Mexico in 1872, President Benito Juárez headed up one of the most enthusiastic receptions ever given a foreigner. Bryant helped give New York a reputation for Hispanophilia, which would in turn encourage further immigration, especially of writers and intellectuals. (And visits, too: when Mexico's de facto poet laureate Guillermo Prieto visited New York in 1877, it was at Bryant's house he stayed.)

Another collection of rebels came after a slave conspiracy in Cuba in 1844 triggered a wave of repression by Spanish authorities. Liberal intellectuals were fired, their books banned, and they themselves exiled. Most opted to come to New York, because it had become both the major U.S. publishing center and a center of the annexationist movement, dedicated to liberating Cuba from Spanish control by having the United States acquire it. John L. O'Sullivan, editor of the *Democratic Review*, had coined the term "manifest destiny" in an 1845 editorial supporting the "Texian" revolt against Mexico. And he worked with Cuban planters, including Cristóbal Madan (who had married O'Sullivan's sister), in advocating that the United States buy Cuba, thus freeing it from autocratic Spanish rule while preserving the autocratic slavery on which planter prosperity rested. Among these annexationists was novelist Cirilo Villaverde, who arrived in 1848, having escaped from a Spanish prison; he promptly established a bilingual pro-annexationist newspaper, *La Verdad*.

Some went beyond peaceable methods to advocate—and attempt—forcible annexation. In 1848 General Narciso López, a former Spanish army officer, fled Cuba to the United States. Making contact with O'Sullivan, López recruited Cuban exiles and Gotham mercenaries (many of them veterans of the recently ended Mexican War), drilled them on Cedar Street, and designed what became Cuba's national flag, which flew for the first time (in 1850) from the offices of the *New York Sun*. But just as López's filibustering expedition was about to embark, the U.S. government seized his ships. López shifted his base to New Orleans and launched two incursions, both of which failed; in 1851 he was caught and garroted by the Spanish.

In 1855 an American named William Walker proved more successful, though not in Cuba. With help from a sizable contingent of New Yorkers, Walker seized control of Nicaragua, installed himself as president, and reinstituted slavery, which Nicaragua had abolished decades earlier. Unwisely, Walker also revoked Commodore Vanderbilt's charter, transferring it to competitors who promised to pay more. Vanderbilt, without setting foot outside Gotham, underwrote an invasion of Nicaragua by four other Central American republics, and Walker was overthrown in 1857.

While the Cuban community expanded in size and rebelliousness, the growing Spanish cluster mostly supported the empire. The tiny group of export-import merchants dealing with Spain and Latin America that had arrived in the 1780s was now bolstered by refugees from the Latin American revolutions (notably exiles from Mexico). Others, long resident in Cuba, moved to New York as an extension of their existing business interests, as was the case with Joseph A. Vega, an Asturian-born wholesale tobacco dealer, who opened an office at Cedar and Pearl streets in 1849. By 1850 the fledgling community of native Spaniards numbered 307. It included merchants, professionals, white-collar workers, and skilled artisans—who settled in Lower Manhattan, notably near the East River where Water and Cherry intersected James and Catherine. It also featured a small body of seamen, a circulating population that stayed for two or three months in Hudson River waterfront boardinghouses along

West Street and Washington from Charlton to Fourteenth Street before setting off again on another vessel.

The Spaniards were slower than the Cubans to establish a public presence in the city, though in 1848 a group of fifty wealthy men of Havana did help underwrite publication of a local newspaper, *La Crónica*. Spain did, however, begin to loom larger—and more benignly— in the wider city's imagination, despite (or perhaps because of) having lost most of its colonies. Most strikingly, New York's preeminent man of letters, Washington Irving, who had given the city its nickname "Gotham" and in a sense invented "New York" with his mock-epic *Knickerbocker's History* (in 1809), now helped invent a new image of "Spain."

Irving got interested early on in things Hispanic. His first book product (1806) was a translation of a Frenchman's visit to the Spanish Main that recounted the "manners and customs of the Spaniards." He mastered *El Quijote* before writing *Knickerbocker*. And he discovered a love for the Spanish language and studied it seriously, enabling him to take a job in Madrid (in 1826) translating a collection of Columbus documents and then produce a spectacularly successful biography of Columbus in 1828 (175 editions by 1900). Irving next turned out the extremely popular *Conquest of Granada* (1829) and *Tales of the Alhambra* (1832), which depicted Spain not as despotic and cruel, but as romantic, picturesque, exotic, languid, sensual—a quasi-Oriental country whose people still bore the imprint of its Moorish past, a past that Spain had tried to expunge as assiduously as it had expelled the Moors themselves. But while the version of Spanish history that Irving helped create was more sympathetic than the Black Legend's, it came at a price. Spain was charming—its bullfights, gypsies, flamenco dancers, and Moorish ruins were well worth a visit—but it was also sleepy and backward, caught in a time warp, seemingly incapable of change. Spain was the opposite of the energetic, progressive United States that was careening into the future. Quaint Granada and kinetic New York were, a fortiori, utterly antithetical cities.

NEW YORK'S LATIN LINKS (1865–98)[7]

Just how go-ahead Gotham was became hyper-evident after the Civil War, when New York businessmen set about expanding their Latin American connections, particularly by forging communication, transportation, and financial links.

In 1866 New Yorker James A. Scrymser's International Ocean Telegraph Company opened the first cable connection from Florida to Cuba, with financial help from Moses Taylor. In 1878 Scrymser got a concession to run cable lines from Mexico City to Veracruz and thence to Texas, where they were spliced into Western Union lines running on to New York and its transatlantic link to Europe. In 1879 Scrymser incorporated the Central and South American Cable Company, with backing from

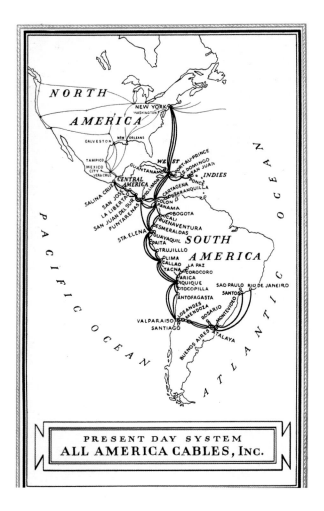

Maps of original 1880 system and 1928 system, All America Cables, Inc. From *A Half Century of Cable Service to the Three Americas 1878–1928*. New York, 1928. Courtesy of Atlantic-Cable.com.

Havana–New York telephone cable landing, Havana Harbor, ca. 1921. Photographer unknown.

Timetable for the New York & Cuba Mail Steamship Company, ca. 1883. Courtesy of Michael Alderson, www.wardline.com.

J. P. Morgan, and sent wires snaking south from Mexico City down the Pacific coast until New York was connected with Valparaíso, Chile. From there, in 1882, he acquired land lines across the Andes to Buenos Aires; and in 1917, having finally overcome a British communication monopoly in Brazil, Scrymser's All-America Company connected up to Rio. By then, having laid 14,300 miles of cable and 2,500 of land wires, he'd girdled the continent and wired the hemispheres together.

In 1865 William R. Grace moved from Callao to New York City and founded his own firm, W. R. Grace and Company. After making a vast fortune in trade (notably by supplying the Peruvian military), he segued into mining, nitrates, guano, railroads, sugar, and banking. As had Havemeyer before him, Grace parlayed the profits from his Latin American connection into municipal political power, becoming New York's first Irish Catholic mayor in 1881. In 1882 he established what would become the Grace Line, linking Peru and New York via sailing vessels; in 1893 he upgraded to steamship service with the descriptively named New York & Pacific Steamship Company.

A plethora of smaller lines webbed Gotham to closer-in Caribbean and Spanish Main ports. In 1881 the Ward Line, established in New York in 1856 as a sailing fleet, was officially renamed (after its shift to steam) as the New York and Cuba Mail Steamship Company but remained popularly known as the Ward Line; its vessels docked at East River Pier 13, south of Pine Street, or at nearby piers. The Clyde Steamship Company provided service to the Dominican Republic, and the New York and Porto Rico Steamship and the Red D Line both touched down at San Juan, with the latter company continuing on to Curaçao and Venezuela.

New York banks and corporations expanded into Latin America, underwriting both transport and mining operations, particularly in Mexico after Porfirio Díaz took power in 1876. During the "Porfiriato" (which would last until the Mexican Revolution) his agents repeatedly made their way to New York, where they dined and made deals at Delmonico's with the likes of James Stillman—a Moses Taylor protégé—who headed what was now called the National City Bank. Mexico also invited investments from J. P. Morgan, Brown Brothers, Grenville M. Dodge, Russell Sage, and Jay Gould, which underwrote among other things the construction of 14,000 miles of rail track. Waters-Pierce—an affiliate of Standard Oil (which relocated from Cleveland to 26 Broadway in 1885)—opened operations in Mexico and by the end of the century led the petroleum field. And Meyer Guggenheim, a textile importer who had moved into mining, built smelters at Puebla, Monterrey, and Aguascalientes to take advantage of cheap Mexican labor and to avoid tariff impositions. By the time Díaz was overthrown in 1911, U.S. direct investment in Mexico totaled $2 billion.

Cuba, too, saw substantial investment by ever-expanding New York firms. In 1887 the current head of the Havemeyer sugar empire—Henry Osborne Havemeyer—on the advice of Elihu Root, longtime legal counsel to the Havemeyers and a pillar of the Manhattan bar, created a consortium of eight New York competitors. Officially the Sugar Refineries Company, informally the Sugar Trust, it was set up, on the model of John D. Rockefeller's Standard Oil Trust, to wring competition out of the industry and enhance profits. Ruled illegal under the antitrust laws in 1891, it reorganized itself (on Root's advice) as a holding company, the American Sugar Refining Company. Under a recently passed law, combining independent competitors in a single enterprise meant they were no longer in restraint of trade. The giant new corporation proceeded to drive most remaining competitors out of business, beat down sugar producers' prices in Cuba, and begin buying plantations itself. The goal was to organize the sugar business vertically (by controlling supply) as it had horizontally (by integrating the refineries). By the mid-1890s, paced by the Sugar Trust (as it remained known in popular parlance), American investment in Cuba surpassed $50 million, $10 million more than Andrew Carnegie's annual profit from steel. With 94 percent of Cuban sugar exports going to the U.S., Spain's claim on Cuba had become more tenuous than ever.

LATINS IN NEW YORK (1865-98)[8]

In 1868 Cuba's struggle for self-determination escalated beyond annexationism and filibustering to all-out war with Spain, a conflict that had a dramatic impact on New York's Cuban community. When landowners in eastern Cuba launched a movement for independence, the Spanish authorities, to reassert imperial control, unleashed the *voluntarios*, a corps of Spanish loyalists who terrorized the populace. The government also froze or confiscated the property of any Cubans whose allegiances were suspect, not sparing economic, professional, or intellectual elites. Refugees streamed out of Cuba, including some of the island's wealthiest men, like Miguel Aldama, and leading academics, like Antonio Bachiller y Morales, senior professor at the University of Havana (and a member, since 1847, of the New-York Historical Society). Within two years, the Cuban-born population in what are now the five boroughs had surpassed 2,700 and was climbing fast.

New York became a base for insurrectionist leaders to outfit expeditions to fight and overthrow the Spanish. One hotbed of militant activity was an old mansion in what is now the Hunts Point area in the Bronx. There exiled author Cirilo Villaverde and his wife, Emilia Casanova, who in 1869 established the Liga de Hijas de Cuba (League of the Daughters of Cuba) to mobilize women for the struggle, converted old vaults into storehouses for arms and ammunition. The matériel was then smuggled out to the East River or Long Island Sound for shipment down to rebels in Cuba. In the end—which came only after ten bloody years of combat—the uprising did not succeed; some affluent exiles went back, while others became permanent residents of Gotham.

Rebellion also broke out in Puerto Rico, spearheaded by Ramón Emeterio Betances. A renowned surgeon, independentista, and abolitionist who had been exiled to New York in 1867, Betances helped launch the insurrection that began in Lares in 1868 ("El Grito de Lares"). It, too, was crushed, though to quell further unrest, Spain's Cortes abolished slavery on the island in 1873. In 1869 Betances returned to New York for a time and worked with other exile leaders like the educator Eugenio María de Hostos, who in 1870 made New York his base (in 1874 he established *La Voz de Puerto Rico* [The Voice of Puerto Rico] in New York); both men advocated an Antillean alliance between Puerto Rico, Cuba, and the Dominican Republic.

Another group of exiles had arrived in town in 1864, after the French, who had invaded Mexico in 1862, installed Maximilian as emperor. The wife and family of President Benito Juárez were sent to New York City. Many republican officials joined them in temporary exile and, establishing the Mexican Club of New York in 1864, worked successfully to win American support for restoring the republic. In 1867, after that was accomplished, most returned home.

The Ten Years' War precipitated a new kind of Cuban immigration, as the owners and workers of devastated tobacco plantations decamped for New York. Back in the 1850s, merchants had imported millions of ready-rolled cigars; now they began importing Cuban tobacco leaves, to be rolled in Gotham by the German immigrants who in the 1860s and 1870s helped make New York the capital of the North American cigar industry. Cuban refugee manufacturers also gained a foothold in the business. They established hundreds of factories around the city, with particular concentrations in the Wall Street area (centered on Pearl Street and Maiden Lane, where a clutch of Cuban restaurants and stores catered to *tabaqueros*) and in what are now SoHo and the South Village.

By the 1880s working class Cuban/Puerto Rican residential communities had grown up near these tobacco-related districts in Manhattan, and in Brooklyn, along Columbia Street and near the Navy Yard. Darker-skinned Hispanics more or less had to live in African American areas like San Juan Hill, then the major black district. Wealthier Cubans continued to live in fashionable neighborhoods around Washington Square or between Fourteenth and Fortieth Streets, while the middle class headed for Chelsea, south central Harlem, and Yorkville.

These communities were partly organized around the Catholic Church, despite the continuing absence of a dedicated Spanish-speaking church or parish in the city. From the 1870s to the 1890s, the leading choice of better-off Cubans for funerals, weddings, and baptisms was St. Francis Xavier (1847) on Sixteenth Street between Fifth and Sixth avenues, named for the Spanish-Basque Jesuit famed for missionary work in East Asia. (Like St. Peter's, it had successfully turned to Mexico for construction funds, one reason, perhaps, that from 1855 on it had offered an 11:00 AM Spanish mass on Sundays, in the lower church.) Working-class exiles from Cuba and Puerto Rico tended instead to build their collective identities around trade union associations and the independence groups set up by exile intellectuals, who continued to arrive and thrive in the 1880s and 1890s, most famously the poet and writer José Martí.

Martí arrived in New York in 1880 from Spain, to which he'd been deported by Havana authorities in 1879 for activities on behalf of independence. Martí supported himself as a journalist, filing insightful copy on New York and U.S. culture and politics (including essays on Whitman, the Brooklyn Bridge, and Coney Island) to newspapers in Caracas, Mexico City, and Buenos Aires, and by doing translations for Appleton. He also continued his own literary work, writing *Versos Sencillos* (1891) and in 1889 editing four issues of *La Edad de Oro*, a magazine of stories, fairy tales, and verses for children, posthumously published as a hugely popular book. Martí also contributed to the new Spanish-language newspapers and journals that sprang up in the city, like *La Revista Ilustrada de Nueva York* (1886–93), whose contributors were a varied mix of Latin Americans (as were its nine thousand far-flung readers in Argentina, Bolivia, Chile, Colombia, Dominican Republic, Honduras, Guatemala, Mexico, Nicaragua, Peru, Puerto Rico, and Uruguay, among other places). *La Revista*'s founder, Elías de Losada, relished publishing (he said in 1892) from "esta metrópoli del mundo, a donde llegan los ecos de todos los pueblos civilizados" (this world metropolis, where the echoes of all civilized peoples can be heard). Many of its articles proposed (with varying degrees of ambivalence) emulating U.S. cultural and technological developments. So did those in *La America*, a magazine—of which Martí assumed the editorship in 1883—that reviewed the latest products of U.S. factories and advertised many of them in its pages for sale to Latin America. Martí also helped found the Spanish-American Literary Society of New York in 1887 and served as president in 1890–91. A Latin American social and literary club, with rooms at 64 Madison Avenue (between Twenty-seventh and Twenty-eighth streets), the society held musical/literary evenings known as "noches Americanas," each dedicated to a different country of the Americas, the goal being to bring writers of various nationalities together and raise their collective profile in the big city. Gotham was becoming a crossroads for writers from widely separated homelands, and a crucible for an emerging pan-Hispanic literary tradition.

Martí was also busy building a revolutionary movement that could launch an armed struggle in Cuba. He founded the Partido Revolucionario Cubano (PRC) in 1892, bypassing the traditional exile leadership in New York because it was soliciting aid from the U.S., which Martí considered an imperial power, too: "Once the United States is in Cuba," he asked, "who will get her out?" Instead he raised grassroots support for his movement in the growing cigar-worker community. Many *tabaqueros* joined his party, bought its newspaper, *Patria*, and flocked to venues like Hardman

Hall on Fifth Avenue and Nineteenth Street, or Clarendon Hall on Thirteenth Street, to listen to the eloquent apostle and his colleagues.

Puerto Ricans signed up too. The PRC had a Puerto Rican section, and several political/cultural clubs worked to foster unity—like Las Dos Antillas (The Two Islands), organized by Arthur Schomburg. Newly arrived in the city in 1891 at age seventeen, Schomburg earned a living as an elevator operator, bellhop, porter, and printer; took night classes at Manhattan Central High; and helped organize the club on Third Avenue to collect money, weapons, and medical supplies for an armed struggle against Spain.

SPANIARDS IN GOTHAM (1865–98)[9]

In these same years, the peninsular Spanish community continued to grow in Gotham, though more slowly than its Latin American counterpart: in 1870, 1880, and 1890 there were, respectively, 682, 1,048, and 1,421 Spanish-born people in New York City.

Some of the new arrivals had been resident for some time in Cuba or elsewhere in Latin America and were simply relocating. Others came directly from Spain, though usually via Cuba as there was no direct service to the U.S. Passengers could take passage from Cádiz to Havana on the Compañia Trasatlántica Española, a.k.a. the Spanish Line, a firm started in Cuba in 1850 and then nurtured by Spain with a mail contract granted in 1861. From Cuba they could switch to local carriers like the Ward Line for travel on to New York, or, after 1886, continue on with the Compañia, which that year added its own feeder service from Havana to Gotham.

As had long been the case, Spanish businessmen were prominent among the newcomers, either as representatives of trading firms (which also recruited Spanish white-collar workers) or as independent export-import merchants. Others made their mark in entrepreneurial pursuits. The Spanish-born José Francisco de Navarro arrived in 1855 after a successful stay in Cuba developing railroads, and rolled his expertise over into founding the company that built New York's Sixth Avenue elevated railroad. Navarro also entered real estate development, completing (in 1884) the Spanish Flats, a vast apartment complex just below Central Park, whose eight buildings were each named for a city in Spain. Rafael Guastavino arrived in 1881 from Barcelona, and in 1889 started the Guastavino Fireproof Construction Company, which, using a traditional Mediterranean technique, made vaults and arches of terra-cotta tiles that would adorn the city's first subway station and, later, many major New York buildings. Antonio and Arturo Cuyás, Catalán brothers, ran the Hotel Barcelona at Bond and Broadway, which their father Antonio had started. They also did translating and publishing. Arturo's Spanish-English-Spanish dictionary, which reflected everyday Spanish-American usage, was first published in 1876 and reissued repeatedly by Appleton (the current edition is available on Kindle).

It was in this post–Civil War period that the Spanish community attained sufficient density and resources to begin creating its own social, cultural, economic, and journalistic organizations. In 1868 members of what the *New York Times* called the "elite Spanish element" formed the Spanish Benevolent Society—La Sociedad Benéfica Española de Socorros Mutuos, known universally as "La Nacional"—whose aim was the relief of destitute Spaniards in the city. Newspapers emerged, representing the full spectrum of political positions inside the community. *La Crónica*, which had been started up in 1848, and *El Cronista*, which succeeded it in 1866, staunchly defended the Spanish empire past and present, attacking Las Casas and Black Legendeers, and defending the *voluntarios*. Liberals who rejected the *Cronista*'s hard line started up *Las Novedades* in 1876, backing the empire in a way less likely to raise hackles in their host country. The Catalonian community's *La Llumanera de Nova York* (1874–81), under editor Arturo Cuyás, had its own quarrels with Spain but still defended colonial rule in Cuba (Cuyás was an ardent opponent of Martí). It was left to *El Despertar* (1891–1902), an anarchist paper, to support the Antillean separatists.

El Cronista also sought to promote a broader Spanish identity that would embrace all Hispanics in the city, and indeed all of Latin America. It advanced the notion of Hispanidad—the argument that Hispanic Americans, despite their differences with the mother country, were (or should be) united by their common language, common heritage, and common culture—the last symbolized by the author of *Don Quijote*. In 1875 the paper called for an annual commemoration of the death of Cervantes, an effort endorsed by the Spanish diplomatic corps and New York's Spanish commercial houses. The first Cervantes Day gathering featured a solemn funeral mass at St. Francis Xavier, held in Spanish, and an evening banquet at which speakers urged colonies and former colonies to unite with Spain in celebrating their "shared glory." (Such local initiatives found favor among Hispanistas in Spain. Juan Valera—poet, lawyer, politician, diplomat—believed Spain had to "become once again a nation worthy of its past, to the point of exercising a certain domination in the New World, above all in the Spanish-speaking world, and the departure point for our activity has to be in New York.")

The conservative elite also used Cervantes Day commemorations to stake out a more visible presence in the city, and did so again in the years surrounding the 1892 Columbian quatrocentennial. In 1890, at the instigation of the consul general of Spain in New York, community leaders organized the Círculo Colón-Cervantes, a social club with a civic agenda. The Círculo's directors, among them Antonio and Arturo Cuyás, set up a clubhouse at 723 Lexington (at Fifty-eighth Street) and held monthly dinners and fashionable balls. They also insisted on participating in the Columbian quatrocentennial events, and succeeded in playing a part in the culminating mammoth pageant-parade, held on the evening of Columbus Day 1892, with Círculo members marching

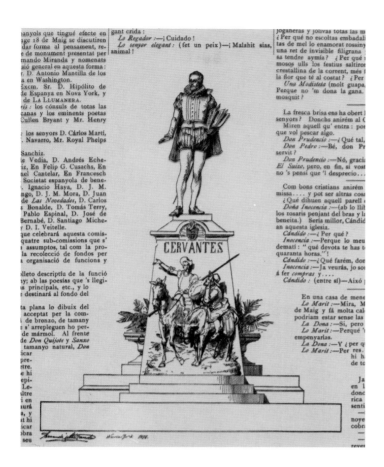

Page from *La Llumanera de Nova York*, no. 1 (November 1874). General Research Division, New York Public Library, Astor, Lenox and Tilden Foundations.

In an effort to put Spain on the metropolitan map, leaders of the Spanish community set out to erect a statue of Cervantes in Central Park, where it would rival those of Schiller and Shakespeare. The project, like the establishment of Cervantes Day in 1872, was also fueled by patriotic fervor in support of Spain's effort to suppress Cuba's insurrection during the Ten Years' War. The sculpture was to have been surrounded by Spanish cannons from the Battle of Lepanto, but fundraising flagged after the war ended, and the expensive ensemble was never built.

Broadside for Central Park bullfights, 1880. Museum of the City of New York.

An attempt to introduce bullfighting in Manhattan—advertised in this 1880 broadside—attracted three to four thousand spectators, including a sizable contingent of Spanish speakers. But the event proved a poor imitation of the real thing as the fighters were denied weapons and the bulls' horns were padded, at the insistence of the Society for the Prevention of Cruelty to Animals, on hand to shut down the affair at the first sign of blood. The SPCA was determined to defend the bulls but even more intent on defending the city's moral culture from debasement by a sport often equated with Black Legend cruelties. A patronizing account in the *New York Times* concluded, "such brutal performances, or even weak imitations of them, will not take root in our healthy soil," and the proprietor was quickly driven out of business.

along Fifth Avenue dressed up as knights and ladies of the Spanish royal court. Even better was the hoopla surrounding the visit in 1893 of the Infanta Eulalie—a real royal —which had all New York society (even Mrs. Astor) in a tizzy about whether or not to follow the rigid rules of Spanish court etiquette (backing and bowing out of the Presence, etc.) until the Círculo managers circumspectly arranged a relaxation of the rules. Apart from this contretemps, from the moment of the infanta's arrival at the Spanish Line's Pier 10 dock, the event was a great success and helped strengthen the elite's public standing.

On the other hand, Círculo leaders were politely rebuffed when they sought to claim a high-profile public space by donating a massive Columbus fountain, to be installed at the entrance to Central Park at Fifth Avenue and Fifty-ninth Street. When told they'd have to settle for Battery Park or Mount Morris, locations they deemed "very unsatisfactory," they withdrew their offer, noticeably peeved at having lost the battle of the bronzes to the Italians, who had captured Columbus Circle.

This blow was offset by the rise of Spanish art in metropolitan estimation in these years, after several New York painters visited the Prado and got transfixed by Velázquez. William Merritt Chase was so taken by the Spanish master that in addition to organizing trips to Madrid for his New York art students, he painted his daughter Helen dressed up as the Infanta Maria Teresa. Still, this burst of Hispanophilia remained in the Irving vein, emphasizing the picturesque, as in Chase's *Sunny Spain* of 1882, and while some first-rate work emerged—both Chase and John Singer Sargent did portraits of a highly popular Spanish dancer, La Carmencita—much of what issued from New York brushes retailed stereotypical images. The era did, however, see sugar king Henry Osborne Havemeyer and his wife, Louisine, embark on amassing an art collection that would be one of the first in New York to include works by Spanish artists, notably Goya and El Greco.

Whatever their impact on New York society and artists (and art market), the Spanish elite's Hispanista discourse did not succeed in winning cultural authority over the increasingly diverse immigrant community. The strategy of glossing over what divided Gotham's Hispanics—notably the resurgence of Cuban nationalism— soon became impossible to overlook.

SPANISH-CUBAN-AMERICAN WAR (1895–98) [10]

In January 1895 José Martí sat down at the desk in his Front Street office (between Wall and Pine streets) and drafted and signed the order to reignite an uprising in Cuba. It was taken—so the story goes—to a waiting Ward Line vessel, docked steps away, rushed down to Key West, rolled in a cigar, and smuggled into Havana. Alas, researchers have declared the story improbable, given the document's sizable dimensions, but the myth nicely captures the spirit of the process. Martí himself headed

José Martí's office at 120–22 Front Street, New York, 1897. Photographer unknown. In *Revista de Cayo Hueso* 1, no. 6 (September 26, 1897), p. 7. Widener Library, Harvard University.

Martí chose this site for his revolutionary headquarters partly because of its strategic placement for communicating with Cuba: It was located close to the pier where the Ward Line docked and next to a Western Union office.

Herman Norman. *José J. Martí* (1853–1895), 1891. Oil on canvas. Cuban Heritage Collection, University of Miami.

south, ending his long New York exile, and was killed in action that May in one of the earliest battles of the renewed hostilities. Despite this and other setbacks, the rebellion soon established itself in Santiago Province. It launched an effective guerrilla campaign that torched mills, ranches, and plantations, some of them American owned. The empire struck back by herding farm families off the land and into "reconcentration camps" where thousands died of disease and malnutrition.

In New York, the insurgent government established a junta to generate U.S. support for the war effort. It was led by Tomás Estrada Palma, who worked out of the office of a sympathetic Wall Street lawyer. A Cuban League was set up to raise money for the war from local supporters, among whom were imperialists like Theodore Roosevelt. Europe, T.R. argued, had inaugurated a new age of imperialism and had swallowed up most of Africa and much of the Far East. The United States must get into the great game and compete vigorously, or risk being cut off from markets and raw materials in a world increasingly carved up into colonies or protectionist blocs.

Gotham's sensationalist press—paced by Joseph Pulitzer and William Randolph Hearst—whipped itself into a competitive frenzy and began to beat the drums for war. For Hearst's *Journal*, the heart of the matter was that villainous Spaniards were brutalizing noble Cubans, and the *heart* of the heart of the matter was that lustful Spanish brutes were ravishing pure (white) Cuban women. New Yorkers were receptive to the message, drawing as it did on the Black Legend schoolbook accounts of inquisitors and conquistadores that had convinced many of the inherent depravity of Spaniards. (In 1898 there appeared in New York a new English edition of Las Casas with the souped-up title *An Historical and True Account of the Cruel Massacre and Slaughter of 20,000,000 People in the West Indies by the Spaniards*.)

Some businessmen, frustrated at Europeans' continuing domination of hemispheric trade and finance, were tempted by war. If "we could wrest the South American
markets from Germany and England and permanently hold them," wrote the *Banker's
Magazine* in 1894, "this would be indeed a conquest worth perhaps a heavy sacrifice."
Others on Wall Street feared war would further interrupt trade and endanger currency stability, but Roosevelt denounced the "craven fear and brutal selfishness of
the mere money-makers," and their reluctance generated nationwide opprobrium.

Some New Yorkers worried that war with Spain might be dangerous, given
that the city itself remained, as it had been for centuries, at the mercy of foreign
fleets. A Spanish armada, *Leslie's Weekly* noted, could anchor off Coney Island and
bomb Madison Square. And when a Spanish cruiser paid a New York courtesy call,
Pulitzer's *World* warned of treachery, claiming "her shells will explode on the Harlem
River and in the suburbs of Brooklyn." But in the late 1880s and early 1890s, two
New York financiers—secretaries of the navy in successive administrations, one
Democrat, one Republican—had overseen the creation of a powerful American fleet
of armored steel battleships, like the *Maine*, launched from the Brooklyn Navy Yard
in 1889. In 1897 this new naval apparatus was to some degree under the control of
Assistant Secretary of the Navy Theodore Roosevelt. And when Brooklyn's *Maine*
exploded in Havana's harbor—almost certainly an accident—jingoes like Roosevelt
seized on it as a casus belli, and the war came.

Hostilities created a crisis for New York's Spanish community. A Junta
Patriótica Española had been established in New York to collect funds for the Spanish
navy, a practice that now seemed treasonous to some, especially when rumors flew

that the steamers of the Compañia Trasatlántica were being armed as cruisers. The Cuyás brothers fled, accused of being spies. Spanish authorities evacuated some prominent residents. But anti-Spanish hysteria hadn't time to build. Within weeks the war was over, both Cuba and Puerto Rico taken.

New Yorkers went wild over America's emergence as an imperial power, with Gotham its de facto capital. The city held a colossal celebration for returning heroes like Admiral Dewey; the artistic community collaborated in creating a mammoth triumphal arch (out of lath and plaster) at Madison Square. New York had come a long, long way from the colonial days when it cowered before the Spanish empire.

In 1898 Rough Rider Roosevelt stumped for the governorship as a war hero, won, served two years, signed on as McKinley's running mate in the successful 1900 campaign, and when McKinley was assassinated the following year, assumed the office. The man whose political fortune had been accumulated in Latin America would focus much of his attention there as president.

NEW EMPIRE (1898–1929)[11]

Victory triggered a race southward by New York investors, somewhat akin to the Oklahoma land rush. It was spurred on by the great merger movement of 1898–1904, which created scores of gigantic new corporations (General Electric, U.S. Steel), most headquartered in New York, most able to raise immense amounts of capital on Wall Street for expansion. A principal investment target was Cuba, now a de facto American protectorate, conveniently being run by Elihu Root, who as newly appointed secretary of war (1899) was overseeing the occupation.

The Domino Sugar sign as seen from the FDR Drive, New York. Photographer unknown. Copyright 2003 The New York Times Company.

In 2004 what was once the world's largest sugar refinery was shut down and sold to developers. The fate of the building, located in Williamsburg, Brooklyn, and its neon sign—reminders of Gotham's three-hundred-year-long sugar-based Caribbean connection—remains under discussion, with preservation a possibility.

The ruins of the old Hotel New York, Havana, 2009. Photograph by Mike Wallace.

Quickest off the mark was Root's longtime client, the Havemeyers' American Sugar Refining Company, which had pioneered the new corporate form; after 1900 it rebranded itself as Domino Sugar, trying to shed its plutocratic image. Together with new rivals like the National Sugar Refining Company (headquartered at 29 Front Street), it began buying up land on the war-devastated island from ruined small planters, sometimes for one twentieth of its value, then transformed the production process itself, erecting state-of-the-art million-dollar mills. New York capital also poured into building the infrastructure—notably railroads and the port—needed to move their product to market.

In the 1920s Prohibition avoidance generated another kind of migration southward. Bars that had been shuttered in Gotham reopened in Havana, as did distilleries

and breweries. To house a flood of thirsty tourists, paced by the glamorous New York social set (Jimmy Walker, Irving Berlin, Gloria Vanderbilt), hotels sprouted—including the Hotel Plaza (modeled on its New York namesake), the Hotel Brooklyn, the Hotel Manhattan, and the Hotel New York, culminating with the Hotel Nacional, designed by New York's premier architectural firm, McKim, Mead & White.

By 1925 American investments in Cuba had reached $1.3 billion, with funds increasingly supplied by New York banks like the House of Morgan, Chase National, J. W. Seligman, and James Stillman's National City Bank.

So it went in Puerto Rico, where, immediately after the invasion, with the legal system restructured to provide security to U.S. investors and tariffs removed on sugar exports to the U.S., New York businesses rushed into banking, communication, transportation, construction, utilities, tobacco growing, cigar manufacture, and, of course, sugar production, which was reorganized and centralized until by the mid-twenties four New York corporations were producing 42 percent of the island's output. The volume of that output had been boosted phenomenally, as it had been in Cuba, and in the Dominican Republic, too, where military occupation in 1916–24 facilitated massive investment in plantation development.

Wall Street investment in Latin America went far beyond the Caribbean and sugar. Much of it was sluiced into securing the raw materials needed by the industrialization under way in the United States.

The electrification of New York, followed by that of cities across the country, created a tremendous demand for copper. A lot was extracted in Arizona—formerly part of Mexico—but much was dug up in Mexico itself after the Guggenheims, who

Cerro de Pasco Copper Corporation stock certificate, ca. 1930. Courtesy of Wendell Wilson, Mineralogical Record Museum of Art.

had smelters there, got into mining to provide themselves with local product and into railroads to carry it; by 1910 the Guggenheims' investments made them the country's largest privately held enterprise. Phelps, Dodge was another pacesetter. Founded in 1834 by New York merchant William Earl Dodge and his father-in-law, Anson Greene Phelps, the firm initially imported tin plate into Brooklyn, then branched out into mining investments in Arizona, then (in 1895) bought the Moctezuma Copper Company in northeastern Sonora, which by 1912 accounted for well over half of Mexico's output. Copper also drew New York capital down to Chile—the Guggenheims bought major mines there after 1909, including the Chuquicamata, the world's largest open pit operation—and to Peru, too. One James Ben Ali Haggin—who owned mines out West and lived in Fifth Avenue splendor—went into partnership with J. P. Morgan, Henry Clay Frick, and Darius Ogden Mills to form the Cerro de Pasco Corporation, headquartered on Broad Street, which invested in Peruvian mining; by the end of the twenties it controlled over 80 percent of the business.

In oil, as well, New Yorkers were major players. In Mexico, the Rockefellers' Standard Oil of New Jersey company began buying up independent outfits in 1912, and by 1920 it was the country's second-largest producer; in 1913, through a subsidiary, it purchased the most important oil fields in Peru; and in 1928, after a 1922 gusher at Lake Maracaibo had demonstrated Venezuela's immense deposits, it acquired Creole Petroleum.

Transportation continued to command New Yorkers' attention. Railroads still drew developers—former Gotham mayor and ironmaster Abram S. Hewitt and a dozen other monied New Yorkers (including a descendent of Peter Stuyvesant) won

Nicaraguan stamp, 1900.

William Nelson Cromwell of the law firm Sullivan and Cromwell, aiming to persuade Congress to switch the proposed canal route from Nicaragua to Panama, sent each member one of these stamps, made in New York by the American Bank Note Company. Cromwell used the stamp to imply that the Nicaraguan course was laden with volcanoes. In fact, the nearest volcano was dormant and 100 miles from the route. But the ploy helped turn the tide.

a contract from the Ecuadorian government to build a line from Guayaquil to Quito. But the biggest postwar goal was to construct a canal across Central America, something devoutly desired by New Yorkers since the days of Commodore Vanderbilt and now more important than ever if the city was to develop two-ocean commerce.

A French company had tried to dig across Panama, a province of Colombia, but failed in 1889. A successor company inherited the right-of-way, which it hoped to sell to the U.S. But Congress was set on a Nicaraguan route. So the new French concern hired William Nelson Cromwell, founder of the corporate law megafirm Sullivan and Cromwell, to do the lobbying. In 1902 Cromwell helped engineer a Congressional change of position, partly by handing out substantial sums to key politicians, and partly by planting false rumors that the Nicaraguan route was strewn with live volcanoes. Cromwell submitted his lobbying bill of $800,000, prematurely as it turned out, because in 1903 Colombia balked at closing the Panama route deal. Cromwell (and J. P. Morgan) then backed an autonomous independence bid by Panamanian rebels. So did President Roosevelt, who sent warships to block any Colombian move to suppress it. The Panama Canal—built between 1904 and 1914, chiefly by imported West Indians (and several thousand Spaniards, mostly Galicians)—ushered in an enormous expansion of transoceanic trade, much of which would stream into Gotham's harbor.

In the 1920s, as New York businessmen pushed deeper into South America, steamship lines added newer and faster vessels, cutting travel time to Rio to thirteen days, to Buenos Aires seventeen. But this was nowhere near fast enough for Gotham's merchants and bankers, who cried out for air service. W. R. Grace tried to start its own airline down the continent's west coast but found itself checked by a youthful New York entrepreneur, Juan Trippe, who had established Pan American Airways in 1927 and sewn up landing rights in key countries, notably Panama. The two sides joined forces, won key government contracts, and brought in assorted Vanderbilts, Rockefellers, Whitneys, and Lehmans in a grand conglomerate of metropolitan capital. In 1929 Trippe, working out of headquarters on Forty-second Street, had Charles Lindbergh pilot a twin-engine Sikorsky flying boat down to Panama, via Nicaragua, in a record-breaking three and a half days. Soon he launched a seven-day service from New York to Buenos Aires, hop-stopping the seven thousand miles at thirty harbors on the way. By the 1930s, with twenty thousand miles of routes in twenty Latin American countries, Pan Am was the world's biggest airline.

Meanwhile, shortly after the 1898 war, Sosthenes Behn, a sugar broker in Puerto Rico, had taken over the primitive Puerto Rican Telephone Company and modernized it; then moved on to Cuba and done the same; then got ATT to lay a cable connecting the two islands; then tackled Spain and Mexico. Behn went on to form a multinational corporation, International Telephone and Telegraph (ITT), which he ran out of space leased on Broad Street. In 1927 ITT bought a 25 percent stake in

Charles Lindbergh and Juan Trippe, ca. 1929. Photographer unknown. Pan American World Airways, Inc. Records, Special Collections, Otto G. Richter Library, University of Miami.

Below: Advertisements for Pan American Airways, ca. 1930. "Days of Tropic Sun" (left) and "The World's Greatest Air Transportation System" (right), from Claude Hudspeth, *Vintage Pan Am*, vol. 1. Copyright © Vintage Pan Am.

DAYS of TROPIC SUN
Quicker travel for short vacations in
HAVANA or NASSAU

NEW YORK to Havana in 39 hours. Panama to Chicago in five days less than by previously available means of transport. New York to Panama in four days.

These are typical of the time savings achieved by travelers who use the Pan American way of travel to and from 21 countries in Central and South America . . . Complete change of scene and climate managed with ease as well as speed.

Famous south-bound trains carry you from your home city to Miami or Brownsville, Texas. Pan American Airliners carry you swiftly southward to your destination in Latin America. Through tickets and reservations, from your nearest rail center to your port of arrival, simplify this service that gives you added days or weeks for sightseeing or business, and brings you home refreshed and rested in the time required for an ordinary outing. Lands difficult of access for centuries are now reached without difficulty or hardship.

Pan American is the most extensive air transport system in the world, flying an average of 88,522 miles weekly along 12,000 miles of airways. Each day 28 to 30 airliners are in scheduled flight simultaneously. Each airliner carries a crew of four, consisting of a steward, radio operator, and two pilots, each with a *minimum of 2,000 hours flying experience*.

For through tickets, reservations, and information, apply to railway ticket offices, leading travel bureaus.

Through Service with These Famous Trains

Direct connections with Pan American Airliners at Miami

from NEW YORK—
39 hours to Havana and Nassau (direct connections from Boston):
Havana Special . . Lv. 6:50 p.m.
Everglades . . . Lv. 10:20 p.m.
Florida Special . . Lv. 8:35 p.m.

from BOSTON—
43 hours to Havana and Nassau:
Everglades . . . Lv. 4:30 p.m.

from CHICAGO—
(44 hours to Havana; 45 to Nassau) and principal cities of Michigan and Ohio:
Dixie Limited . . Lv. 2:00 p.m.
Floridan . . . . Lv. 3:45 p.m.
Flamingo . . . Lv. 11:35 a.m.

from ST. LOUIS—
40 hours to Havana and Nassau:
Dixie Limited . . Lv. 4:22 p.m.
Floridan . . . . Lv. 6:20 p.m.
Connecting at Brownsville for Mexico City—Daily

from NEW YORK—
68 hours 30 minutes to Mexico City:
The American—Penn. R. R.
Crescent Ltd.—Southern Ry.

from CHICAGO—
51 hours to Mexico City:
La Salle . . . Lv. 11:25 a.m.
Daylight Special Lv. 11:45 a.m.

from ST. LOUIS—
44 hours to Mexico City:
Sunshine Special, Lv. 6:30 p.m.
Seven Airliners daily from Havana—one daily from Nassau—for home bound travelers.

PAN AMERICAN AIRWAYS, Inc., 122 East 42nd St., New York City

PAN AMERICAN AIRWAYS

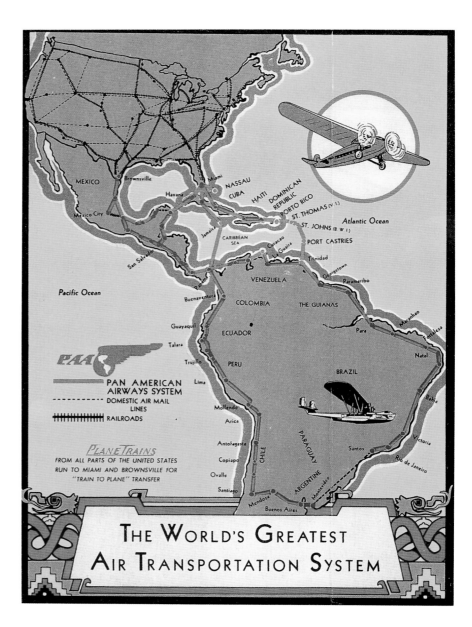

PAA
PAN AMERICAN AIRWAYS SYSTEM
--------- DOMESTIC AIR MAIL LINES
+++++++ RAILROADS

PlaneTrains
FROM ALL PARTS OF THE UNITED STATES RUN TO MIAMI AND BROWNSVILLE FOR "TRAIN TO PLANE" TRANSFER

THE WORLD'S GREATEST AIR TRANSPORTATION SYSTEM

Scrymser's All America, and in 1928 bought New Yorker Clarence MacKay's Postal Telegraph and Cable Corporation, which had established working connections with All America back in 1922; the whole ensemble was housed in a 1928 skyscraper at 67 Broad Street.

Financing for all these initiatives was provided either by the corporations themselves raising capital on Wall Street's industrial securities markets or, increasingly, by Gotham-based banks that now advanced into Central and South America—territories long the domain of European financiers—to service their U.S. industrial and mercantile clients. When World War I broke out and the English and Germans were occupied elsewhere, Gotham's financiers moved to fill the breach. First National City Bank opened its first Latin American operation in Argentina in 1914; five years later it boasted forty-two branches. Wall Street investment bankers also floated billions worth of bonds issued by Brazilian, Peruvian, Cuban, Chilean, and other governments; by decade's end New York had replaced London as Latin America's primary source of capital.

New York's position at the center of this web of commercial and financial relationships was underscored when, in 1912, the Pan-American Society was created in Gotham. Led by, among others, J. P. Morgan and Elihu Root, now a senator and a pillar of the New York establishment, it was aimed at fostering inter-American relations by entertaining distinguished Latin Americans when they came to town. The Pan-American Society drew hundreds of distinguished New Yorkers from banks, bond houses, industrial organizations, and steamship lines, businessmen who were keen to cement the city's and country's standing in Latin America. By 1929 the society numbered over one thousand; and eminent South Americans—diplomats, businessmen, journalists, intellectuals—unless they had official business with an embassy in Washington, beelined for Gotham because, as the *Times* reported that year in "New York A Centre of Pan-American Life," it was the place from which "most of the activities pertaining to the neighboring continent radiate," and a place where visitors could comfortably mingle with New Yorkers of a Latin American background.

There did indeed develop an admiration for New York (and the U.S.) in Latin America, particularly among modernizing elites, who often hailed Gotham as a model. In the early 1900s when Buenos Aires planners envisioned their city's future, it looked like New York, not Paris; in the 1920s Lima imported everything from Gotham dress designers to architects and engineers, who erected (very) miniature versions of New York skyscrapers to house the New York corporations; and in Chile, Santiago's financial district was located on Calle Nueva York.

But New York, or more precisely Wall Street, also aroused terrific resentments. The massive transformations proposed or achieved in the economies and societies and cultures of one country after another repeatedly provoked resistance—from labor, from indigenous cultures, from peasants and small businessmen, from local regimes

Calle Nueva York, Santiago, Chile, 2007.
Photograph by Mike Wallace.

Since the 1910s Santiago's financial district—Chile's Wall Street—has been located on Calle Nueva York.

or would-be regimes—opposition that was often overcome, at least in the short run, by the use of force, provided by complicit local governments or the U.S. Marines. In addition, the extension of credit on such a massive scale to fragile states and fluctuating economies repeatedly engendered financial crises, and when local regimes proved unable or unwilling to come up with their interest payments, bankers increasingly called on Washington and the U.S. Navy to serve as debt collectors. The new American empire could not be run solely out of New York; it would need one foot in Gotham, the other in D.C.

Theodore Roosevelt—who himself had a foot in each city—set the pace, both in the Panama Canal endeavor and immediately afterwards, when he sent the Navy to the Dominican Republic in 1904. The intervention was on behalf of the New York-based Santo Domingo Improvement Company (SDIC), a collection of Wall Street crony capitalists, who in collusion with Dominican dictator Ulises Heureaux had milked the treasury and run up huge debts to Europeans. After Heureaux was assassinated in 1899, the economy and polity tumbled into chaos, the SDIC was expelled, and Europeans (notably the Germans) threatened at gunpoint to collect what they were owed. Roosevelt sent in the Caribbean Squadron, arranged for new loans from deep-pocketed New York banks to pay off old debt, took control of the Dominican customs house and channeled its revenues to creditors, and imposed financial oversight (barring tax increases or government spending without a U.S. okay). This model was applied again in 1909 in Nicaragua, where troops ousted an unamenable dictator, and the U.S. arranged a loan from Brown Brothers and J. & W. Seligman, secured by control of the National Bank of Nicaragua (the country's currency would henceforth be countersigned by a Brown Brothers representative). But when dollar diplomacy failed to produce the desired "stability," the fallback position was force, and the Dominican Republic was occupied during 1916–24. Washington had enlisted to ride shotgun on Wall Street's stagecoach, and the Marines splashed ashore in Latin America repeatedly in these decades.

LITTLE SPAIN (1900–29) [12]

In the decades after 1898, though Spain had lost its imperial foothold in the hemi-sphere, its presence in New York increased significantly and the Spanish community acquired a substantial working class. After 1901 the Spanish Line offered direct service straight to South Street's Pier 8, at the foot of James Street, and immigration from Spain picked up steam, though the influx remained tiny in comparison to the torrent arriving from other parts of Europe. The number disembarking surged during the First World War, when sailors and stokers (especially from coastal Asturias and Galicia) were attracted to Gotham by its boom in shipping, and the war-enhanced industrial and commercial sectors provided jobs for laborers, tobacco workers, clerks, and accountants. By 1920 there were 14,659 Spanish-born residents in New York. By 1930 there were 22,501—most of whom arrived before 1924, when the Johnson-Reed Act, aimed at restricting incoming Jews and Italians, had a drastic impact on Spaniards as well by setting an *annual* quota of 131.

A major destination for newcomers was Little Spain, an Hispanic neighborhood that crystallized around 1900 in the northwest corner of Greenwich Village, near the Hudson River docks. Fourteenth Street was its spinal thoroughfare. Here, in 1902, Archbishop Corrigan opened Our Lady of Guadalupe Church in a row house at 229 West Fourteenth Street, between Seventh and Eighth avenues, and established a "national" parish with the same name; it was the first one dedicated to serving Spanish-speaking Catholics of the Archdiocese. (Protestants quickly moved to counter this initiative: In 1912 the New York City Mission Society organized the First Spanish Evangelical Church.) Other institutions now arrived on the street, including the Casa María (a Spanish settlement house run by the Servants of Mary), the Spanish Benevolent Society, St. Raphael's Spanish Immigrant Society, and the Spanish American Workers Alliance. Soon the surrounding blocks were home to a slew of Spanish grocery stores, barbershops, taverns, restaurants, bodegas (grocery stores), and boardinghouses (even a Hotel Español). In the 1920s this community migrated farther north, into Chelsea, up to roughly Twenty-sixth Street. Nevertheless, the Fourteenth Street institutions continued to serve the dispersing population, and new ones continued to open, like Casa Moneo (1929), whose owners sold goods imported from Spain.

Many Spaniards organized themselves around region of origin (as had the Italians, Jews, and Irish). A Basque community took root around Cherry and Water streets, at the foot of the Brooklyn Bridge, near the Spanish Line's dock; it featured a Basque hotel, grocery stores, and restaurants. For major religious ceremonies, like weddings, residents had to travel to Our Lady of Guadalupe, the only place a Basque priest was available. In 1913 the Basques formed the Centro Vasco-Americano Sociedad de Beneficiencia y Recreo, a mutual benefit and charity organization.

Soon New York included a Casa Galicia, Centro Andaluz, Centro Aragonés, Centro Asturiano, Centro Balear, Centre Nacionalista Català, and Círculo Valenciano, along with a growing number of Spanish boardinghouses, restaurants, and grocery stores catering to regional tastes.

Efforts were made to develop pan-Hispanic institutions as well. In 1914, in hopes of consolidating the myriad societies into one strong federation, a Unión Benéfica Española was established. It grew from an initial 250 members to 2,200 in 1920, and in 1924 opened a headquarters on Fourteenth Street, although it never supplanted the regional associations. In 1929 the Hispanic Naturopath Society, whose members embraced nature and vegetarianism, acquired land on Staten Island's southern shore and set up Spanish Camp, where they vacationed in the summer, living in tents (later bungalows). An "Official Spanish Chamber of Commerce" opened in 1910, and in 1917 announced grand plans to build a home for itself—La Casa de España—that also would house Spanish banks, an exposition of Spanish produce, Spain's consulate, and the Spanish Club, among other Iberian-inflected institutions; the enterprise fell through, but the effort was emblematic of growing ambitions. And the community finally received statuary recognition in a strategic public place when in 1905 Cass Gilbert, architect of the Customs House at Bowling Green, selected Queen Isabella to represent Spain on the facade's nod to "Seafaring Nations."

The community was now large enough to support its own weekly newspaper, *La Prensa*, founded in 1913 by Rafael Viera, a Spaniard. The magazine *El Gráfico: Revista mensual illustrada de literatura, arte, ciencias, política, viajes, modas, etc.* appeared in 1916. And a bookstore arrived (La Librería de los Latinos), at 118 East Twenty-eighth Street, founded by José Juan Tablada, a Mexican poet who moved to New York in 1914.

A new round of literary luminaries began to visit, and to take New York as a subject. The great Nicaraguan poet Rubén Darío came to New York in 1914, when he penned *La Gran Cosmópolis* (he had been here in 1893, when he was hailed by Martí as "¡Hijo!" ["Son!"] and visited Niagara Falls, partly in homage to Heredia's verses). Two years later, in 1916, the Andalusian Nobel Prize–winner-to-be Juan Ramón Jiménez came to Gotham to court and marry Zenobia Camprubí, sister of the owner of *La Prensa*; his *Diario de un poeta recién casado* (Diary of a Newlywed Poet), which he began writing in Gotham, includes striking images of the cityscape. Federico García Lorca visited the city in 1929–30, ostensibly to study English at Columbia University. He reacted violently against what he saw as an inhuman and soulless metropolis—especially detesting Wall Street, where "rivers of gold arrived from all parts of the earth, and with it death." His powerful posthumous collection, *Poet in New York*, spared only Harlem ("Oda al Rey de Harlem") his denunciations.

No one was more fervent in promoting Spanish culture than Archer Milton

Our Lady of Guadalupe Church, ca. 2006.
Photograph by David Dunlap. University Archives,
Columbia University in the City of New York.

Nuestra Señora de la Guadalupe, founded in 1902
to serve the Spanish-speaking population of New
York, was created in an existing row house (the
former home of restaurateur Charles Delmonico) at
229 West Fourteenth Street. The Spanish Baroque
facade was added in 1921. By the early 2000s,
the small church could no longer accommodate the
growing Mexican population, and in 2003 the congregation moved to nearby St. Bernard's Church at
328 West Fourteenth Street, which was renamed
Our Lady of Guadalupe at St. Bernard's.

Queen Isabella statue, U.S. Custom House, New
York. Photograph by Andrew Dolkart.

Queen Isabella, sculpted by François and Mary
Lawrence Tonetti for Cass Gilbert's Custom House
(now the National Museum of the American Indian),
rests her right hand on a globe displaying the New
World.

Huntington, who founded the Hispanic Society of America (HSA) in 1904. Uninter-
ested in taking over his stepfather Collis Huntington's railroad business, he had discovered his true calling when he first encountered Hispanic culture on a visit to Mexico
City in 1889 (where the family dined in Chapultepec Castle with Huntington-père's
business associate Porfirio Díaz, for whom he was building the Mexican International
Railroad). Archer now set out with "feverish eagerness" to collect Hispanica and
establish a museum and library. Given his inherited fortune, one of the country's largest, he was able to amass the greatest such collection outside Spain. His HSA, which
opened in 1908 at 155th Street and Broadway, also brought major Spanish artists to
the city. In February 1909 Huntington mounted an exhibition of Valencian painter
Joaquín Sorolla's work, his first in the United States. It was a spectacular success,
drawing 160,000 uptown in its first four weeks; one art dealer wrote: "Spain sank low
in our defeat of her, she has replied with the lightnings of art."

Huntington involved himself in other metropolitan Hispanic affairs. He underwrote the building—a block from his society—of Nuestra Señora de la Esperanza, a
church that anchored the city's second Hispanic parish, established in 1912 at the
suggestion of the wife of a former Spanish consul general. Huntington also supported
the teaching of Spanish in the schools, as did Federico de Onís, a philologist at the
University of Salamanca who, in 1916, was recruited to set up a department of
Hispanic Studies at Columbia University. The surge of interest in studying Spanish
was in part a function of the World War I-era rejection of the German language

Joaquín Sorolla y Bastida (1863–1923). *Vision of Spain: Castilla*, 1913. Oil on canvas. 138⅝ x 548⅝ in. (351.5 x 1393.5 cm). Hispanic Society of America, New York (A1815).

as subversive. When the Board of Education banned German from the city's high schools, Spanish became the primary substitute. In addition, because trade with Latin America had boomed during wartime while that with Europe had diminished, Spanish (as de Onís noted) seemed the more useful career choice, and by 1924 there were forty thousand students taking it in public schools. University studies boomed, too; by 1929 New York University had over a thousand registered for Spanish classes, up from less than a hundred a decade earlier. And at Columbia another thousand undergraduates were enrolled, with hundreds more working under de Onís researching Hispanic life and literature, and listening to visiting lecturers from Spain and Spanish America.

The boom in Spanish language and cultural studies was part of a larger phenomenon. Spain, hoping to recoup the position at the apex of the Spanish-speaking world it had lost in 1898—universally known in Iberia as "El Desastre"—was once again promoting the notion of Hispanidad that had been floated in the 1870s. Writers, philosophers, journalists, and organizations like the Madrid-based Unión Ibero-Americana argued that the peoples of Spain and Latin America together constituted a common *raza*, held together by a shared culture, heritage, and purity of spirit that sharply distinguished their civilization from that of the grubby, materialistic Anglo-Saxon civilization, of which the United States was currently the leading avatar. The

empire per se was no more, but there was hope that a reconciliation between Spain and its former colonies could be established, and a pan-Hispanicism could be developed that would counter the pan-Americanism emanating from New York. Promoting Spain's language and culture was part of this initiative.

Many in Latin America rejected this approach, believing Spain's legacy in the hemisphere on balance a disastrous one, and were open to embracing Yankee modernity. Others, however, saw post-1898 U.S. expansion as signaling the rise of a new imperialism—cultural, economic, and political—and were attracted by the notion of reestablishing links to Spain via an affirmation of Hispanidad. One way to do so was to jointly celebrate their Hispanicity on an annual basis. New York's Cervantes Day had sought to do this in the 1870s, and New York's Columbus Day—since 1909 an official holiday at the urging of the Italian community—provided a working model. In 1913 the Unión Ibero-Americana started a campaign to create a Día de la Raza, to be held throughout the Spanish-speaking world on October 12, in effect recasting the meaning of Columbus Day. One of the first places to take up the practice was Gotham, when in 1917 the New York consular representatives of Spain and all Spanish American nations marked the Día with a banquet on behalf of the Unión Benéfica Española. Even more grandly, plans were unveiled in 1927 to establish a Casa de las Españas, a trade and consular center for all Spanish-speaking countries that would include facilities to celebrate their national cultures. It won the backing of King Alfonso of Spain and many Latin American government leaders, but the real estate deal fell through.

EL BARRIO (1900-29)[13]

The surge in immigration to Gotham from Spain was trumped by the influx from its former empire. The economic transformations wrought throughout Latin America by Wall Street–backed initiatives dislodged many small farmers from the land; some relocated to local cities, others migrated from the periphery of America's new empire to its center. By 1920 Gotham residents from Mexico numbered 2,572, from Central and South America 7,777, and from Cuba and the West Indies 9,722, but the big demographic development involved Puerto Rico. In 1917, over the unanimous objection of the Puerto Rican House of Delegates, the Jones Act granted the island's residents U.S. citizenship but left the island's colonial status largely intact. By 1920 there were 7,364 Puerto Ricans in New York, and over the ensuing decade, passengers disembarking from New York and Porto Rico Steamship vessels helped drive the 1930 total to 44,908. Puerto Ricans thus became the biggest Spanish-speaking group in the city, followed by Spain's 22,501, Cuba and the West Indies' 19,774, Central and South America's 18,748, and Mexico's 4,292.

A booming economy awaited the newcomers. Though the old standby of cigar manufacturing was being eroded by the switchover to mechanized production of cigarettes, labor was needed in many other areas, thanks to the immigration restrictions that had throttled the inflow of Europeans. Puerto Ricans entered factory work (especially garment manufacture) and took jobs on the waterfront, in hotels and restaurants, in domestic service and laundries, and in white-collar positions as bookkeepers and cashiers (especially Puerto Rican women who had learned English in island schools).

Some settled down wherever work was. When Greenpoint's American Manufacturing Company, which made rope from Philippine hemp, recruited hundreds of migrants directly from Puerto Rico, a small community of rooming houses, bodegas, and restaurants sprang up to service the factory. Others were drawn to established Hispanic areas: near the Manhattan foot of the Brooklyn Bridge; around the Lower East Side (then emptying out as Jews moved to Brooklyn and the Bronx); and in Brooklyn around the Navy Yard, along the waterfront (down Columbia Street through Red Hook all the way to the Erie Basin), and inland, toward the Gowanus Canal, where they coexisted with Italians.

But the major destination for working-class Puerto Ricans and other Latins was Harlem—especially the blocks fanned out around the northeast corner of Central Park—where they intermixed with Italians, Jews, Irish, and African Americans. These blue-collar workers in turn supported a growing entrepreneurial and profes-

sional class: The 1923 *Guía Hispana* listed some 275 businesses and 150 profession-als. By the late 1920s the area boasted cafés and restaurants serving distinctive Puerto Rican specialties and some two hundred bodegas. The Jewish proprietors of stalls in the open-air market on upper Park Avenue began to sell Caribbean foods and spices, and slowly Puerto Ricans began to take over these stands. Botanicas (selling herbs and religious articles), boardinghouses, bakers, and barbershops flourished as well, with the last giving birth to the *bolita*, known as the "numbers" by black West Indians, who were among the early patrons.

This expansion touched off a backlash. Prior inhabitants—irritated at the encroachment of Spanish-speakers who were racially mixed to boot, and dismayed at the competition for jobs and resources—occasionally harassed the newcomers. In July 1926, during a heat wave, a riot broke out between older and newer residents. Such tensions hastened the formation of mutual defense and mutual aid societies, notably the Porto Rican Brotherhood (1923) and La Liga Puertorriqueña e Hispana (1926). On the other hand, the Harlem Renaissance was under way, and links were estab-lished—political and cultural—between African American and Afro-Caribbean commu-nities. There was growing interest among Cubans and Puerto Ricans in Garveyism and pan-Africanism, and much political attention was focused on affairs in their homelands. But mainstream political clubs also were established, like the Club Demo-crático de Brooklyn, and activist workers could join labor, anarchist, or socialist asso-ciations like La Resistencia or the Círculo de Tabaqueros.

Local newsstands offered *La Prensa*—brought out on a daily basis after 1918—along with working-class journals like *Cultura Proletaria* or *Gráfico*, a magazine published in 1927–31 by Bernardo Vega, which he subtitled "A Weekly Defender of the Hispanic Race." Vega, a *tabaquero*, a trade union and socialist militant, a community activist (he helped found La Liga), and a proponent of Puerto Rican independence, was also a local chronicler whose *Memoirs* are an indispensable guide to El Barrio's first decades.

From 1929, librarian Pura Belpré made the New York Public Library branch at 115th Street a center for the Spanish-speaking community. Schools routinely placed new arrivals one or two years behind their grade level on the island, or into classes for "retarded" children and slow learners. The colonia fought this and proposed bilingual education, an idea whose time had not yet come.

Local theaters offered Spanish-language films (Mexican and Argentinian) and Spanish vaudeville shows. A thriving theater movement emerged, with troupes of Puerto Rican players and performers of *bufos cubanos* (musical comedies) attracting wide followings, especially as they often advocated Puerto Rican independence. Professional touring zarzuela companies from Spain, Mexico, and Cuba included New York on their performance circuit, and there were local zarzuela groups like Manuel Noriega's troupe, Compañía Dramática Española.

The growth of these various Hispanic communities provided a market for authentic Latin music and provided the immigrant composers to produce it. Many

of them developed fruitful connections with black musicians and the New York music industry. Rafael Hernández moved to New York after the war, played in Broadway pit bands and jazz orchestras, and collaborated with black ragtime and jazz greats. In 1927 his sister Victoria opened the first Puerto Rican–owned record store (on Madison Avenue between 113th and 114th streets), which became a place where Latin musicians could get jobs and recording dates. It was also where in 1929 Rafael composed the song "Lamento Borincano," about the travails of a Puerto Rican *jíbaro* (subsistence farmer); recorded in 1930 by RCA Victor, it became an immigrant (and unofficial national) anthem.

Since the turn of the century, the metropolitan-area recording industry—notably the Columbia Phonograph, Victor Talking Machine, and Edison National Phonograph companies—had been sending talent scouts and recording engineers on expeditions to the Spanish-speaking south: first to Mexico in 1904; by 1910 to Havana, Buenos Aires, and San Juan; and by 1915 to virtually all of Latin America. As in the U.S., the goal was to sell record players, which necessitated producing records for people to play. An extractive industry of a sort, the studios would search out local musicians, record them in makeshift studios in their home countries (which had no facilities of their own), press the records back in New York or New Jersey (selecting or even altering the music to fit presumed *norteño* tastes), then sell the refined product back south, having in the process built up yet another Gotham-based line of business. In the late 1920s, with the development of a resident community of music-makers, Columbia and Victor turned to recording this material, which was then exported southward, or sold locally through outlets like Victoria Hernández's shop. Finally, Latin American artists from Cuba, Mexico, and Argentina began coming to Gotham to record, making the city the point of confluence for musicians it had long been for writers and political exiles.

The new music spread outside the barrio and beyond Spanish-language radio programming (initiated by WNYC in 1924) into mainstream cultural channels. During Prohibition, Havana became a favorite escape for the liquor-deprived, as noted in the 1920 Irving Berlin ditty "I'll See You in Cuba" (whose refrain asked: "Since Prohibition, tell me, pal, have you been / A very frightened little feller?" and answered: "Why don't you do your drinking like a Cuban / Instead of hiding in a cellar?"). Nightclub patrons returned home with a taste for Cuban music, and Tin Pan Alley took notice. New York publishers began bringing out sheet music of Cuban Habanera songs, like those of Cuban composer Ernesto Lecuona ("Siboney," "Say Si Si"), and Gotham songsters brought out their own compositions, like George Gershwin's "Argentina" and Richard Rodgers's "Havana."

Latin American literature—all but unknown in the U.S.—got an airing, too, when Waldo Frank, resident expert on Spain, turned his attention southward. Frank had been a pre–World War I Greenwich Village bohemian who rejected U.S. materialism and puritanism and sought a cultural revolution, only to have his hopes dashed by the postwar return to "normalcy" and Babbitry. But in the 1920s, when his peers went to Paris, Frank went to Spain, where he found a picturesque people, rooted in the land and moored in tradition. In the New York Hispanophile tradition of Bryant, Irving, and Chase, he reported in *Virgin Spain: Scenes from the Spiritual Drama of a Great People* (1926) that the country's culture seemed to offer an antidote to civilization. Frank visited Cuba in 1926 with his protégé Hart Crane, and in 1929 spent six months traveling through Latin America, then published his responses in *The Re-discovery of America* (1929) and *America Hispana: South of Us* (1930). Frank again hailed Latin culture as a spiritual antidote to the hyper-materialist U.S.—very much in the mode of Hispanista sentiment—even as he urged that there were lessons Latin America could learn from the North. He proposed a hemispheric partnership, a cooperative and egalitarian variant of pan-Americanism, in which two "half-worlds" could become an organic whole that combined the best of each.

Audiences in the south enthusiastically received this somewhat mystical vision, in part because Frank was capable of critiquing U.S. culture, not simply purveying it. But Frank also worked in a more grounded way to help introduce each culture to the other, by translating figures like Whitman, Melville, and William Carlos Williams into Spanish, and arranging (with John Farrar in 1930) to translate and publish Spanish works in English. He also urged Argentine intellectual Victoria Ocampo to start a literary magazine that could bridge North and South America. Ocampo came to New York in 1930 to discuss the project—she was blown away by the city's energy and openness, finding it "the most extraordinary and intriguing spectacle that can be seen in our day"—and what evolved was *Sur* (South), the most prominent cultural review in Latin America; it would publish Mary McCarthy, e. e. cummings, and Marianne Moore, in translations by Borges and Bioy Casares. But if Frank had his pulse on Latin American dynamics, his view of Spain as quaint and static was about to take a beating.

DEPRESSION (1929–39)[14]

The global depression brought disaster to Latin American countries. World prices for their export commodities plummeted. They couldn't meet payments on their massive debts. Beginning with Bolivia in 1931, virtually every nation defaulted. New York investors retreated throughout the 1930s. The result was misery, protest, repression.

Puerto Rico was among the hardest hit. Export-oriented sugar and manufacturing sectors tumbled into crisis, and by 1935 the economy had virtually collapsed. Starvation was rampant. So were strikes and nationalist anti-Americanism, the latter led by Pedro Albizu Campos, whom Federal agents would arrest on charges of sedition. A protest march in Ponce on Palm Sunday 1937 was fired on by police, leaving 19 dead and 150 wounded. Many nationalists were hunted down and rounded up; others headed for exile in New York City.

Despite these and other disorders, the Big Stick policy of Teddy Roosevelt was laid aside for the Good Neighbor policy of Franklin Roosevelt. (It had actually first been tried out by Herbert Hoover's secretary of state, Henry Stimson, a New York corporate lawyer.) Adjudging three decades of armed intervention a failure, the U.S. pulled out troops where they remained and refused to send new ones, even in 1938 when Mexico nationalized U.S. oil companies.* On the other hand, the administration acquiesced in (or supported) the establishment of local dictators ("our" sons-of-bitches)—Batista, Somoza, Trujillo, et al.—who were prepared to act as surrogates. It was El Jefe time: by 1933 dictators ruled fifteen of the twenty republics.

In New York, times were hard in the barrios, where the Depression brought great suffering. Immigration slowed, as was usual during downturns. The numbers of Cubans, Mexicans, Spaniards, and Central and South Americans residing in New York in 1940 was very slightly higher than what they had been in 1930. Even the Puerto Rican population went only from 44,908 in 1930 to 61,463 in 1940, a significant increase—driven by desperation—but not the sizzling pace of the previous decade.

*Few of the critics were harsher than one of interventionism's most active agents, Major General Smedley Darlington Butler. The man in charge of various Marine occupations, Butler was disturbed by the Corps' usage as underwriter of New York bank profits. As early as 1912, when he was only a major, he had written his wife that "It is terrible that we should be losing so many men fighting the battles of these d–d spigs – all because Brown Bros. have some money down here." In 1935, now retired, he argued the point publicly, in books and lectures of Brechtian flair: "I spent 33 years and four months in active military service and during that period I spent most of my time as a high class muscle man for Big Business, for Wall Street and the bankers. In short, I was a racketeer, a gangster for capitalism. I helped make Mexico and especially Tampico safe for American oil interests in 1914. I helped make Haiti and Cuba a decent place for the National City Bank boys to collect revenues in. I helped in the raping of half a dozen Central American republics for the benefit of Wall Street. I helped purify Nicaragua for the International Banking House of Brown Brothers in 1902-1912. I brought light to the Dominican Republic for the American sugar interests in 1916. I helped make Honduras right for the American fruit companies in 1903. . . . Looking back on it, I might have given Al Capone a few hints."

Organizer Jesús Colón speaks to the Sociedad Fraternal Cervantes, the Spanish-language division of the International Workers Order, at the Park Palace, in October 1938.

Hispanic communities responded in a variety of ways to depression difficulties: self-help through mutual aid societies; nationalist politics (in August 1936, over ten thousand joined a march for Puerto Rican independence); local party politics (Oscar García Rivera became the first Puerto Rican elected to public office in New York in 1937); labor organizing (by 1935, the International Ladies Garment Workers had constituted a separate Spanish Department for the now 2,000 Puerto Rican dress trade operatives); and participation in New Deal and American Labor Party initiatives, with the latter led by Vito Marcantonio, East Harlem's leftist Congressman, who was a powerful protector of his constituents and a passionate supporter of Puerto Rico. There were even some entrepreneurial initiatives: In 1936 Prudencio Unanue began selling local Hispanics olives, oils, and sardines imported from Spain under the brand name Goya.

But during the Depression decade nothing so roiled Hispanic communities as the arrival of Jefe time in Spain, in 1936, when Franco set out to overthrow the Republic (making a hash of Waldo Frank's veneration of Spain's timeless and unchanging essence). From the opening days of the Spanish Civil War, the Irish Catholic hierarchy in New York City, already hypersensitized to violent anticlericalism by the Cristero War in Mexico, unequivocally supported Franco's insurrection. The general also had backers in the upper echelons of Gotham-based Spanish shipping and commercial circles, some of whom in early 1937 organized the Casa de España (House of Spain)—the first U.S. affiliate of the Falange Exterior—and set up headquarters in the Park Central Hotel, in an office dominated by a large painting of Franco.

Obrero ambulance, ca. 1938. Photographer unknown. University Archives, Columbia University in the City of New York.

East Harlem's Club Obrero Español—Puerto Rican IWO Lodge 4763—donated this ambulance to the anti-Fascist cause in Spain.

Gotham's barrios, on the other hand, were aboil with loyalist activities. Emigrant mutual aid societies backed the Republic. So did leftist Hispanic groups like the Grupo Antifascista del Bronx, the Frente Popular Español in Queens, and the Spanish-speaking lodges of the International Workers Order, confederated in the Sociedad Fraternal Cervantes, led by Jesús Colón (like Vega, one of the community's leading activists and chroniclers). During the conflict many of these associations banded together to form the Sociedades Hispanas Confederadas, which in 1937 established a newspaper, *Frente Popular,* that reported on pro-loyalist initiatives and also organized citywide rallies in Madison Square Garden. East Harlem's Spanish-language theater/cinemas (the Hispano, the Granada, and the Latino) screened documentaries about the fighting. Thousands of Spanish speakers took to the streets in the summer of 1936 to protest the bombardment of Madrid, where many had relatives. Defense of the Republic established a bond between many Spaniards and Latin Americans on very different grounds than those advocated by the Hispanidad movement (of which Franco became an advocate).

After Franco's victory, the community turned to raising money to aid the quarter-million loyalists who had fled to exile in France, where they languished in internment camps. Some managed to get to New York, but Gotham's most famous refugee was a painting. New York's Spanish Refugee Relief Campaign invited Picasso to send *Guernica* on a U.S. tour to raise funds for those in the camps. (The Spanish-born painter had gained a significant following in the U.S. when his work appeared in the New York Armory Show of 1913, after which the U.S. became his

single biggest market). When *Guernica* arrived in 1939, art dealer Sidney Janis and a committee that included Eleanor Roosevelt, Mayor La Guardia, and Ernest Hemingway arranged a showing at a Fifty-seventh Street gallery. After war broke out, it was agreed that the Museum of Modern Art would take charge of *Guernica* until the time was right for its return. And U.S. relations with Spain now entered the deep freeze.

If the art of Spain had a powerful impact in New York during the 1930s, so did that of Mexico. Painters who would constitute the New York Abstract Expressionist school, one of Gotham's foremost contributions to the world of art, paid close attention to work done in Gotham by a series of renowned visiting muralists. Jackson Pollock met José Clemente Orozco in 1930 when the latter was working on a mural for the New School. He watched in 1933 as Diego Rivera painted the mural for Rockefeller Center that was famously destroyed after it sprouted a head of Lenin (after which Rivera's commission was handed by Nelson Rockefeller to Spanish muralist Josep María Sert). In 1936 Pollock joined the Experimental Workshop that David Alfaro Siqueiros set up in a Fourteenth Street loft, where members poured Duco paint onto panels laid out on the floor, or used sticks to splatter and drip it on the surface below. He visited *Guernica* at the Valentine Gallery (as did Willem de Kooning and Arshile Gorky) and returned to see it repeatedly, taking in as well the 1940 Picasso retrospective at MoMA.

Pollock was fascinated, too, by the museum's colossal *Twenty Centuries of Mexican Art* exhibit that year, arranged by MoMA president Nelson Rockefeller and Mexican president Lázaro Cárdenas, in part as a cultural correlative of the Good

En la ciudad de Nueva York el día 21 del mes de Octubre de 1938, a las seis de la mañana, se suicidó la señora DOROTHY HALE tirándose desde una ventana muy alta del edificio Hampshire House. En su recuerdo [...] este retablo, habiéndolo ejecutado FRIDA KAHLO.

Carlos Gardel in New York, ca. 1933. Photographer unknown.

Carlos Gardel, the French-born Argentine, was already a star in the Spanish-speaking world when he arrived in Gotham in 1933, and the films he made in Queens were received enthusiastically throughout Latin America. (Most notable was *El Tango en Broadway* [The Tango on Broadway], a comedy about an Argentine playboy in New York.) Although Paramount wanted to make him a crossover star, Gardel proved unable to master English. He died in 1935 in a plane crash shortly after returning to Argentina, and was mourned by millions of people around the world, including New York.

Neighbor and pan-American initiatives. More than one thousand items filled the entire museum, ranging from pre-Columbian artifacts through Modernist pieces. The modern portion was curated by Mexican artist Miguel Covarrubias, a New York resident since 1923 and a well-known caricaturist for magazines like *Vanity Fair*, the *New Yorker*, *Fortune*, and *Vogue*, and book publishers like Alfred A. Knopf. Artists in the show included Frida Kahlo, Rufino Tamayo, and Orozco, who, just after the Nazis blitzkrieged France, painted in public a portable mural called *Dive Bomber and Tank*, with Pollock among the onlookers taking notes. The influence worked both ways, however: Tamayo, then living in Gotham, was profoundly affected by modernists he met in the city—Duchamp, de Kooning, Gorky, and Stuart Davis. "I went to New York to get to know what painting really was," he said. "We were blind here [in Mexico], and New York made me aware of all the trends and currents that existed in those years. It showed me what art was."

New York in the 1930s was also spellbound by Latin music. There had been a tango mania in the 1900s and 1910s, when the import from Buenos Aires had swept working-class dance halls and spread up the social ladder to Times Square cabarets. Semi-suppressed as indecent, the tango craze had reignited in 1934 when Carlos Gardel, the French-born Argentinian international star, came to New York to shoot movies at Paramount's studios in Astoria, Queens. Gardel was received with ecstatic enthusiasm in New York, and his films, like *El tango en Broadway* (featuring the song "Rubias [Blondes] de New York"), were a smash in Gotham and throughout Latin America.

Advertisement for Trans Caribbean World Airways, ca. 1940.

But the Depression decade belonged to the rumba (actually an Afro-Cuban *son*). As the *New York Times* observed in 1939, the rumba had roared out of Gotham's Cuban community and "invaded New York's night life in general." A Latin American craze swept theaters and spawned nightclubs with a Cuban atmosphere (Havana-Madrid, La Martinique, La Conga). Explanations for the phenomenon ranged from FDR's Good Neighbor policy, to Hollywood's featuring of exotic Latin imagery, to the deepening first-hand acquaintance with hemispheric cultures gleaned from growing tourism, the latter in part a result of the Depression and fear of impending war. Hard times had redirected much tourism from Europe to South of the Border (cruise passengers went from 2,567 in 1929 to 64,103 in 1937), and with the outbreak of hostilities in 1939, traffic to South America and the Caribbean—heavily promoted by Grace Lines and Pan Am—rose yet again.

Again, a significant traffic flowed in the other direction, as rumba and conga bands from Havana were drawn north, as were samba singers from Brazil and celebrated Argentinian and Mexican crooners, who came to play the new clubs and to make recordings and movies. New York was once again a confluence point for Latin American artists. And at the same time, in the late 1930s and early 1940s, New York's Spanish-speaking communities were crucibling another new music in interaction with African Americans, as when Cugat vocalist Frank Grillo (better known as Machito) and Mario Bauzá, a classically trained musician who worked with Dizzy Gillespie, blended Latin and jazz rhythms and founded the Afro-Cubans in 1940, which drew in talented young barrio-born Puerto Ricans like Tito Puente.

WAR (1939–45)[15]

In 1940 Diego Rivera, long since reconciled with Nelson Rockefeller, was in San Francisco working on a mural called *Pan American Unity*. His project represented a larger hemispheric development—an alliance, under the banner of anti-Fascism, that Rockefeller was instrumental in fashioning, and which would have significant consequences for New York City.

Rockefeller had made his first visit to Latin America in 1933, spending a month in Mexico collecting art. In 1937 he toured Venezuela, where Creole Petroleum's Lake Maracaibo fields had helped make that country the second biggest oil producer on earth, and contributed greatly to the profits of Standard Oil of New Jersey, of which it was a subsidiary. Rockefeller was appalled to find American oil executives aping the most arrogant British colonialists. Living inside barbed-wire compounds, aloof from all but the richest locals, and seldom bothering to learn Spanish, they treated with supercilious disdain their workers, who lived in oil towns bereft of sewers, clinics, or schools. His travels elsewhere in South America that year left him shaken by the poverty.

Back in New York, the idealistic young millionaire lectured some three hundred Standard executives on their obligation to improve local conditions for "the people in the host country"; adding that, ethics aside, if better relations weren't cultivated, "they will take away our ownership." Oil officials were unmoved until Cárdenas nationalized their holdings in 1938, after which, to forestall a similar fate in Venezuela, Creole let Rockefeller have his reforms. Returning in 1939 with twelve New York Berlitz teachers in tow, he introduced mandatory Spanish lessons (having himself developed a passable facility); had the barbed wire removed; phased out job discrimination against Venezuelans; and introduced some schools and public health clinics modeled on those established by the Rockefeller Foundation's International Division. He also launched the Compañía de Fomento Venezolano (Venezuela Development Company) to undertake programs—water drilling, mining, low-cost housing—that would demonstrate the benignity of capitalism, the compatibility of profit and progress. The only venture that got airborne, however, before war-spawned economic crisis grounded such visionary flights, was the luxury-class Hotel Ávila for the Caracas elite and visiting American businessmen.

The war in Europe severed South America from its major markets; exports dropped 40 to 60 percent, leaving Brazil awash in coffee, Chile in copper, Argentina in wheat and meat. And it raised the question of which side Latins would be on if war came to the Western Hemisphere. German commercial influence had grown during the Depression when U.S. trade with Central and South America had declined, and German commercial houses had seized the opportunity, selling ever more manufactured goods to Brazil, Chile, Mexico, and Venezuela while buying ever more grain, meat, and raw materials. German airlines' 16,500-mile (and growing) network had closed fast on Pan Am's 25,000-mile system, and a German media blitz of shortwave broadcasts and newsreel presentations now was reaching large areas. Moreover, there were pockets of potential sympathizers throughout the area: Nearly 1.4 million German-born immigrants lived in South America, along with an even bigger second-generation cohort, and there were substantial Italian communities as well, notably in Argentina. Might not some countries be tempted by proffered Nazi deals? Roosevelt harped on this danger repeatedly, at one point announcing he possessed "a secret map, made in Germany by Hitler's Government, by planners of the new world order. It is a map of South America and part of central America as Hitler proposes to organize it." In FDR's worst-case scenario, Hitler would establish footholds in Latin America with the help of Fifth Columnists, and develop the capacity to attack the U.S. directly.

Nelson Rockefeller proposed to Roosevelt that to forestall such possibilities, he create an independent government agency, to be advised by private industry. Modeled on his own Venezuelan venture, it would promote "hemispheric solidarity" and also

The "secret map" showing South America and part of Central America reapportioned into five republics, ca. 1940. Franklin Delano Roosevelt Presidential Library and Museum.

The original of this map was put up in Nazi Party headquarters in Buenos Aires in 1940, as a signal to certain Latin American republics that if they backed the Third Reich they would be rewarded with territories carved out of neighboring countries. British intelligence obtained a copy of the map, touched it up to magnify the proposed alterations, then passed it in October 1941 to FDR, who used it to promote repeal of neutrality laws. The handwritten notes, in German, pertain to the production, storage, and shipment of fuel.

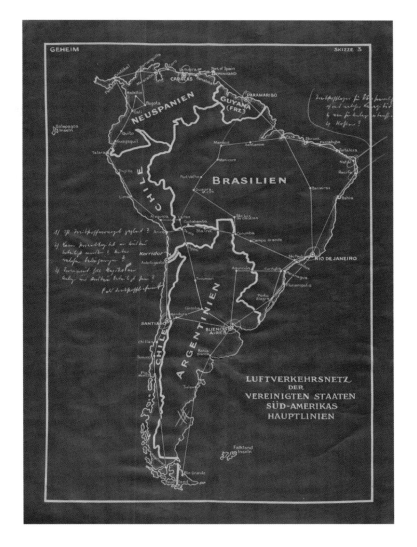

"lessen the dependency of Latin America upon Europe as a market for raw materials and a source of manufactured articles." Rockefeller had England in his sights as well, seeing a chance for the United States to replace Britain as the hemisphere's long-standing dominant trading partner. At one point he recommended asking England to put up their holdings in Argentina and Chile as collateral for wartime aid—"good properties in the British portfolio," as an aide put it, that "we might as well pick up now."

In 1941 Roosevelt set up the Office of Inter-American Affairs (OIAA), made Rockefeller its coordinator, and asked him to wage an anti-Nazi Kulturkampf. This he did, calling on a network of New Yorkers in banking, culture, media, advertising, architecture, and the academy, in ways that built upon and strengthened the old pan-American networks and strengthened New York City's hemispheric position.

Rockefeller's OIAA undertook a variety of initiatives—including establishing a boycott of Latin American companies that made deals with German enterprises, an effort that proved wildly successful at driving German competitors out of the marketplace—but his major focus was forging a North-South cultural alliance. This, in turn, required improving the U.S. image (many Latins still considered the Yankees materialist-minded barbarians) and enhancing its presence. Setting up operations in Gotham, he quickly got to work. A communication division purchased huge amounts of advertising space in 350 Latin American papers and provided them with newsprint otherwise in short supply, thus filling their coffers and keeping their presses running at a desperate moment while simultaneously filling their pages with pro-U.S. propaganda. He set up, with the help of *Life* editors, a glossy newsweekly, *En Guardia*, which though blatantly propagandistic was an instant hit, its circulation soon soaring to over half a million. He dispatched newsreel crews from New York studios to set up operations in Santiago and Rio. To counter shortwave broadcasts from Radio Berlin, he called on William Paley of CBS to put together the Cadena de las Americas (Network of the Americas), which signed up sixty-four stations. Perhaps its most popular program was *Viva America*, which featured renowned musicians and orchestras from North and South America.

The OIAA also sponsored South American tours by Lincoln Kirstein's American Ballet Caravan (George Balanchine, the company's artistic director, created four new ballets for the trip, and composer Aaron Copland flew down to Lima to conduct *Billy the Kid*). The Museum of Modern Art, in cooperation with the OIAA, arranged a traveling exhibition—*Exposition of Contemporary North American Painting*—put together from holdings of MoMA, the Metropolitan Museum of Art, the Whitney Museum of American Art, and the Brooklyn Museum.

Rockefeller encouraged initiatives from the private sector, which had its own interest in penetrating new markets at a time when old ones were in disrepair. RCA chief David Sarnoff took Toscanini and his NBC Symphony Orchestra on tour. *Time* started a syndication service (in Spanish) that generated each week an eight-thousand-word summary of the current issue, which was then printed in twenty Latin American papers. In December 1940 *Selecciones del Reader's Digest* was launched, and soon, with a circulation of 350,000, it had become the largest-selling Spanish-language magazine in the world. Juan Trippe's planes airlifted south reels of the Spanish (and OIAA-subsidized) version of *The March of Time* (*La Marcha del Tiempo)*, and soon it was playing in five hundred Latin American movie houses. Then the OIAA began producing its own newsreels—newsreel crews from New York studios set up operations in Santiago and Rio—along with cartoons, documentaries, and features (short and long) on the sunnier side of North American life, and heroic episodes from South American history (*The Life of Simón Bolívar*). Production was handled in conjunction with MoMA'S Film Library, whose president, John Hay Whitney, hired refugee movie professionals like Luis Buñuel to subtitle or dub U.S. productions into Spanish.

Rockefeller also did his best to whip up New Yorkers' interest in Latin American

On October 20, 1945, accompanied by Chilean president Ríos, Mayor La Guardia officially changed Manhattan's Sixth Avenue to the Avenue of the Americas. At the renaming ceremony, La Guardia dedicated the avenue to "the peace and solidarity of the Western Hemisphere." He also used the occasion to hail recently deceased president Franklin Roosevelt's Good Neighbor Policy, which, the mayor said, had previously been "limited to and believed to have been fulfilled when American money went down there [to Latin America] to exploit people. I hope that policy will not be repeated and will soon be forgotten."

neighbors, backing everything from an Inter-American Music Day to a Latin American Fair at Macy's, which was visited by fifty thousand and broadcast live to South America. (Gimbel's, as was its wont, followed suit with an exhibition of the "Ancient Arts and Crafts of South America," complete with "native Cuzco Indian music and dancing.")

Rockefeller also supported an effort, begun in 1941, by the Sixth Avenue Association to change the street's name to Avenue of the Americas, which they hoped would extend down to Thirty-fourth Street the kind of real estate upgrading that had taken place above Fiftieth Street (notably at Rockefeller Center). The notion was to have all the Latin American countries move their consulates there—most had long hung their hats in the Whitehall Building at Manhattan's lower tip—and to build hotels to house the increased flow of businesspeople. Despite some last-minute opposition—it was "an awful mouthful," one opponent testified—the City Council and Mayor La Guardia approved the change in 1945.

Rockefeller's dreams for Sixth Avenue (as most New Yorkers would doggedly continue to call it) did not come to pass. No bevy of Spanish-inflected institutions came to roost on their namesake boulevard—though in time a clutch of statuary Latin liberators (Simón Bolívar, José de San Martín, and José Martí, all astride steeds) would congregate at its northern terminus at Central Park South—not far from the Maine Monument at Columbus Circle. Instead, something much more remarkable was under way in the years after V-J Day, evidenced in the growing number of Pan Am flights touching down at La Guardia Airport carrying Puerto Rican newcomers: Not an Avenue of the Americas, but a City of the Americas, was busy being born.

NOTES

1. Thanks to the kindness of friends and far-flung scholars, I have committed many fewer errors of commission and omission than I would have if left to my own limited devices, being no more expert in Spanish and Latin American history than in the many other national stories with which a historian of New York City must grapple. My readers' and counselors' generosity, I believe, was due in part to our shared conviction that Gotham has not paid sufficient attention to the emergence of Nueva York, a fact brought home to me, quite literally, by my marriage to Carmen Boullosa. Herself a distinguished representative of Mexican and Latin American letters, Carmen was startled at the near invisibility, in the city's cultural canon, of the many superlative writers who have lived in New York and written in Spanish. Her efforts—in conjunction with a circle of Cuban, Argentinian, Bolivian, Spanish, Mexican, and other colleagues—to excavate and celebrate that tradition inspired me to propose a wider commemoration of the city's lengthy interaction with the Spanish-speaking world. This seemed particularly appropriate at a time when Gotham was approaching the demographic milestone of becoming one third Hispanic; when a surge of anti-immigrant sentiment was once again abroad in the land; and when the entire Spanish-speaking world, including Spain, was marking the 2010 bicentennial of the Wars of Independence. Happily, Louise Mirrer and Julian Zugazagoitia agreed that a full-scale exhibition was warranted, and they, their staff, and—crucially—curator Marci Reaven together made it happen.

The following individuals helped me in various ways with researching and writing this essay and assembling images, and I am deeply grateful. While insisting that they are not responsible in the slightest degree for any remaining errors or infelicities, I offer my heartfelt thanks to Michael Louis (my righthand man), and to Sarah Armstrong, Jean Ashton, Tony Bechara, Laura Benton, Laird Bergad, Carmen Boullosa, Jane Bowers, Luisa Campuzano, Juan Carlos Mercado, Juan Carlos Calderón, Barry Carr, Mario Coyula, Inmaculada de Habsburgo, Arcadio Díaz Quiñones, Anne Eller, Alejandro Espejel, Carlos Espinosa, Eli Faber, Marc Favreau, Jim Fernández, Juan Flores, Lloyd Gardner, Charly Gehring, Noah Gelfand, Frances Goldin, Juan Gonzalez, Greg Grandin, Nuria Grégori Torada, Gabriel Guerra, Margarita Gutman, Gabriel Haslip-Viera, David Healey, Sarah Henry, Peter Hudson, Kathleen Hulser, Miriam Jiménez-Román, Peter Johnson, Richard Kagan, Eduardo Lago, Eusebio Leal, Isaías Lerner, Jay Levenson, Sandy Levinson, Clara Lida, Mario Linares, Enrique López Mesa, Ana Maria Varela-Lago, Milagros Martínez, Elena Martínez, Cathy Matson, Erendira Matzumura, Ann Meyerson, Louise Mirrer, Valerie Paley, Lisandro Pérez, Julia Preston, Richard Rabinowitz, Sergio Ramirez, Marci Reaven, Claudio Remeseira, David Rockefeller, Alicia Rodríguez, Salvador Rueda Smithers, Chris Sabatini, Joe Salvo, Linda Salvucci, Virginia Sánchez Korrol, Arturo Sarukhan, Andre Schiffrin, Christopher Schmidt-Nowara, Robert Smith, Sam Stoloff, Edward Sullivan, David Sumberg, Barbara Tenenbaum, Silvio Torres-Saillant, Susana Torruella Leval, Jeremy Travis, Suzanne Wasserman, Barbara Weinstein, Oscar Zanetti, and Raul Zorilla.

2. **Colonies, Empires, Rebellions (1500s-1825)**
Albion 1970; Berlin and Harris 2005; Bernardini and Fiering 2001; Brown 2006; Chavez 2002; Chernow 2004; Coatsworth 1967; Cuenca Esteban 1984; DeGuzmán 2005; Doolen 2004; Duncan 2005; Dushkin 1918; Elliott 2006; Faber 1998; Foy 2008; Gehring, Schiltkamp, and Stuyvesant 1987; Gelfand 2009; González 2000; Godfriend 2005; Herbermann and Pace et al., 1913; Hodges 1999; Horsmanden and Zabin 2004; Jacobs 2005; Kamen 2003; Lepore 2005; Lewis 1984; Linderman 1974; Lynch 1986; Moya Pons 2007; National Portrait Gallery 2007; Neumann 1947; Pérez [2010]; Racine 2003; Robertson 1929; Ryan 1935; Salvucci 1984; Salvucci 2005; Schama 1987; Schmidt 2001; Shattuck 2009; Shea 1978; Shorto 2004; Singleton 1909; Swierenga 1994; Thomas 2006; Whitaker 1962; Whitaker 1968; Williams 1968; Williams 2001.

3. **The Bolivarian Moment (1806-25)**
Albion 1970; Cleveland 1850; González 2000; Lynch 1986; Porter 1931; Racine 2003; Robertson 1929; Salvucci 1984.

4. **Venturing South (1825-65)**
Albion 1970; Ely 1964; González 2000; Lynch 1986; Moreno Fraginals 1976.

5. **Metropolitan Spinoffs (1825-65)**
Albion 1970; Brickhouse 2001; Burgos 2001; Chaffin 2003; Dallett 1960; de Onís 1957; Haslip-Viera 1996; Jaksic 2007; Kanellos and Dworkin et al. 2002; Kanellos and Martell 2000; Kanellos 2008; Lazo 2005; Mirabal 2000; Mirabal 2001; Montes Huidobro 1995; Muller 2008; Peterson 1933; Pérez [2010]; Tucker and Boston Athenaeum 1980; Wilder 2000.

6. Colonias (1825–65)

Adorno 2002; Bender 1987; Bigelow 1980; Brown 2002; Bryant and Voss 1975–92; Burstein 2007; de Secada 1985; DeGuzmán 2005; Foner 1962; González 2000; Irwin 2008; Kagan 2002; López Mesa 2002; McCadden 1964; McCadden and McCadden 1984; Moore 1950; Muller 2008; Pérez [2010]; Poyo 1989; Sampson 2003; Sánchez Korrol 1994; Schell 2001; Scroggs 1916; Stein 2002; Varela-Lago 2008; Williams 1968.

7. New York's Latin Links (1865–98)

All America Cables 1928; Brown and Knight 1992; Eichner 1969; González 2000; Mirabal 2000; Quirarte 2006–07; Rotker 2000; Sánchez Korrol 1994; Scrymser 1915; Zimmermann 2002.

8. Latins in New York (1865–98)

Antón and Hernández 2002; Chamberlin and Schulman 1976; Colon 1975; González 2000; Haslip-Viera 1996; Hoffnung-Garskof 2001; Kanellos 2008; Kanellos and Dworkin et al. 2002; Kanellos and Martell 2000; Kirk 1977; Martí and Foner 1975; Molloy 1996; Ramos 2001; Rotker 2000; Sánchez Korrol 1994; Vázquez Pérez, 2008; Vega and Andreu Iglesias 1984.

9. Spaniards in Gotham (1865–98)

Boone 2007; Casanovas 1998; Kamen 2007; Sheinin 2000; Varela-Lago 2008.

10. Spanish-Cuban-American War (1895–98)

Castonguay 1999; Kamen 2007; Linderman 1974; Pérez 1998; Schoonover 2003; Varela-Lago 2008.

11. New Empire (1898–1929)

Ameringer 1963; Ayala 1995; Ayala and Bergad 2002; Baker 1966; Bunau-Varilla 1913; Calder 2006; Castro-Klaren 2003; Chernow 1990; Díaz Espino 2001; Ferrer 1998; Ferrer 1999; García-Muniz 1997; Gaulin 1990; González 2000; Grandin 2006; Gutman 1999; LaFeber 1989; McAvoy 2003; O'Brien 1989; O'Brien 1996; Pérez 2008; Powell 1971; Rosenberg 1982; Rosenberg 2003; Schmitz 1986; Schwartz 2004; Taylor and Lindeman 1976; Uggen 2003; Uggen 2008; Unger and Unger 2005.

12. Little Spain (1900–29)

Bercovici 1924; Boone 2007; Davis 2005; Fay 1942; Federal Writers' Project 1984; Fernández 2002; Galasso 2008; García Lorca 2008; Kagan 2002; Kamen 2007; Klein 1992; O'Brien 1999; Ogorzaly 1994; Pérez 2008; Rachum 2004; Remeseira 2002; Rostagno 1989; Sheinin 2000; Shelley 2003; Sturman 2000; Taylor and Lindeman 1976; Totoricaguena 2005; Totoricaguena and Sarriugarte Doyaga et al. 2003; Unger and Unger 2005; Van Vechten 1918; Varela-Lago 2008; Veeser 2002; Young 2001; Zimmermann 2002.

13. El Barrio (1900–29)

Ayala and Bernabe 2007; Burnett 2001; Cabranes 1978; Colón 1975; Colón López 2002; Delgado 2005; Federal Writers' Project 1984; Fernández 2002; Flores 2000; Glasser 1995; González 1959; González 2000; González 2004; Haslip-Viera 1996; Mátos-Rodriguez and Hernández 2001; Mirabal 2000; Ortiz 1990; Rivera Ramos 2007; Sánchez Korrol 1994; Statham 2002; Thomas 2002; Varela-Lago 2008; Vega and Andreu Iglesias 1984.

14. Depression (1929–39)

Anreus 2001; Beer 2001; Butler 1974; Carroll and Fernández 2007; Chase 1943; Chenault 1970; Collier 1986; Colon 1975; Figueroa 2007; Glasser 1995; González 2000; Hurlburt 1976; Hurlburt 1989; Kanellos 1997; Kanellos and Martell 2000; Meyer and Ocampo 1990; Meyer 1992; O'Connor 1986; Ogorzaly 1994; Ojeda Reyes and Marcantonio 1978; Polcari 1992; Roberts 1999; Roorda 1998; Rostagno 1989; Ruíz and Sánchez Korrol 2006; Sánchez Korrol 1994; Schmidt 1987; Schwartz 2004; Stein 2002; Sublette 2004; Thomas 2002; Van Hensbergen and Picasso 2004; Vega and Andreu Iglesias 1984; White 1975.

15. War (1939–45)

Colby and Dennett 1995; Erb 1982; Friedman 2003; Kamen 2007; Mewburn 1998; Meyer 2000; O'Connor 1986; Oles and Ferragut et al. 1993; Polcari 1992; Reich 1996; Rivas 2002; Sánchez Korrol 1994; United States and Office of Inter-American Affairs 1947; Van Hensbergen and Picasso 2004; Varela-Lago 2008.

PERMEABLE EMPIRES:

Commercial Exchanges between New York and Spanish Possessions before 1800

CATHY MATSON

For over a century after its initial conquests in the Caribbean, the Spanish empire's dominion over native peoples, vast territories, and the environmental resources of the Western Hemisphere was relatively unchallenged by competing European empires. Long before the tiny outpost of New Amsterdam was planted at the mouth of the Hudson River, plundering Spanish armies and merchants established Santo Domingo, Cuba, Puerto Rico, Jamaica, and Hispaniola. Beginning in the 1490s, these islands became staging grounds for conquistadores venturing onto the mainlands of North and South America. Within a generation, Spanish imperialists had spun out threads of settlement from the Caribbean and cast a great imperial net covering the Mayan Yucatan, central Mexico, Panama, Ecuador/Peru, Florida, and the southwest interior of North America.

In their search for precious metals and cheap agricultural exports, Spanish conquerors migrated quickly from their possessions in the Caribbean to take over mines and Native American labor from Mexico to Argentina. Some early Spanish possessions were abandoned or taken over by a new series of conquerors: Pernambuco became Portuguese once again in 1654; Jamaica was turned over to the British in 1655; western Hispaniola became French by 1670. But on the mainland, unprecedented transformations unfolded. Potosí became the world's premier site for the extraction of silver and forced subjugation of native populations. As death caused by devastating diseases, harsh work regimes, and forced internal migrations reduced native populations to a fraction of their former sizes, Spanish mining authorities and landowners turned to importing African slaves. Massive ships convoyed silver from the New World mines to Spain, and particular shipping lines were established from Cartagena and Porto Bello to the staging ground at Havana, where they set out across the Atlantic. Veracruz became another shipping conduit for silver from Peru across the Pacific Ocean to Manila.

Spain's forcible extraction of great wealth from Mexico and Peru during the 1500s had a profound effect on the economies and cultures of Europe, and spurred efforts by rival Dutch, French, and British adventurers to grab what they could from

Artist unknown. *Cerro de Potosí, Bolivia*, 1584. Print. Schomburg Center for Research in Black Culture, New York Public Library.

the Spanish galleons. Under the influence of the Black Legend, a propaganda campaign in Europe designed to turn masses of people against purported Spanish cruelties in the New World, as well as gain the blessing of Queen Elizabeth, pirates such as the "sea dog" Sir Francis Drake preyed on Spanish ships and ports, including his capture of the great silver convoy at Nobre de Dios in 1573 and the sacking of San Juan in 1595. A generation later, Piet Hein, a Dutch West India Company agent and captain, underscored the growing intensity of imperial rivalries in the Caribbean. In 1628 Hein commanded a large privateering fleet of thirty-one ships and four thousand men on his third voyage to the West Indies, a force that captured eleven Spanish silver ships in the bay of Matanzas near Havana, netting his Dutch employers some twelve million guilders, an immense profit. Indeed, European pirates overran Spanish island ports and stripped Spanish ships of gold and silver regularly by the early 1600s.

During these uncertain times, the Spanish "plantation complex" also was sinking deep roots. Spaniards grew and processed sugar with forced labor near Mexico City beginning in the mid-1550s, and soon Spanish landlords set up sugar plantations in the Andean valleys. The most important islands to remain Spanish possessions, Cuba and Puerto Rico became the sites of tobacco and sugar plantations that imported thousands of slaves before 1650. Regular but not yet extensive trading of food and livestock developed by the early 1600s between these Spanish islands and the new French and British ones. By 1650 Peru's new capital city of Lima also had an African population of many thousands, who were brought huge distances to work in the gold and silver mines alongside native peoples. Meanwhile, viceroys and *encomenderos* divided vast territories in the name of the Spanish crown, imposed new political authority and law, forced new systems of land usage on prior occupants, and introduced new currencies and social customs—all in efforts to establish the authority of Spanish newcomers over populations now declared the "subjects" and "inferiors" of the empire.

Far north of Spain's expanding presence in the Western Hemisphere, New Amsterdam was only a tiny outpost of the Dutch empire in the early 1600s. Founded more than a century after Spanish conquests in Mexico and Peru, the diminutive port at the mouth of the Hudson River was intended to be a supply station for Dutch vessels engaged in slave and staples trading throughout the Atlantic world. New Amsterdam's fur exports provided modest profits for Dutch West India Company shareholders, but there were few agricultural settlements at this early date and the region was unsuited to plantation production and labor.

Still, by the 1650s New Amsterdam had become a crossroads of people from throughout the Atlantic world, including the Spanish colonies. Dutch traders brought slaves seized from Spanish ships by privateers or purchased off Spanish ships landing at Curaçao, providing the first slave labor in the colony. In 1613, runaway slave Jan Rodrigues of Santo Domingo sought refuge in New Amsterdam. During the

1700s, reports of government officials noted the presence of "Spanish slaves" and "Spanish Indian slaves" in New York's growing population of forced labor, which heightened existing fears about the impact of peoples from Catholic colonies on the city. Sailors from many nations, indentured servants of the Dutch West India Company, a few aspiring landed estate owners, ship captains, and some families starting over in the New World also populated the Dutch outpost. New Amsterdam also became a regular stopping place for the company's agents and "interloping" independent shippers. Some of the Jews expelled from Brazil in the mid-1650s fled to New Amsterdam, further embellishing the Spanish-based culture, language, and foodways in the small Hudson River port. Governor Peter Stuyvesant came to New Amsterdam after years of service in Curaçao (a Dutch possession), where regular contact with Spanish slave traders, smugglers, and imperial officials taught him a pattern of open commerce among numerous nations. Stuyvesant emulated this open trade in New Amsterdam from the 1640s to the 1660s.

By the late 1600s, New York City was no longer a small Dutch outpost. Its colonists were firmly enmeshed in the interimperial commerce and wars that marked the British empire's rise. Mercantilism, the loosely woven net of regulating policies that favored rising new men of commerce in the British empire, also shaped the contours of colonization and provided guidelines about how colonists were expected to treat the Spanish empire's peoples as "strangers" outside their orbit of commerce. Of course, reality was quite different. Servants and slaves from Spanish colonies were brought to New York on trading vessels with regularity in the early 1700s and joined the pool of bound labor in New York. For example, the infant son of "a Spanish mollatta woman named Dianna," a slave in the household of Governor Edward Hyde, Viscount Cornbury, was sold to a New Yorker for five shillings.[1]

Religion still figured prominently in the imperial rivalries, law, and cultural perceptions keeping British and Spanish peoples separated, but commerce, the slave trade, wars, and territorial expansion made imperial boundaries a practical impossibility. As New York City became dependent on its coastal and Caribbean trade by the late 1600s, it began to depend on open exchanges going on at Spanish ports, especially by around 1700, after the global reach of piracy was reduced due to active imperial efforts to channel commerce into regulated mercantilist routes, and Spanish Caribbean ports became more accessible to New York's shipping community. The "Spanish trade," as merchants called it, involved both exchanges of goods across porous interimperial boundaries, which were nearly always balanced in New Yorkers' favor, and the gold and silver coin that British colonists desperately needed and Spanish peoples had aplenty.

Most New York merchants believed that the Spanish trade was essential to their prosperity. Sugar and rum exports from British Barbados and Jamaica were

A brig of the sort used at Nueva York for trade with Caribbean islands and the Spanish Main.

insufficient to fill the ships New Yorkers could provide for this trade by the early 1700s, and therefore could not yield high enough payments for New Yorkers to pay their debts to English manufacturers for colonists' imports. In the breach, Spanish islanders beckoned New Yorkers to bring food, textiles, and construction materials to them, and in return promised to sell their tobacco, sugar, coffee, and rum cheaply to New Yorkers. For thirty years after the Peace of Utrecht in 1713, the Spanish also granted their *asiento* to England—a monopoly of supplying the Spanish colonies with slaves and the allowance of one English ship a year trading goods to the Spanish islands—which proved especially lucrative to slave traders. But despite the clearance of one official ship per year, New Yorkers engaged in significant illicit commerce outside of the *asiento*.

By the 1720s, British ships called at all Spanish colonial ports, but three places attracted many New York City traders. One of these, the Bay of Campeche, was less a port city than a veritable nest of pirates, smugglers, corrupt Spanish officials, and a few servants and slaves, where ships could anchor away from the shoreline and be met with agents selling dyewood, spices, drugs, and contraband from around the Caribbean. Alternatively, New York merchants landed at Jamaica, where under cover of legal commerce within the British empire, they loaded up Spanish dyewood (also called "Campeche wood") and silver coin, or made contact with Honduran logwood cutters who brought contraband trade to New Yorkers. This smuggling flourished in a transnational environment of permissiveness, attracting into the Spanish Caribbean such New Yorkers as the Ludlows, Bayards, Livingstons, Beekmans, and many lesser merchants.

Although ports of the Spanish colonies were officially closed to North Americans for most of the eighteenth century, the Honduras smuggling spread quickly to other ports of call. When direct trade into New York City proved difficult, Honduras wood was shipped directly to Amsterdam, Spanish sugar to coastal North American cities, and silver to London. From the Spanish imperial point of view, these "encroachments" threatened the stability of their possessions, especially when the British founded Georgia during the 1730s and colonists systematically violated the terms of the *asiento*, which Spain revoked in 1739. British Admiral Edward Vernon's expedition of a few British forces against Porto Bello that year fueled animosities in both empires that led into the War of Jenkins' Ear from 1739 to 1748. But British efforts to capture Cuba and Panama proved to be expensive failures, as was an attempt on St. Augustine, Spain's most northerly outpost. The siege of Cartagena in 1741 also was a disastrous British military failure, though it was an extremely popular campaign in the British colonies; some 3,600 North American volunteers served in that long war. Equally significant, this war was far more than a diplomatic conflict; it was the first major inter-European contest that began as a Caribbean dispute focused primarily on commerce. The war brought British and Spanish sailors and commanders

into regular contact with each other, keeping alive anti-Catholicism and fueling ideological divisions in New York. Yet interimperial wars rarely had clear lines of national identity, and New Yorkers' logwood smuggling actually grew during the hostilities. Moreover, flags of truce, which were issued to exchange prisoners between nations, spurred additional Spanish trade with New Yorkers in otherwise forbidden ports such as the Bay of Campeche.

A second Spanish port, Monte Cristi, on the north coast of Hispaniola, became a favored stopping place for New York ships during the eighteenth century. Colonial merchants declared Spanish salt, sugar, and silver "necessary" for North American commercial survival, and London policy makers were hard-pressed to disagree. After losing the *asiento* in 1739 and as war talk rose to a fever pitch, new British legislation attempted to cut off trade to Spanish possessions. Some of the slave trade on British vessels to Spanish islands did, in fact, decline for a few years. But London officials treaded cautiously in suppressing the "Mountmen" at Monte Cristi, fearing they would take their sugar and coffee to French islands. As a result, New York merchants continued to send large amounts of food and manufactured goods to this Spanish port. A Spanish decree of 1752 making Monte Cristi (and Havana) free ports deepened the presence of New Yorkers and gave a new boost to their extensive credit networks with the Mountmen. By 1757, Monte Cristi was one of the busiest shipping centers in the Atlantic. As many as 180 foreign vessels were sighted in the bay at a time, greeted by Spanish coasting vessels that hauled away New York's provisions and manufactured items, to be sold to Spanish retailers on shore or French buyers at Cape François (also called Le Cap). Mountmen paid for these imports with sugar, coffee, indigo, and other island produce.

Elias Durnford (1739–1794). *A View of the Market-Place in the City of the Havana*, ca. 1768. Engraving. 14¼ x 20⅞ in. (36 x 53 cm). John Bowles, Robert Sayer, Thos. Jefferys, Carington Bowles, and Henry Parker, publishers, London. Archive of Early American Images, John Carter Brown Library (04515).

The third port favored by New Yorkers by the early 1700s was Havana, where New York ship captains bought tobacco and, increasingly, sugar. The island's deep natural harbors and low export prices (compared to British planters' prices) proved irresistible to rising ambitious merchants as well as the great slave traders. But what truly tipped the balance was Havana's position as the official staging port for Spain's transport of silver from the New World. When the *asiento* was revoked in 1739, the Spanish crown gave trading rights with its colonies back to the *guarda costas*, government-appointed traders who were in charge of exchanges within the Spanish empire and often bore commissions from island governors to seize illegal foreign vessels. In 1740 the *guarda costas* were ordered to protect the new Havana Company, which was made up of Cuban merchants who held a royal monopoly to ship tobacco to Spain. The company also received a huge subsidy of silver from Mexico to pay for provisions shipped off to St. Augustine and Cuba. The silver was spent in New York, Charleston, and Jamaica, technically still enemy ports. Outside this new officially sanctioned set of privileges, however, Spanish Caribbean planters and North American smugglers also colluded to trade sugar and tobacco for provisions and slaves.

Driving forward these informal and illicit arrangements between Spanish traders and New Yorkers was the relentless rise of consumer demand for tropical goods

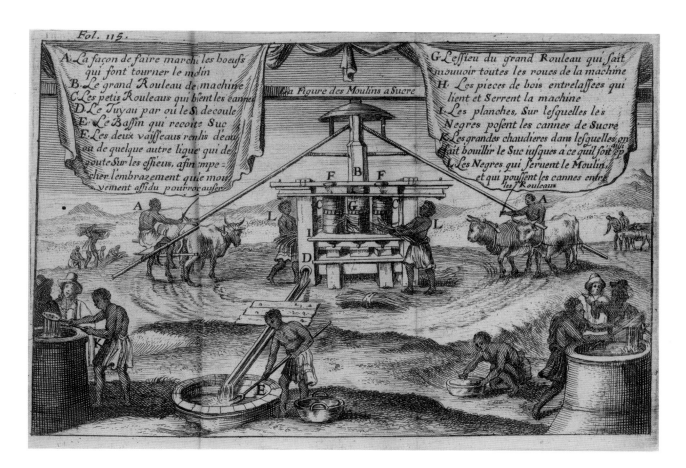

Artist unknown. *La Figure des Moulins à Sucre*, ca. 1667. Engraving. 5¾ x 7½ in. (14.4 x 19.1 cm). [Christofle Fourmy], publisher. Archive of Early American Images, John Carter Brown Library (01618).

produced on plantations. Not only in New York, but throughout the British empire, the appetite for sugar grew exponentially during the 1700s. By the 1740s, New Yorkers imported more sugar than the colony could consume, and so its merchants developed a strong reexporting business to Amsterdam and London, with the result that New York's trade with Spanish possessions became a multilateral network of credit and debt over expansive parts of both empires. Despite the continuing fears of "papacy" on their frontiers, or "Spanish negroes" leading slave conspiracies and rebellions within the city in 1712 and 1741, or the proximity of Spanish colonies to which slaves could run for their freedom, New Yorkers refused to give up the pleasures of sugar, tobacco, rum, and other goods from their Spanish trading partners. By the 1740s, "Spanish sugar" was in highest demand in the city because of its whiteness and low prices. Particular brands or qualities of Spanish colonial sugar, coffee, and tobacco entered the city in ever larger quantities. Demand soared not only for what critics already called a "noxious leaf" (especially among women), but also for colorful paraphernalia and rituals of consumption such as pipes and snuff boxes. Sugar made an even deeper impact, as a sweetener in bitter drinks such as chocolate (popular in Spain and imported into New York by the 1720s); as a part of the rituals of tea or coffee consumption; as candy; and as a meat garnish. Coffee houses, tea parties, entire dish sets, and metal goods to make and serve sweet drinks proliferated. Spices, dried exotic fruits, and medicinal plants from Spanish possessions also became a part of the foodways, market activities, and broader culture of New York City. Clothing and household textiles imported from Mexico and Cuba became highly desirable items of cultural refinement.

Intellectually, the richer material culture of New York City also raised new discussions about the meanings of such goods for interimperial relations, sparking debates about the wisdom of imperial restrictions on trade with foreign empires. In the 1750s, New York City merchants appealed for an end to Spanish and British, as well as French, regulations governing their trade with the Caribbean. One of their resolutions underscored that trade with foreign peoples served the public welfare, since British islanders could not supply tropical goods in great enough quantities, and these goods provided valuable staples to refiners and distillers in addition to employment for dockside workers. This trade was also seen as "necessary" for selling New York's flour and provisions where markets were good and where payments in silver could be used to pay colonial debts to English manufacturers.

The Seven Years' War seemed to prove these arguments, as it brought New York's merchants previously unheard-of opportunities to prosper in privateering and smuggling with Spanish possessions. By then, England had a far more powerful imperial presence in the Western Hemisphere, and demand for sugar, coffee, and other Caribbean commodities was rising so rapidly in England that many of its merchants no longer feared competition from lower-priced Spanish and French goods. So, for North American colonists who boasted of a flourishing trade through Jamaica, where merchants secured Spanish goods and insurance for voyages to Havana, Porto Bello, Cartagena, and other Spanish ports around the gulf region, the chaos of global warfare during the 1750s simply opened up these opportunities more.

New York trader John Watts, for example, praised the Monte Cristi trade during the Seven Years' War. He remarked in 1762 that "We have an odd kind of Mungrell Commerce here call'd the Mount Trade," which "the Lawyers say it is legal & contrary to no Statute," but "the [British] Men of Warr say it is illegal."[2] British naval attacks on this trade, continued Watts, made the trade risky. "[If] A Stranger [were] to form a Judgment from [these seizures, he] would imagine that the Nation in its Jurisdiction had neither Rule [of] Law or probity & yet the Evil is suffer'd to go on without any determination."[3] Meanwhile, every merchant who ventured to "the Mount" to trade risked being "tor[n] to pieces by Robbers, Lawyers & all sorts of Vermin."[4] Still, some scholars estimate that between 1748 and 1763, over three million pounds sterling worth of Spanish bullion was taken into the British colonies, most of which was then sent to English merchants and bankers to balance colonial debts.

New Yorkers increasingly focused their attention on Havana. During the Seven

Years' War, demand for slaves began to rise rapidly among the island's expanding sugar planters, a demand that New York traders were anxious to fulfill. When the British overran Manila and captured Havana in 1762, a majority of the colonial volunteers who supplemented Redcoat forces in Cuba were from New York and New Jersey. Although most of the volunteers succumbed to yellow fever, New York's merchants remained optimistic about the commercial opportunities in Cuba. John Watts sent numerous ships full of flour to hungry islanders; Henry and John Cruger supplied clothing and provisions. Watts complained in late 1762 that "His Lordship [Commander Albemarle] is playing the Devil with us at the Havanna, [because he] obliges all Comers to part with their Bread and flour at his own price which [was far under] the first Cost and Charges, & when the inhabitants would give the double for it, an Advantage it seems he takes to himself."[5] To compound problems, Cuban officials forced New Yorkers to take only sugar in payment for flour, rather than the preferred silver coin.[6] So, while the military leaders of the campaign benefited, soldiers and merchants suffered from "the Melancholy affair" of fixed prices and yellow fever.

Nevertheless, when Cuba was returned to Spain in 1763 under the terms of the Treaty of Paris, North Americans resumed cutting logwood at the Bay of Campeche and supplying goods and slaves to Cuba. A handful of New Yorkers sent agents to Havana regularly, processing some ten thousand slaves during the early 1760s. British seized the Havana Company's property and rationalized plantation development in a few short months while extending numerous written invitations to New York and Philadelphia merchants to hurry supplies and food to the island and hastening the threefold increase in sugar production during the next twenty years. Coffee, too, became an important product exported from Cuba and Puerto Rico by the late 1760s, typically on North American and English vessels.

By the end of the war in 1763, some seven hundred English and mid-Atlantic ships were landing each year at Cuban ports, and the Spanish crown's open port policy brought huge returns to New York's postwar traders to Havana, Porto Bello, Vera Cruz, and Cartagena during the next years. Moreover, ports such as St. Augustine and New Orleans became part of New Yorkers' regular circuit of stops for sugar, tobacco, and dyewoods. By the end of the Seven Years' War, the Spanish crown also was ordering large shipments of silver sent from Mexico to Venezuela to stimulate the economy of the latter, and soon much of that silver found its way into New York City and Philadelphia, whose merchants eagerly routed flour to Venezuela. Food shortages in Caracas and Santo Domingo also spurred Spanish officials to open up trade with North Americans under special permissions; during the late 1760s, numerous New York ships stopped at Jamaica, Curaçao, and other British ports to drop off flour and provisions, in exchange for silver payments and Spanish sugar. Buenos Aires now also became a stop-off for some North Americans, as well as Bogotá, although those two cities would capture significant American trade only after 1800. So, although Parliament tried to assert mercantilist principles more firmly after the war, especially by seizing Spanish ships carrying contraband to and from British possessions, their efforts largely failed. Giving in, Parliament passed the Free Port Act of 1766, which opened up four Jamaican ports (among other British ones) for the Spanish trade.

By the time of the American Revolution, habits of exchange and deep networks of credit linked the Spanish and British empires. In 1776, Spanish royal officials opened Havana to North American trade in essential food and naval stores, which were paid for with silver that was channeled into American insurgents' coffers. Within a few months, Spain granted the new American states most favored nation status in Havana. In addition, the Spanish arranged lines of credit for Americans through bankers in Amsterdam and Paris, and Spanish colonists in New Orleans provided thousands of barrels of gunpowder, while merchants in Bilbao, according to Benjamin Franklin, stood ready to ship blankets, clothing, and other necessities to revolutionary Americans. Some scholars believe that Spain raised over three million pesos in aid for American patriots—one third from Mexico and another third from Cuba—which was to be repaid in American exports to needy Spanish Caribbean islands. For their part, Americans anticipated that their independence would initiate an open commerce and extensive diplomatic friendship with the Spanish Caribbean, Venezuela, Peru, and Mexico. These expectations were palpable in the press, correspondence, and diplomatic writings of both sides from 1778 onward, so when the Spanish crown decreed a generalized *reglamento* that year—a measure that allowed all trade within the Spanish empire to flow freely without port duties—North Americans pushed through British blockades and rushed to satisfy Spanish colonial needs. The effect was to temporarily increase American patriots' scarcities of food and fuel, but by 1781 the longer-term effect was to stimulate flour exports from the new mid-Atlantic states.

The American Revolution also raised opportunities for diplomatic relations between patriots and Spanish possessions. For example, Juan de Miralles, a rapidly rising Spanish merchant-diplomat, traveled from port to port in North America orchestrating commerce to Cuba. Miralles was already a familiar figure to prominent Americans, and he spent time in George Washington's army camps. During the Revolution, a few American patriot merchants' captains also visited Santo Domingo, Havana, and New Orleans. Other New York merchants used the services of Spanish officials at Caribbean ports to expedite loans from Cuban and Mexican lenders; sometimes, these networks also shared the proceeds of captured privateering vessels that were taken into Havana or New Orleans. Thus, from 1778 to 1782 the open port policies of the Spanish empire proved mutually beneficial to American revolutionaries and Caribbean Spanish peoples alike. By 1782, the only silver and gold coin of consequence circulating in revolutionary North America had originated in Spanish America.

In Spain, Diego de Gardoqui of Bilbao became the crown appointee for expediting loans to patriots, using his own commercial connections with Spanish possessions as a conduit to patriot leaders. Gardoqui, already linked to Aaron Lopez of Newport, Robert Morris of Philadelphia, and other trading partners, fervently sought ways to benefit in trade as he served the interests of patriots in North America. Following the Revolution, Gardoqui resided in New York City as a consul with the power to license ships that sold flour to Spanish colonies, reaping his own commission fees for organizing the licensed trade. In Havana, the first American consul was Robert Smith of Baltimore, appointed in 1781 and in close touch with Robert Livingston, the first American Secretary of Foreign Affairs and an established New York merchant. Although Spain closed its ports to foreign trade in 1783, the two men shared political news and granted each other credit for commercial exchanges. Oliver Pollack —already established as a Havana merchant since the early 1760s—replaced Smith that year, and Livingston easily transferred his private Havana accounts to Pollack. Already assured by Robert Morris that his American diplomatic appointment in Havana would advance his own business interests, Pollack took a large load of contraband goods on the ship that carried him to Havana.

During the early 1780s a consortium of merchants including Pollack, Smith, James Seagrove, and Francisco de Miranda—who soon would move from Cuba to New York to promote Latin American independence—brought goods and slaves into Havana against Spanish crown policy, paying for them with silver that was quickly returned to New York and Philadelphia. New York merchants filled the bottom half of flour barrels with contraband, while Cuban merchants stuffed the bottoms of barrels with silver pesos and topped off the containers with sugar. Bribing port officials at Havana proved easy, and a thick network of bankers on different continents facilitated this trade. David Parish of Philadelphia and New York, the Barings of London, the Hopes of Amsterdam, the Rothschilds of London and Paris, and even Napoleon's private bankers brokered widespread transatlantic exchanges going through Havana and New York. Although Spain shut down its colonial ports to foreigners officially from 1783 to 1797, people in New Orleans and Buenos Aires bought more American flour and wheat; Venezuelans and Santo Domingans placed orders for extensive lists of manufactured items and construction materials. By 1788, American whaling vessels touched at Patagonia, often bringing slaves and flour to colonists there and smuggling out all manner of South American products. Vessels rounding the tip of South America also landed for fuel, food, and silver before proceeding to China. By the 1800s, Parish was procuring silver from New Orleans and Vera Cruz, some of which was used to buy neutral American goods for consumers in Napoleonic Europe, and some of which was sent to China to purchase tea and porcelain wares. New York's

Archibald Gracie was at the center of a multicity consortium of merchants that took millions of pounds sterling in silver from Mexico, outfitted ships to transport the specie to Europe or North America, and secured return supplies of food and manufactured goods for Spanish Americans.

Voyages lengthened and networks of credit thickened in New York's postrevolutionary trade with Spanish colonists. Seaman & Company, as well as the Rhinelander brothers, built sugar-boiling works in New York in 1799 as a direct result of trade with Havana. As Haitian revolutionaries destroyed sugar and coffee plantations, Cuba took over first place among Caribbean sugar-producing islands; during the same years, New York's overall level of trade with Cuba and Puerto Rico took first place away from Philadelphia. By the 1820s New Yorkers carried away more Cuban sugar and silver than any other group of merchants.

American revolutionary ideas reverberated throughout the Spanish Caribbean and South America, aided by long-term commercial contacts and the self-conscious exchange of ideas made possible by the maturing print culture of the Atlantic world. Yet until the early 1800s, when South Americans would initiate their own independence movements, direct cultural and diplomatic exchanges between New York and the Spanish empire were still tentative. While collaboration to defeat a mutual enemy—England—put chinks in the walls between Protestants and Catholics, there was not yet any large-scale immigration into North America of people from Spanish-speaking islands and countries. Lingering antipapal sentiments surfaced in New York from time to time, although it became legal to practice Catholicism in the city. An important exception to New York's previous generations of anti-Catholicism occurred when the Spanish consul (led by the efforts of Thomas Stoughton) was authorized to build St. Peter's in New York City in 1785, the completion of which was made possible by the finances of royal officials under King Charles III in Spain, royalists in Mexico, and merchants in Cuba. Diplomatic connections with Don Diego de Gardoqui and with Francisco de Miranda helped turn long-standing commercial connections into closer cultural ones.

In 1806, when Miranda loaded up some New York ships with arms, food, and soldiers, set sail for Venezuela, got caught by Spanish royalists, and lost his ship and soldiers, the American press followed his story closely and applauded the export of their revolutionary ideals to southern neighbors. By then, New York's merchants and financiers were less connected culturally and economically to continental Spain and far more invested in the prosperity of Spain's colonies. As Spanish colonial independence movements took shape, interimperial quarrels over regulation and the spoils of warfare diminished, and discussions about the mutual benefits of open trade in the Western Hemisphere deepened. When Spain reopened its colonial ports to North Americans in 1797, New York merchants were poised to rush to Latin America with flour and other essential commodities, including large orders for British manufactures reexported out of North America. The same North American shippers also reexported Spanish American goods to England and Europe, typically under the cloak of neutral ships, neutral commodities, and neutral silver. And especially after Napoleon's armies entered Spain in 1809, American merchants became ever more committed to linking Latin American commerce to their own prosperity, as newspaper advertisements for trade goods from Havana, Vera Cruz, and Cartagena regularly reminded New Yorkers. Archibald Gracie loaded up his ships with flour for New Orleans, Havana, and Vera Cruz; LeRoy, Bayard, and McEvers sent flour and textiles to Chile, guns to Bolivia, and slaves to Havana. A dozen fast-rising fortunes were made by New Yorkers who deepened the flour-and-slaves-for-sugar trade through Cuba's flourishing ports during the early 1800s.

The Spanish and British empires had never been independent of each other, despite imperial commercial regulations and divergent cultures. New Yorkers and Spanish colonists had always crossed porous boundaries in the Western Hemisphere, traded legally and illegally, and built communities that were multicultural crossroads of people and material goods. The empires became interdependent, evidenced very early in the slave trade and commerce in staple crops, and grew stronger over time in the cultural crosscurrents and material goods that people in both empires enjoyed despite imperial rules and long before true neighborhoods of Spanish, Cubans, Puerto Ricans, and other peoples of Hispanic origins became visible in New York.

NOTES

1. Quoted in Joyce D. Goodfriend, *Before the Melting Pot: Society and Culture in Colonial New York City, 1664–1730* (Princeton, NJ: Princeton University Press, 1992), 116.

2. John Watts, *The Letter Book of John Watts, Merchant and Councillor of New York*, 27, Collections of The New-York Historical Society (New York: The New-York Historical Society, 1928).

3. Ibid.

4. Ibid.

5. Ibid., 88.

6. Ibid., 229–31.

CUBANS IN NINETEENTH-CENTURY NEW YORK:

A Story of Sugar, War, and Revolution

LISANDRO PÉREZ

In Cuba, as far as I know, is where you can find the largest number of Cubans; but besides Cuba nowhere else are there more Cubans than on the docks of the Columbia or the Marion on sailing days. Someone said that it appears as if New York is a neighborhood of Havana, and I could not disagree.
—Simón Camacho, *Cosas de los Estados Unidos*, 1864[1]

Cristóbal Madan y Madan was a teenager when he arrived in New York aboard the brigantine *Emma* from the Cuban port of Matanzas on June 24, 1822. His family's origins were in Waterford, Ireland, where the name was probably spelled Madden. Cristóbal's grandfather migrated to Havana by way of the Canary Islands around the time of the British occupation of the city, the right moment to get in on the ground floor of the island's sugar boom. The family lived in Havana, but their mills were in the Matanzas region. Cristóbal was named after his maternal grandfather, who was also his father's uncle. Cristóbal's father, Joaquín, had married a first cousin, Josefa Nicasia Madan. Joaquín and Josefa had six children, of which Cristóbal was the youngest and the only male. After his wife died, Joaquín married yet another first cousin, Josefa's sister. They had no children.

As with many other young men from Cuba's sugarocracy, the young Cristóbal went to New York to learn English, study, and gain experience in the city's mercantile world. Arrangements were made for him to intern as a clerk in the countinghouse of Jonathan Goodhue, a New Englander who had moved to South Street from Salem and was engaged in importing sugar from the mills of the Madans and other Cuban producers.

On a cold day in December 1823, the sixteen-year-old Madan heard Goodhue, in an excited voice, summon him to the front of the office at 44 South Street. There, in a lightweight coat peppered with snow, stood Father Félix Varela, an acquaintance of

Goodhue and Madan's former philosophy teacher in Havana. The Cuban priest and intellectual had gone directly from the gangplank of the cargo ship *Draper* to the one place in the city where he knew he could find people from his days in Havana: a South Street countinghouse. Madan arranged lodging for Varela at a boardinghouse on Broadway. For days thereafter he took his former teacher on walks near the piers, steadying him as Varela became accustomed to walking on the icy streets.

Although Father Félix Varela was only in his mid-thirties when he arrived in New York, he already had an established reputation as an educator, a philosopher, and an advocate of Cuban separatism. In 1822 he had traveled to Madrid as one of three elected deputies from the island to present proposals before the Spanish parliament that were intended to reform how Spain governed its island colony. The reinstatement of King Ferdinand to the throne, however, meant an end to all progressive reform initiatives, and the Cuban priest became a target for the monarch's reprisals, forcing Varela to take refuge in Gibraltar. He disembarked in New York from the *Draper*, the first ship he could find out of Gibraltar. During the first two years that he lived in the United States, he wrote extensively about Cuba, arguing for a change in the political status of the island and the need to abolish slavery. Varela's bold essays calling for a new social and political order for Cuba reached the island and had a tremendous impact. But the Spanish Crown did not want Cubans thinking about change. The island's colonial governor, Francisco Vives, was given extraordinary emergency powers to deal with any manifestations of civil unrest or disloyalty to His Majesty. Varela had already been sentenced to death in absentia for his role in the liberal movement, and Vives decided to apply the sentence, dispatching an assassin to New York in the spring of 1825. One of Varela's biographers identified him as "One-Eyed Morejón" of the Havana police and one of Vives's "thugs." Varela's sympathizers in Havana alerted their friends in New York, and the plot was foiled by the vigilance of Varela's Irish parishioners, who had befriended the priest and had no sympathy for colonialists. The one-eyed Spanish-speaking stranger no doubt had difficulty passing unnoticed in the Irish neighborhood, and returned to Havana, presumably without earning the thirty thousand pesos Vives promised him for the job. Although the attempt on Varela's life did not take place, it was clear that he could not return to Havana.

That same year, the President of Mexico, Guadalupe Victoria, invited Varela to sail to Veracruz aboard a Mexican warship that was due to arrive in New York. The president offered the protection of his government for as long as Varela wished to live in Mexico. The priest declined the generous invitation, preferring to stay in New York. It was a decision that spoke volumes about the place that New York had come to occupy in the Cuban economic, political, and cultural landscapes. No doubt Varela would have felt more comfortable leaving New York. During those first years in the city he did not adjust well to the cold weather or to the language, which he found hard

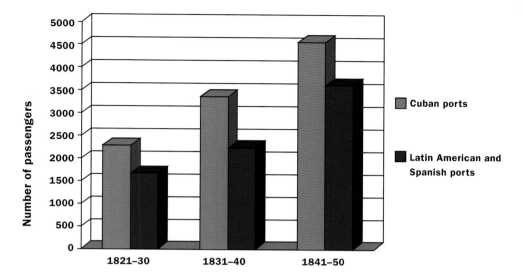

The number of passengers arriving in New York from Cuban ports and from Latin American and Spanish ports, 1821–50, by decade.

to learn. "The whistling sound of English," he wrote at the time, "rings in my ears like impertinent flies, making it hard to write comfortably in Spanish."[2] And yet, when offered a privileged opportunity to move to a warmer Spanish-speaking country, he chose to face New York's climate and language. Varela would remain in the city for almost thirty years, eventually conquering English to the point where he spoke it almost without an accent. The founder of two downtown churches and an eloquent defender of the rights of Catholics and the Irish at a time when they faced serious challenges from "nativists" and "anti-papists," the Cuban priest played a critical role in the development of the New York archdiocese.

The choice to live in New York City was to be repeated in subsequent decades by Cuban exiles who wished to stay close to their native island and remain active in its affairs. In terms of economic, political, and sociopsychological distance, the closest place to Cuba was New York, and it was New York's commerce with the island that made that distance appear so short. The commercial ties and the intense ship traffic served to attract and sustain a growing expatriate community. Only one week after Varela arrived in Manhattan, a young exiled poet from Matanzas also made his way to Goodhue and Company and was greeted by the young Cristóbal Madan. José María Heredia came to the same conclusion, and for the same reasons, that Varela reached when he arrived in the city. In the first letter the poet wrote from New York, he told his mother that "one reason I am inclined to remain here is the constant communication there is with Havana; it is where I can easily and frequently receive news of my family."[3]

In 1823, the same year that both the priest and the poet made their way to Manhattan, ninety-seven passenger ships had arrived directly from seven different Cuban ports, more than half of them from Havana.[4] Several ships were engaged regularly in transporting passengers to and from the island. In that decade, from 1821 to 1830, there were more passengers arriving in New York from Cuban ports than the number of passengers arriving from all the other ports of Latin America and Spain combined, a trend that continued throughout the first half of the nineteenth century. In 1830 alone, 936 U.S. ships entered Cuban ports. By 1835, commerce with Cuba had reached such proportions that it became an important factor in the total U.S. trade picture. Between 1835 and 1865, Cuba consistently ranked third or fourth among U.S. trade partners in the combined value of exports and imports.

At first, New Orleans, Boston, Philadelphia, and Baltimore vied with New York for the flourishing Cuba trade. But ultimately, New York ended up with the lion's share of the commerce with the island, especially in sugar. By 1860, the port of New York was handling almost two-thirds of all sugar entering the U.S. The key to New York's dominance was its capacity to turn a hefty profit through the further industrial processing of the raw sugar. Cuba exported raw brown sugar that was marketable only to the poorest consumers. The real profit was made by selling it as refined white sugar packaged in a large cone or loaf. The profitable refining process was done in New York, the nation's established refining center since even before the Cuba trade. In 1689 New York had the first sugar refinery of the North American colonies, and by 1855 it had fourteen plants operating. From 1845 to 1860 the port of New York exported an average of 1.8 million pounds of refined sugar annually. In 1860 alone it exported 4.7 million pounds.

Besides raw sugar, New York also was interested in Cuban cigars, which became fashionable among the men in the city. In 1860, 243 million cigars—more than half of all U.S. cigar imports—came in through New York harbor, most of them from Havana. New York would also import Cuban tobacco leaves as the number of cigar factories multiplied in Lower Manhattan; and New Yorkers, especially German immigrants, once again turned Cuba's unprocessed imports into a manufactured product.

New York's exports to Cuba were, of course, much more diverse than the products arriving from Cuban ports. As noted earlier, the island's increased population and wealth and its dramatic shift to a single-crop economy meant that the demand for a wide range of products that New York could provide increased sharply. Cuba had to import practically everything. The sugarocrats bought machinery for their mills, fine linen and clothing for themselves, furnishings for their new mansions, carriages in which to be seen around Havana, and large amounts of foodstuffs, especially flour, to feed their slaves.

The protagonists of that trade were countinghouses such as Goodhue and Company and its successor at 44 South Street, Moses Taylor and Company. A combination of trading office, warehouse, accounting firm, credit agency, bank, and investment managers, the countinghouses that lined South and Wall Streets were key players in New York's trade with Cuba. They cultivated relations with the Cuban planters, extending them credit, acting as their shipping and commission agents, selling their sugar, and purchasing manufactured goods in New York on their behalf. The countinghouses and their agents forged links between Cuba and New York that went beyond the commercial sphere, establishing the basis for a profound and extensive exchange of not only goods and money, but also of people and culture. Cubans started coming in greater numbers to New York.

Spearheading that flow were boys and young men from wealthy families seeking an education and work experience, and the countinghouses had a direct role in bringing them from Cuba. In many cases, the New York merchants, at the request of their Cuban clients, would make the arrangements for the sons of the planters to be enrolled in boarding schools in the area. The countinghouse was responsible for meeting the young men at the dock, enrolling them in a boarding school and transporting them to it, outfitting them with winter clothing and other necessities, and making arrangements for periodic disbursements of tuition, board, and allowances. The countinghouses would also temporarily employ young Cuban men in their own operations in New York, as Goodhue had done with Cristóbal Madan, in a sort of internship that would enable them to learn English and become familiar with modern business operations. As early as 1850, one New Yorker estimated that nearly two thousand young Cubans had already been educated in U.S. schools, adding that "their ideas and customs upon returning to the island are more North American than Spanish."[5]

The business of the South Street countinghouses created a bridge between Lower Manhattan and Cuba. On the back of New York's Cuba trade rode an extensive network of social contacts that would cement the New York–Cuba connection and begin the process by which New York, and by extension the United States, replaced Spain as the "other" place in the Cuban consciousness. That substitution, which had already occurred in the commercial arena before the end of the eighteenth century, would rapidly expand to the social, cultural, and political spheres. It was the basis for the rise of a community in Manhattan that for most of the nineteenth century remained the largest concentration of Cubans in the United States and the largest community of Latin Americans east of the Mississippi. New York became the place of refuge, exile, banishment, or escape for Cubans, that world outside the homeland where they went for an education, opportunity, or wealth, to start a new life or forget an old one, to evade royal authority, plot a revolution, experience freedom, or buy and sell. At mid-nineteenth century, as the island was on the verge of tumbling into the tumultuous decades that were to define the Cuban nation, it was unavoidable that New York would take center stage as Cuba's struggle to separate from Spain intensified.

There is no better symbol of New York's role in the Cuban separatist movement than the extraordinary event that occurred exactly at mid-century, on May 11, 1850, at the corner of Nassau and Fulton Streets, the location of the *New York Sun.* Then and there, a flag identified in that day's edition of the *Sun* as the "Flag of Free Cuba" was flying over Lower Manhattan.[6] No one had ever seen this nor any other piece of cloth identified as a flag of Cuba. And it was not just any Cuban flag, but *the* Cuban flag, the one that would be adopted by the separatist movement and remains to this day, despite a turbulent history, the flag of Cuba. It was on that day, in New York, that it flew for the first time anywhere, reportedly designed and sewn in a Manhattan boardinghouse.

The flying of that flag heralded the launch of an armed expedition, largely organized in New York, to wrest control of Cuba from the Spanish. The expedition was supported and funded by Cubans and Americans who favored the annexation of Cuba to the Union. Annexationism had its heyday in the 1840s and 1850s and its origins, as well as the motivations of its proponents, were varied and often contradictory. One condition that led to the rise of the movement was Spain's steadfast refusal to relax colonial controls and grant Cubans a role in determining the island's affairs.

Spain's intransigence led some progressive Cubans to regard annexation to the United States as a desired alternative to Spanish rule. Becoming a U.S. state seemed a pragmatic and dignified path for Cuba, especially given the relative autonomy enjoyed by the states in the American federal system and the progressive spirit of the United States. But the core of the annexationist movement was not composed of progressive Cubans, but rather sugar planters in the island eager to save the basis of their wealth: slavery. Becoming a U.S. slave state seemed to offer the best guarantee for continuing the institution, since at the time the United States had shown itself to be a powerful defender of slavery in their own nation, rebuffing British attempts to end it immediately.

One of the most notable efforts of the annexationists in New York was the establishment of a pro-annexation bilingual newspaper, *La Verdad*, which appeared biweekly from 1848 to 1853. It was printed at the *Sun* and the editor was one Cora Montgomery, a pseudonym for Mrs. W. L. Cazneau, a relative of Moses Yale Beach, the editor of the *Sun*. Beach was a strong advocate for the annexation of Cuba. *La Verdad* was a newspaper supported by wealthy annexationists and produced by, and for, elites and intellectuals. It was the voice of a movement and not a commercial venture, carrying virtually no advertising and distributed free of charge to readers. Typically, *La Verdad* had four pages plus a supplement in English, all of it crammed with long pro-annexation tracts printed in small type. The articles were usually unsigned, but many were probably written by Cristóbal Madan, by now in his forties, a lawyer, and one of the leading annexationists, representing in New York the interests of his family and other sugar planters. Madan maintained a home in the city when he was not in Cuba, as did many other Cuban New Yorkers who were able to live transnational lives, taking advantage of the traffic between South Street and the Cuban ports to cement business, professional, family, and political ties in both places.

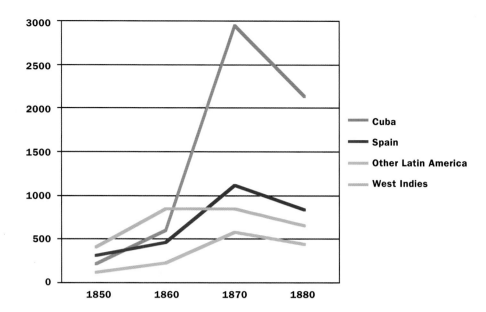

The birthplace of the Hispanic population of New York according to the U.S. decennial censuses, 1850–80.

The annexationist movement lingered for several years after the failure of the armed expeditions that were dispatched to Cuba. But it started to decline around 1855 as many of its proponents realized that the U.S. government was unwilling to risk its relations with Europe to annex Cuba and that it would oppose the launching of expeditions from its own soil. The movement was nonexistent by the time of the American Civil War. For the rest of the century, New York would be the setting for many other émigré revolutionary activities and movements, most of them rejecting annexation and pursuing nothing short of total independence for Cuba. But the activities of the annexationists in New York marked the beginning of organized efforts on the part of Cubans in the city to effect changes in their homeland. The movement was a harbinger of things to come as Cuban New York became more and more affected by the emerging conflict between Cubans and Spaniards over the future of the island, as other separatist movements arose and Spain countered with greater repression.

By the end of the American Civil War, Cristóbal Madan and the other sugar planters of Havana and Matanzas were trying, without much success, to extract concessions from the Madrid government that would allow the Cubans some measure of autonomy in governing the island. But on October 10, 1868, all efforts to peacefully reform Cuba's colonial status ended. War broke out. In its intensity and scope it was unlike anything that had been experienced before through conspiracies, expeditions, and local insurrections. It came unexpectedly, literally out of nowhere, for it did not originate in the usual places. It was not hatched in the meeting halls or newspaper offices of émigrés in New York, nor in the sugar plantations of Matanzas, and not even in the Havana homes of impatient intellectuals, merchants, or sugar planters. It came from the backwater that was eastern Cuba, spearheaded by long-neglected and resentful landowners, most of whom were virtually unknown in Havana or Matanzas or New York. But in 1868, when those easterners decided they had had enough of Spanish rule and were willing to risk everything to end it, Cuba, as well as its émigré community in New York, would not be the same again.

The eastern landowners had endured generations of neglect from colonial authorities. They had few sentimental or economic ties to Spain. To them, colonial rule meant only oppression and taxes. The sugar boom that occurred in the western provinces had bypassed them and consequently they had few trade connections with New York. The eastern elites remained stuck in a more modest and diversified agricultural economy. Without a great dependence on slavery and sugar, and therefore devoid of an economic stake in the continuation of the colonial or slave regime, eastern patricians had no use for annexationist or reformist formulas. The only thing that made sense to them was independence, and unlike their cautious Havana compatriots who feared the consequences of violence for their economic interests, the easterners had relatively little to lose and were willing to risk all of it. The desire for freedom and independence was stoked by the privileged education they received, including boarding schools in Havana, and trips to Europe and the United States, where they were exposed to liberal and democratic ideals.

When the easterners decided that Cuba's colonial status had to be resolved with firepower, the sugar planters of Havana and Matanzas were swept up in the wake of forces unleashed by a war they had not started and were powerless to control. The Spanish, and especially the *voluntarios*, a paramilitary unit loyal to the Crown, countered with repression and persecution against those perceived as enemies of Spanish colonialism. Cuban planters such as Madan, who had long advocated changes in the island's colonial status, were especially suspect and vulnerable to the intimidation and terrorism the *voluntarios* unleashed in the capital. Fearing for their personal safety, many of Havana's elite families fled the country during the first few months of 1869. Others were deported.

The resulting exodus had a special impact on New York. The fleeing elite families, most of whom had longstanding trade and financial connections to the city and were therefore likely to have accounts in South Street countinghouses, overwhelmingly favored New York as their destination. The influx dwarfed the earlier migrations of Cubans to the city. Moreover, it was a true migration, not just the comings and goings of sojourners, transnational merchants, or students. It involved entire families who were leaving the island without knowing when, and if, they would ever return. This large wave of Cubans arriving in New York was reflected in the results of the 1870 census as the number of Cuban-born persons living in what are now the five boroughs reached nearly three thousand, with about 2,600 enumerated in Manhattan alone. The total number of Cuban New Yorkers far surpassed the total number of all Latin Americans and Spaniards living in the city that year.

CUBAN LADIES IN COUNCIL AT THE HOUSE OF SENORA R. HOURRITINER, NEW YORK CITY.—[Sketched by Theo. R. Davis.]

With the boom in the city's Cuban population and with a war raging in the island, New York's role as the most important setting for émigré separatist activism became even more prominent and took on a greater urgency as external support for the rebels became a critical piece in the struggle. The volume and intensity of Cuban émigré activities in New York were turned up substantially and became a more visible element in the city's landscape. The war would last until 1878, and during those war years many more Cubans would seek refuge in New York, including some of the easterners who had been on the battlefield, or their widows and children.

The war did not result in the independence of Cuba, but the treaty that ended it did allow Cuban New Yorkers to return to the island. Some of them, such as Cristóbal Madan, by now nearly seventy years old, returned with the intention of recovering their estates, which had been confiscated by the Spanish authorities. It would be a fruitless endeavor. Yet many Cubans chose to remain in the city. For those who were laborers, cigar workers, former slaves and indentured servants, domestic workers, and even some real estate investors and professionals, life in New York had meant new opportunities to improve their lives. They had nothing to recover and nothing to gain by returning to a Cuba ravaged by war.

But New York was not finished as the setting for Cuban separatist activities. In fact, its best-known chapter was yet to come, the one that would finally lead to the establishment of the Cuban nation-state in the twentieth century. That chapter

opened with the arrival in New York on January 3, 1880, of a young Cuban lawyer and writer by the name of José Martí.

Martí is the towering figure of Cuban history, and he spent most of his adult life in New York. Shortly after his arrival he wrote that in New York "one can breathe freely" and "feel proud of one's species."[7] The city gave him experiences he could not have found anywhere else, experiences that allowed him to develop politically, intellectually, and personally, and made it possible for him to sharpen his vision of the world and his strategy for achieving an independent Cuba. It was in New York that he did his best writing and earned a living from it. It was in New York that he accomplished what no other Cuban émigré had been able to do: build a unified civilian movement that would take a sustainable armed struggle to Cuba. And it was in New York that he was exposed to the best, and the worst, of what the most important city in the world, the one at the cutting edge of urban modernity, had to offer.

As with Varela, Heredia, and so many Cubans who preceded him in New York, Martí chose to remain in the city to carry out what he always knew to be his destiny: the creation of an independent Cuba. It was in New York, despite the unfamiliar language and the hostile climate, where he felt closest to Cuba. He remained in New York for fifteen years until he left for the island at the head of the movement he had painstakingly organized. Only three months after leaving, Martí was struck by a volley of Spanish bullets in the Cuban countryside, a moment captured in the equestrian statue of him in his adopted city at Sixth Avenue and Central Park South. As happened with so many Cubans who throughout the nineteenth century lived in New York and made the city the most important staging ground for the building of the Cuban nation, he did not live to see his homeland freed from Spanish colonialism.

NOTES

1. Simón Camacho, *Cosas de los Estados Unidos* (New York: Imprenta de "El Porvenir," 1864), 205.

2. Quoted, without reference, by José Ignacio Rodríguez, *Vida del presbítero Don Félix Varela*, 2nd ed. (1878; reprint, Havana: Arellano y Cía., 1944), 144.

3. Letter to María Mercedes Heredia Campuzano, New York, December 24, 1823, in *Epistolario de José María Heredia*, ed. Angel Augier (Havana: Editorial Letras Cubanas, 2005), 90.

4. Bradley W. Steuart, ed., *Passenger Ships Arriving in New York Harbor*, vol. 1, *1820–1850* (Bountiful, Utah: Precision Indexing, 1991), 11–14.

5. J. S. Thrasher, "Preliminary Essay," in Alejandro de Humboldt, *Ensayo político sobre la isla de Cuba*, rev. and trans. ed. (Havana: Publicaciones del Archivo Nacional de Cuba, 1960), 425 (translation mine).

6. *New York Sun*, May 11, 1850, 2.

7. José Martí, "Impressions in America (By a Very Fresh Spaniard)," *The Hour* 2, no. 1 (July 10, 1880): 164.

PUERTO RICANS IN "OLDE" NUEVA YORK:

Migrant *Colonias* of the Nineteenth and Twentieth Centuries

VIRGINIA SÁNCHEZ KORROL

In 1889, during the heat and humidity of the wettest July on record, a pair of newly-weds arrived in New York from Puerto Rico. Bringing the accoutrements of his printing trade, they settled in their new lodgings at 284 and 286 Pearl Street, the new home of the publishing house Imprenta América. The bride, Inocencia Martínez Santaella, was a native of Ponce, Puerto Rico. The groom, Sotero Figueroa, an ardent advocate of the island's separation from Spain, shared a dangerous preoccupation in a repressive colony. The bride cultivated a love of Spanish romances but an aversion to domesticity. The groom was a self-made man known for his erudition and fiery discourses. As the starry-eyed couple envisioned a bright future in New York, the match was doomed in the eyes of her parents because of his color and slave ancestry. But the free-spirited bride defied convention and wed the dashing revolutionary on June 28, 1889.

The New York that the couple encountered that July was a noisy, energetic city teeming with immigrants, a virtual "Iron Tower of Babel," according to cigar maker Bernardo Vega, where politics permeated the couple's daily existence. Although their story forms an important part of Puerto Rican history in New York, the Figueroas were not the first Puerto Ricans to emigrate. The broader narrative spans most of the nineteenth century, when the city became a haven for exiles harboring antigovernment convictions and a smattering of agents representing commercial enterprises that traded the island's raw materials for American manufactured goods. Brokerage associations reflected a steady growth of exchange networks between the United States and the Hispanic Caribbean during the antebellum years. By mid-century, American ships plied Atlantic waters laden with tobacco, rum, sugar, and molasses from the Antilles. Briny-aired brothels, beer joints, and boardinghouses in New York greedily beckoned the Antillean sailors and merchants who often accompanied trade goods. Spanish-owned boardinghouses tucked amidst dark alleys and narrow streets or on the waterfront courted business using language and cultural

Elisa Santiago Baeza, New York, ca. 1927. Photographer unknown. Collection of Virginia Sánchez Korrol.

familiarity, although they sought to attract merchant seamen and dockworkers of all nationalities.

Beginning in the 1820s, Spanish-language publishing houses printed scores of books read throughout the Americas, a venture that fostered commerce and defined a national consciousness. Radical-minded émigrés during the 1850s and 1860s wrote for Spanish-language or bilingual presses. They aimed to influence the politics of the homeland and disseminate their ideas to a wide reading public. Such was the case with the 1858 literary collection *El Laúd del Desterrado* (The Exile's Lute), compiled by Miguel Teurbe Tolón, an editor at the *New York Herald*. Writing from the oasis of American freedom, the land of Jefferson and Adams, exiled Cuban authors mourned the tragic loss of their colonized homeland from a distance. *El Laúd* inspired patriotism, and Cuban students were said to pass along dog-eared copies of the volume. As exiles moved from country to country, the foundational thinkers on Puerto Rican nationhood and liberation, among them Eugenio María de Hostos, Francisco "Pachín" Marín, and Lola Rodríguez de Tió, found fertile ground for their ideology.

The immediate background to the Figueroas' relocation was the movement for Antillean liberation that intensified in 1868 with the rebellion known as El Grito de Lares in Puerto Rico. Planned in conjunction with a companion uprising in Cuba, El Grito de Yara, the Puerto Rican strike was quickly crushed by Spanish authorities, but the Cuban rebellion became the Ten Years' War (1868–78), erupting again into hostilities from 1895 until 1898, the year of the Spanish-American War. For four decades, New York City would play a crucial role in this movement as a base for planning and mobilizing revolution.

Fired with the fervor for independence, Martínez de Figueroa would have known the legendary role of earlier émigrés who helped ignite from afar and maintain rebellion in motion from the city she now called home. Since the wars for Latin American independence (1810–25), Puerto Ricans and Cubans in the U.S. stirred conspiratorial intrigue with fellow sympathizers from the circum-Caribbean. A coalition of influential Cuban and Puerto Rican expatriates in New York formed the Sociedad Republicana de Cuba y Puerto Rico in 1865 to end Spanish colonialism and seek support from Latin Americans in their struggle. Following the successful Cuban uprising in 1868, it adopted the name Junta Revolucionaria de Cuba y Puerto Rico and essentially became a government in exile. An impressive confluence of Puerto Rican leaders, artisans, and tobacco workers in New York endorsed the junta because it represented a step toward liberation for Puerto Rico. Junta support came from Antillean cigar workers, small businesses, hostels, and restaurants.

Although less politically experienced than her husband, Martínez de Figueroa would have heard or read about the effects of the Ten Years' War on New York's Antillean communities. War-related familial ruptures, enforced emigration, and instability became common expatriate experiences. Widows and orphans faced overwhelming hardships in the city where life as they had known it suddenly disintegrated. Sharply defined norms and class distinctions fluctuated, and the affluent were often reduced to penny pinching. Emilia Casanova de Villaverde, who would become Martínez de Figueroa's compatriot in the 1890s struggles, was the first Latina to petition the U.S. Congress to support Cuban independence. Casanova de Villaverde had come to New York in 1854, and much of her family's plantation wealth went into the war effort. But the palatial halls of the Casanova mansion, the family estate in the Oak Point (Mott Haven) section of the Bronx, did not blind her to the troubling plight of her countrymen. In a letter to a compatriot, she described the situation circa 1870: "Here there is more misery than you could imagine among the immigrant Cubans. Not only the men, but women and children, naked, barefoot, and without bread to take to their mouths."[1]

Brought to an end by a Spanish victory in 1878, the revolutionary agenda of the Ten Years' War would not fully resurface until José Martí, the writer/philosopher, appeared in the snowbound city of New York during the bitterly cold January of 1880. The revolutionary siren calls issued by Martí and his supporters during this heady period may well have lured Sotero Figueroa and his wife to the city. As with other émigrés driven by deep convictions that everyone was entitled to live in freedom, the Figueroas' life in New York centered on this mission.

In just one short month after his arrival in the city, to renew the enthusiasm for Antillean liberation Sotero Figueroa organized the Club Borinquen with some two hundred Puerto Ricans residing in New York. Figueroa also joined the Club Los Independientes, the launching site of José Martí's Cuban Revolutionary Party (PRC), and Las Dos Antillas, a newly formed group headed by the young Afro-Puerto Rican Arturo Schomburg and Rosendo Rodríguez. Figueroa's revolutionary soulmate, Martí named him secretary of the New York Council and editor of *Patria*, the PRC's official newspaper. In Martí's absence, Figueroa often served as the voice of the movement.

The renaissance of revolutionary-club formation within and outside of the PRC structure ranged from tobacco workers' organizations to women's clubs. In the spirit of liberation, clubs funded military expeditions sending weapons, medicine, bandages, clothing, and other scarce materials to Cuba. As it had during the Ten Years' War, the financial backbone of the movement rested on the shoulders of Antillean tobacco workers and other artisans, fundraisers for the cause in the city's cigar factories.

Puerto Rican cigar workers found jobs as rollers and strippers in some five hundred factories owned by Spaniards and Latin Americans and concentrated in Manhattan's Chelsea neighborhood, the Lower East Side, and around Adams, Johnson, and Jefferson streets in Brooklyn. During hard times, cigar makers, along with their wives and children, turned their homes into domestic factories, selling the finished

Hamilton Avenue in Brooklyn as seen from Union Street, 1924. Photographer unknown. Jesús Colón Papers, Archives of the Puerto Rican Diaspora, Centro de Estudios Puertorriqueños, Hunter College, CUNY.

products to cigar stands and other factories. In his memoirs, Vega recounts, "One room . . . is used as the bedroom and work area. The next room . . . serves as both a bedroom and kitchen. And the third room . . . is for children and storing the tobacco."[2] Dank, airless, unsanitary, and overcrowded living conditions were not unfamiliar to the bulk of the working class who, in turn, comprised the greater part of the *colonias*.

Imprenta América provided revenue for the growing Figueroa family. Martínez de Figueroa probably donned the full-length apron of the trade on occasion and worked alongside her husband, plucking type letters from wooden cases or proofreading broadsides, pamphlets, and articles. But she also honed her own social circles, and on February 21, 1892, she founded the first women's organization within the PRC, the Club Mercedes Varona. The only women's club to fully exercise its right to vote within the PRC administrative structure, it was also the first venue where New York women cast their vote in a political organization. Members included Casanova de Villaverde and Rodríguez de Tió, whose inspirational verses—"Cuba y Puerto Rico son / de un pájaro las dos alas" (Cuba and Puerto Rico are the two wings of one bird)—defined the core of the movement. Seven PRC women's clubs sprouted in the city on the heels of Mercedes Varona; by 1897 there were eleven.

Martínez de Figueroa's personal life, however, was not without tragedy. Fifteen months after launching Mercedes Varona, she gave birth to a healthy baby boy. But the felicitous occasion was marred by grief as she witnessed the painful passings of her three young daughters, victims perhaps of the typhus or cholera epidemics that

Members of the Puerto Rican section of the Cuban Revolutionary Party, 1896. Photographer unknown. General Collection, Archives of the Puerto Rican Diaspora, Centro de Estudios Puertorriqueños, Hunter College, CUNY.

Left to right: Manuel Besosa, Juan de M. Terreforte, Aurelio Méndez Martinez, Dr. José J. Henna, Sotero Figueroa, Roberto H. Todd.

gripped the city. By year's end, the emotional roller coasters careening through their personal and high-profile political lives shattered the Figueroa marriage.

On December 22, 1895, the Puerto Rican section of the PRC, led principally by J. J. Henna, Juan de M. Terreforte, Manuel Besosa, and Sotero Figueroa, was created. Two years later, to honor the esteemed Puerto Rican commander Juan Ríus Rivera, Martínez de Figueroa organized her last club, El Club Hermanas de Ríus Rivera. The club was successful, but the U.S. invasion of the islands in 1898 destroyed all hope for independence. Profoundly disillusioned, the Figueroas left the city for Havana, where they spent the rest of their years, officially dissolving their marriage in 1909. Like leaves scattered to the wind, the dissolution of the Puerto Rican section of the PRC on August 2, 1898, also signaled the end of an era but ushered in a new period in the flowering of the city's Puerto Rican *colonias.*

Numerous Puerto Ricans remained in the city after 1898. Their leadership skills, labor, and organizational experiences would help structure distinct and vibrant *colonias.* Some, like the cigar makers Bernardo Vega and Jesús Colón, engaged directly in community or trade union organizing, and shaped city and *barrio* politics; others, like Victoria and Rafael Hernández, pioneered in the worlds of music, the arts, and entrepreneurship; still others, skilled and unskilled workers' families, transmitted traditions and forged community through generations of lived experience.

Consider the story of Amelia Agostini del Rio, a woman who is rarely found in the history books but was similar to other Puerto Ricans who came to study in the city early in the 1900s. She arrived in 1918 and stayed to build an impressive career in academia. Agostini del Rio advanced her education at Vassar College, earned a master's degree from Columbia University, and in 1929 secured a faculty appointment at Barnard College, eventually heading the Spanish department. She wrote more than forty-five books, but one important textbook that she coauthored connected her to the schooling of generations of New Yorkers: *Antología General de la Literatura Española* (1954), a classic text familiar to multitudes of undergraduate majors for its wide use in the instruction of Spanish literature.

Puerto Rico became entrenched within the U.S. political and economic structure. An American-dominated, mechanized sugar monopoly and the demise of coffee cultivation unleashed vast unemployment, setting the stage for emigration. American citizenship under the Jones Act of 1917 facilitated the relocation of thousands of Puerto Ricans to mainland communities. The economic boom following World War I drew most Puerto Ricans to work in the lowest-paying sectors of production: manufacturing and light factory work, hotel and restaurants, cigar making, domestic service, and laundries. By the 1930s, some 61,463 Puerto Ricans comprised more than 40 percent of New York City's Latino population of 134,000 individuals.

The dynamics of migration were inextricably linked to economic considerations.

In a poverty-stretched, neglected colony, those who could scrape together the price of a steamship ticket could dream of leaving; others opted to sign contracts as seasonal workers, pawns in the international circulation of a colonized labor force. Such was the case with the 130 women from "good families" recruited to work in Brooklyn's American Manufacturing Company in 1920 (they later appealed for repatriation due to a breach of contract), and thousands of exploited agricultural workers who tilled and harvested the crops along the Atlantic seaboard. Workers like these succeeded in planting the seeds for new migrant *colonias* in places like New Jersey, Connecticut, and Pennsylvania.

What motivated men and women in their most productive years to exchange the brilliant hues of *Boricua* tropics for the city's drab concrete slabs, and the proximity of extended family for anonymity? They came because the shift from small subsistence family-owned farms to absentee-owned American conglomerates denied them the means to engage in fair market competition; because they searched for adventure and decent wages; or because family members pooled their resources to allow a favorite son or daughter an educational opportunity. They came to make their fortunes, to escape bleak personal circumstances, or to join migrant husbands or parents, the first in the family to plant stakes in the city.

In 1916 Bernardo Vega, the thirty-year-old, ruddy-faced chronicler of more than forty years of Puerto Rican life in New York, left Cayey "heavy of heart, but ready to face a new life." Shipboard conversations revealed similar goals among the traveling migrants. "First savings would be for sending for close relatives. Years later the time would come to return home with pots of money."[3]

At sixteen, Jesús Colón, the Afro–Puerto Rican cigar maker, hungered for excitement and opportunity. A prolific writer and future political activist, he left in 1918 following proper legal channels but wove a tale reflecting the plight of others in his essay "Stowaway."

> *Thus passed the days and nights traveling under strict war regulations, darkness during the night—for the United States was at war with Germany. During the day, I was shining dishes and pans or collecting china from the tables. . . . As the ship dropped anchor alongside a Brooklyn dock and a plank connecting dock and ship was securely fastened in place, I went ashore as unobtrusively as I had come into the boat in San Juan Bay in Puerto Rico.*[4]

The city's first Puerto Rican librarian, Pura Belpré, had no intention of remaining in New York when she attended her sister Elisa's wedding in 1920, but the lure of the city was irresistible. The petite, brown-skinned, twenty-one-year-old hoped to become a teacher in Puerto Rico but instead became a librarian, folklorist, writer, and storyteller. "I grew up in a home of storytellers listening to stories which had been handed down by word of mouth for generations," she recalled.[5] One story, in particu-

Bernardo Vega, 1916. Photographer unknown. Jesús Colón Papers, Archives of the Puerto Rican Diaspora, Centro de Estudios Puertorriqueños, Hunter College, CUNY.

Jesús Colón's war zone pass, 1918. Jesús Colón Papers, Archives of the Puerto Rican Diaspora, Centro de Estudios Puertorriqueños, Hunter College, CUNY.

Pura Belpré, n.d. Photographer unknown. Pura Belpré Papers, Archives of the Puerto Rican Diaspora, Centro de Estudios Puertorriqueños, Hunter College, CUNY.

lar, would forever be etched in Belpré lore. The 1932 publication of *Pérez and Martina: A Porto Rican Folk Tale,* a beloved story of the courtship and marriage of a lovesick mouse for a beautiful cockroach, was Belpré's gift to generations of schoolchildren. The tale stands among the earliest books to be published in English by a Puerto Rican.

The attractive twenty-year-old daughter of an impoverished *jíbaro* (peasant) peddler and an Indian-featured mother, Elisa Santiago was abandoned by her boyfriend when his upper-crust family forced him to marry another woman. Anticipating an untenable future, she left for New York in 1930 because "I was invited to go to New York to care for my cousin's children. I went and I stayed."[6]

The migrant world created by this diversity of experiences, particularly during the years between the world wars, cut across class and color lines in a racially delineated city and laid the multilayered foundations of Puerto Rican New York. Cheap housing, employment, and access to public transportation often determined where working-class barrios would form. The crowded cold-water flats in Manhattan, Brooklyn, and the South Bronx that had sheltered earlier immigrants now anchored Puerto Rican *colonias* with distinct characteristics, not the least of which were the Spanish language and cultural touchstones.

Predominantly in the city's poorer neighborhoods, Puerto Rican *colonias* boasted a richly layered infrastructure of restaurants, bodegas, botanicas, small businesses, mutual aid societies, lodges, professional organizations, cultural groups, and political, religious, and labor-oriented associations. From burial societies to beauty pageants, these institutions reinforced, coalesced, and redefined traditions, providing the barrios with cultural and consumer needs unavailable through other means.

The Liga Puertorriqueña e Hispana (1927), a confederation of citywide organizations, and the Porto Rican Brotherhood (1923), a political working-class club, sponsored an extensive array of activities, including baseball teams, that helped stitch tightly knit, self-sustaining barrios, promote class interests, and build a Puerto Rican heritage. Workers' groups such as Alianza Obrera (ca. 1922) and its cultural arm, Ateneo Obrero (1926), emphasized employment and workers' rights, while Puerto Rico Literario (1929) and the Asociación de Escritores y Periodistas Puertorriqueños (ca. 1930) attracted writers and intellectuals. Other groups combined different functions, giving cultural maintenance priority.

Named for cities and towns in Puerto Rico, the hometown clubs that would in recent years become the core of New York's largest cultural pride manifestation, the Puerto Rican Day Parade, were among the earliest Puerto Rican organizations in New York. The Club Caborrojeño, for example, was founded in the 1920s and named for the town of Cabo Rojo. In a period when ritual kinship networks substituted for extended family, the hometown clubs formed a bonding nucleus, drawing members who either knew one another from their island towns or knew about one another through familial connections. A home away from home, this private intergenerational space was where religious, social, and cultural celebrations reproduced the Puerto Rican nation in absentia; clubs also bridged the wider society, providing a fount of information for newcomers.

Information was spread by word of mouth and through a prolific network of Spanish-language radio and print media. Citywide newspapers, community presses, periodicals, organization newsletters, and illustrated magazines carried local and international news. These not only covered current events but connected Spanish-speaking communities around common concerns.

Gráfico, Semanario Defensor de la Raza Hispana (1926–31), a local weekly edited by Ramón La Villa and later Bernardo Vega, printed social commentary, satire, and bilingual editorials on issues of citizenship, race, and ethnicity. The March 27, 1927, issue questioned the lack of Puerto Rican civil rights: "While citizens of other countries have their consulates and diplomats to represent them, the children of

Flyer for baseball games at Howard Field, Brooklyn, 1924. Jesús Colón Papers, Archives of the Puerto Rican Diaspora, Centro de Estudios Puertorriqueños, Hunter College, CUNY. Benigo Giboyeaux for the Estate of Jesús Colón.

Borinquen have no one."[7] Soon thereafter, Gráfico called for unity among all Hispanics: "We should so unite our energies as to make us respected. . . . If it is impossible to create . . . a single organization that can defend and work for our group—then it is imperative that we seek . . . contact in our fight for the betterment of our social and economic condition."[8]

At the other end of the scale, New York's monthly journal *Revista de Artes y Letras* (1933–45) appealed to an international readership but did not ignore the affairs of the *colonia hispana* with which it strongly identified. Its creator, Josefina Silva de Cintrón, emphasized women's participation in the production, content selection, and writing of the journal. Its editors and writers represented a broad Hispanic constituency and included writers Pedro Caballero, Clotilde Betances de Jaeger, and Juan La Barthe. Within its glossy pages, *Artes y Letras* stressed the arts, but essential community concerns and a strong feminist perspective also were well represented.

Young Puerto Rican and Hispanic women preparing to stage *Colegiales*, 1928. Photographer unknown. Erasmo Vando Papers, Archives of the Puerto Rican Diaspora, Centro de Estudios Puertorriqueños, Hunter College, CUNY.

While most women followed traditional paths as homemakers and mothers, others were intrigued by the alternatives posed by feminism and women's rights. New York offered a daring array of possibilities to young Puerto Ricans sheltered under strict parental supervision. Bobbed hair, made-up faces, and skirts at mid-calf argued for women's modernity, and the variety of cultural events offered by Hispanic clubs engaged Puerto Rican women in an active social life. For the small group of ambitious risk takers, avowed feminists, artists, and/or activists, New York was the place to be.

The Puerto Rican feminist and international labor organizer Luisa Capetillo practiced iconoclastic beliefs when she lived in the city in 1912 and in 1919. Perhaps the only woman reader (*lectora*) hired in the cigar factories,[9] Capetillo ran a vegetarian restaurant and boardinghouse on Twenty-second Street and Eighth Avenue, par-

laying her status as housekeeper into a bully pulpit from which she badgered her
lodgers with revolutionary and anarchistic ideology. A resolute advocate for women's
and working-class rights, Capetillo espoused the virtues of yoga, Swedish calisthenics,
and meditation.

In the mid-twenties, Jesús Colón warned his future wife that Puerto Rican
women in New York were not like those in the homeland: They were too American-
ized, a characteristic that he hoped she would not acquire. But he also advised her
not to come to New York before completing her education, as it would determine
her quality of life and employment in the city.

Indeed, the images of Puerto Rican women in the 1920s and 1930s challenge
conventional notions about women's roles. One black-and-white photograph immortal-
izes seven coquettish young women seated bare-legged on an empty stage; each
wears a French beret, a white open-necked blouse, and knee-length pants. The cap-
tion reads: "Young Puerto Rican and Hispanic Women Preparing to Stage *Colegiales*,
1928." *Colegiales* was a *zarzuela* (Spanish light opera) in three acts. And captioned
"Brooklyn Women's Committee of the Liga Puertorriqueña e Hispana, 1932," another
image captures sixteen smartly dressed club women smiling at the camera, resplen-
dent in their high heels and jewelry.

Intent on making a living, the majority of female migrants were young working-
class homemakers or single women who labored as seamstresses, unskilled workers,
domestics, or home needle workers. And yet class barriers blurred in more ways than
one. Among this group, many also ran informal businesses, caring for children of
working mothers or managing boardinghouses. It was not unusual for accomplished

women to work in blue-collar occupations, the few jobs available to them, as they pursued professional, business, or political options.

Before becoming a businesswoman, Victoria Hernández worked in a factory. The sister of Rafael Hernández, composer of "Lamento Borincano," the immortal homage to the perseverance of the island's peasants, Victoria opened Almacenes Hernández, the first Puerto Rican music store in El Barrio, at 1735 Madison Avenue in 1927. The business proved a family success. The brains behind the venture, Victoria soon parlayed the small shop into a larger establishment. Her third store, Casa Hernández, opened in 1941 at 786 Prospect Avenue in the Bronx. Sold to composer Mike Amadeo in 1969, it became Casa Amadeo; in 2001 it was listed in the State and National Registers of Historic Places as the city's oldest Latin music store.

As the 1939 World's Fair prepared to launch the "world of tomorrow," *colonias* were hotbeds of radical politics. Socialists, Communists, and nationalists courted barrio endorsement, but it was a coalition of the American Labor, Republican, and City Fusion parties that elected the first Puerto Rican, Oscar García Rivera, to the New York State Legislature in 1937. His wife, Eloisa, believed a woman's place was to support the man, not to take center stage. She mounted a strategic campaign, trained college students to register voters, provided babysitters so mothers could vote, and instructed citizens on taking the required tests. Representing the Seventeenth District until 1940, García Rivera opened the door for dozens of Puerto Ricans to serve in public office. However, it would take seven decades before Puerto Ricans in public service achieved national prominence. That happened in 2009 with the confirmation of the Honorable Sonia Sotomayor to the U.S. Supreme Court. And therein lies the rest of the story.

Victoria and Rafael Hernández, 1930. Photographer unknown. Jesús Colón Papers, Archives of the Puerto Rican Diaspora, Centro de Estudios Puertorriqueños, Hunter College, CUNY. Courtesy of Miguel S. Amadeo.

Oscar García Rivera with friends, ca. 1937. Photographer unknown. Oscar García Rivera Papers, Archives of the Puerto Rican Diaspora, Centro de Estudios Puertorriqueños, Hunter College, CUNY.

NOTES

1. Emilia Casanova de Villaverde, letter to Concepción C. de López, New York, April 1, 1870, in *Apuntes biográficos de Emilia Casanova de Villaverde, escrito por un contemporáneo* (New York, 1974), 9–10.

2. Bernardo Vega, *Memoirs of Bernardo Vega*, ed. César Andreu Iglesias, trans. Juan Flores (New York: Monthly Review Press, 1984), 73–74.

3. Ibid., 6.

4. Jesús Colón, *A Puerto Rican in New York, and Other Sketches* (New York: International Publishers, 1982), 24.

5. Nelida Pérez, "Belpré, Pura (1899–1982)," in *Latinas in the United States: A Historical Encyclopedia*, ed. Vicki L. Ruiz and Virginia Sánchez Korrol (Bloomington: Indiana University Press, 2006), 83–84.

6. Elisa Santiago Baeza, interview with the author, Mayaguez, Puerto Rico, July 1977.

7. *Gráfico, Semanario Defensor de la Raza Hispana* (New York), ed. Ramón La Villa, March 27, 1927, 2.

8. Ibid.

9. Capetillo was employed as a reader in a cigar factory. Paid by the workers as they engaged in the various tasks of making cigars, she entertained and enlightened her audience by reading novels, newspapers, and political and philosophical essays aloud. This prestigious position, held in high esteem among cigar workers in New York and the Caribbean, was seldom given to women.

Setados: Al frente: Ch. Ramsey; Primera línea de izq. a derech — 1. Acosta
2. César Soler 3. O. García-Rivera 4. E. Michelli 5. G. Soler. De pie. 1ra línea
1. R. Rodríguez 2. Ledo. W. Ramos 3. R. Matos 4. H. tol. Cruz
5. R. Medina 6. Laíno. 2da línea. 1. F. Martínez 2. 3. Vincentro 1-6
7. C. González 8. R. Rodríguez-Archilla 9. Dr. A. Figarella.

LIBRERIA DE LOS LATINOS
JOSE JUAN TABLADA & CO.
STATIONERY AND PRINTING
SPANISH BOOKS
LIBROS REVISTAS PERIODICOS
SPANISH MUSIC
LIBRERIA DE LOS LATINOS
JOSÉ JUAN TABLADA & Co.
LIBRERIA DE LOS LATINOS

NOTES ON WRITING IN SPANISH IN NEW YORK

CARMEN BOULLOSA

Translated from the Spanish by Samantha Schnee

No one knows for sure who authored the first literary works written in Spanish in New York. It might have been that one of the Sephardic Jews who arrived in New Amsterdam from Brazil in 1654 was a poet, whose writings in the New World did not survive his or her ongoing peregrinations. Or perhaps one of the "Spanish Negroes"—seamen captured by an English privateer in 1740 and sold into slavery in New York City—had inherited Africa's griot tradition as well as Iberian and Caribbean storytelling strategies, and recited stanzas and couplets aloud from memory, enriching them by improvisation (additions, changes, reimaginings), before being hung the following year as an accused insurrectionary. But the supposition that such poems and stories existed is no more than a conjecture, a piece of fictionalized literary history (like those that Borges and Bolaño loved).

What we do know for sure is that in the early nineteenth century, waves of Latin American literati arrived on New York's shores, driven from their countries as rebels against the Spanish empire, drawn to Gotham by its tolerance of political expression, its status as the American publishing hub, and the possibility it offered of winning moral and financial support. The first group of these exiles came in the 1820s from Cuba, which, like Puerto Rico, had failed to obtain its freedom in the wars of independence.

The priest, philosopher, and writer Félix Varela arrived in New York in 1823, in flight from Spain and unable to return to Cuba, where he had been condemned to death by the Spanish crown. Varela became a political and theological activist and author of articles and tracts, but what interests us here is a literary work, the 1826 historical novel *Xicoténcatl*, produced in Philadelphia by a publisher Varela had met while visiting in 1824. The book, a story of the conquest of Mexico, was published anonymously—no surprise, given that it cast Cortés as a monster and Spain's empire as tyrannical. The case for Varela's authorship is strong, and if correct, makes it the first known novel in Spanish by a writer living in New York.

José María Heredia also arrived in New York in 1823 (within weeks of Varela), and also in flight from Cuba, where he had been connected with a revolutionary group called the Rational Gentlemen. Heredia installed himself at 44 Broadway,

Exterior of Librería de los Latinos, José Juan Tablada & Co., n.d. Photographer unknown. Archivo Tablada, UNAM Mexico.

THE CENTRAL REPUBLICAN JUNTA OF CUBA AND PORTO RICO IN SESSION AT NEW YORK CITY.—[SKETCHED BY THEO. R. DAVIS.]

where he wrote his celebrated romantic poem "Niagara," about the spectacle of the great falls, making him a candidate for the author of the first poem written in Spanish in New York. Heredia championed among his peers the language's continued use, even in Anglo-exile. His stay proved a short one, and in 1825 he relocated to Mexico, where he had been offered sanctuary.

Most of the remarkable number of poets who arrived in New York as exiles from Cuba over the next three decades did write in their native language, and in a romantic and militant mode. Among them was Juan Clemente Zenea, who spent two periods in New York, where he wrote a novel, *Far From Homeland* (1859), set in the city. (He would later be executed in Cuba.) This wave of writers produced enough work to warrant the publication—in New York in 1858—of an anthology of their writings, *El Laúd del Desterrado* (The Exile's Lute), which included a poem of Heredia's. ("Tyrants and despots will laugh at our enthusiasm," says the book's prologue.)[1] One of the book's leading contributors, Miguel Tolón, wrote and published poems in English as well as Spanish, and he was the only member of his generation to work for an English-language newspaper, the *New York Herald*, editing its Latin American section.

Not all of the epoch's exiled literati came from Cuba. The Puerto Rican Eugenio María de Hostos, author of a romantic novel written in Spain, *The Peregrinations of Bayoán* (1863), moved to New York in 1870 to campaign for the independence of Cuba and Puerto Rico. Another prominent Latin American, the Argentinian intellectual and politician Domingo Faustino Sarmiento, visited the city in 1847 (on behalf of the Argentinian government), settling there in 1865 as plenipotentiary minister to

the United States. After writing a book on Abraham Lincoln, he left for good in 1868.

Pedro Santacilia was a Cuban, also included in *The Exile's Lute*, who came to New York by a circuitous route. He had been exiled to New Orleans, where he had met the future Mexican president Benito Juárez, struck up an enduring friendship based on their political compatibility, married Juárez's daughter, and resettled in Mexico. When his father-in-law's family had to flee during the reign of Maximilian, he moved with them to New York (they lived at 208 East Thirteenth Street). Santacilia spent three years there, during which time he wrote poems and fraternized with Cuban colleagues. Along with other liberal Juaristas, including Francisco Zarco, he helped found the Mexican Club of New York in 1864.[2]

After the American Civil War and the Ten Years' War in Cuba, a new generation of exile writers arrived, most famous among them José Martí, who lived in New York from 1880 to 1895. A "poet and hero," Martí stands out among that era's many Spanish-speaking writers, activists, journalists, and editors in the city who produced a sea of newspapers, literary magazines, pamphlets, and books in Spanish. Martí, like Heredia, rejected the idea of writing in English, and was quite insistent about the "difference of language" of "the Latin race of America."[3]

Martí was as brilliant an activist as he was a poet, and he kept the two roles distinct, never confusing a poem with a tract. Some writers, like Octavio Paz, have argued that Martí's poetic genius lay in his knowing how to awaken the secret power of colloquial language—perhaps the language he honed in his political work with New York's cigar workers. Certainly his work was considerably more urbane than that of the earlier romantic exiles, and its simplicity changed the landscape of Hispano-American poetry. According to Dionisio Cañas, it was during his time in New York that Martí brought modernity to the Latin American literary tradition.[4]

Along with Martí, there were a host of other Latin American writers in New York who engaged in conversation with one another in literary societies or through their writings in Spanish-language journals and newspapers. In 1881, the Colombian José María Vargas Vila, a pamphleteer and the celebrated author of a series of best-selling novels, arrived in the city after the president of Colombia put a price on his head for publishing a diatribe ridiculing the government (*Scribblings on the Last Colombian Revolution: Wartime Sketches*). Vargas Vila wrote that he went to New York "to fight, with my magazine, *Nemesis*, a noisy and romantic battle, against the illiterate, sinister dictatorships that were devastating certain Latin American countries, as well against the hydra of Yankee imperialism, which reared its head between the wings of an eagle, beneath the starry flag waving in the wind in front of the semi-Greek facade of Washington's Capitol."[5] He also published novels, in serial format, to considerable popular success, although he was dismissed by critics. Still read today by a general audience, his books have yet to be admitted to the literary canon.

In contrast, Cirilo Villaverde's *Cecilia Valdés*, published in New York in 1882, is considered the best Cuban novel of the nineteenth century. Villaverde had arrived in New York in 1849, after he escaped from prison in Cuba and became secretary to filibusterer Narciso López ("the best-known *filibustero* prior to William Walker," according to Rodrigo J. Lazo[6]). Later he became an editor and Spanish translator of many literary works, including Dickens's *David Copperfield*.

Puerto Rican writers also took refuge in New York. One was Francisco González Marín (aka Pachín) who visited New York on several occasions between 1882 and 1886. A poet who had been a typographer, and a friend of José Martí's, González is sometimes credited with designing the Puerto Rican flag. He later enlisted in the Cuban Liberation Army, and fought and died in the Cuban war of independence. Another Puerto Rican patriot, Lola Rodríguez de Tío, stayed in New York in 1892, and again from 1895 to 1898. She was the author of "The Boriqueña," considered by some the national anthem of Puerto Rico: "Wake up, boriqueño /

they've given the sign! / Wake up from your sleep / it's time to fight!" With the dramaturg Sotero Figueroa, who was a member of the revolutionary junta, Rodríguez de Tío founded the Imprenta América, which published Martí's journal, *Patria,* and also launched the separatist group Club Borinquen in 1892 and the Puerto Rican section of the Cuban Revolutionary Party in 1895.

After the Spanish-Cuban-American War, independentistas lost their primacy among the writers who lived in New York and wrote in Spanish, as new kinds of visitors or immigrants were added to the literary mix. Some came on diplomatic assignments, such as Fabio Fiallo, reinventor of Dominican poetry, who arrived as consul in 1905. Fiallo published his *Fragile Stories* (1908), complete with Art Deco illustrations, with the H. Braeunlich Press of 63 Cliff Street in lower Manhattan. Interestingly, the prologue underscores the author's affiliations with European writers including Lamartine, Hugo, Boileau, Musset, and the Spaniard Zorrilla, but does not mention a single North American author.

Others passed through New York en route to other destinations, but were influenced by their time there. Such was the case with the Nicaraguan Rubén Darío, whose first two visits occurred on his way to Madrid and Buenos Aires. When Darío met Martí at a revolutionary gathering in New York on May 24, 1893, in Hardman Hall, Martí introduced him to the audience, calling him "Son!"—and the crowd broke into lengthy applause.

It is said that with Darío's work, the caravels returned to Spain, as the poet conquered Hispanic literature with his voice. Though Darío was raised in a provincial environment, his work was resonantly cosmopolitan. His fresh style appropriated forms from French poetry while refusing to accept the marginalization of Latin America, or its literary-topographic status as an exotic corner of the world. He wrote with such authority that he constituted his language and culture as another center, one of many in a truly cosmopolitan cosmology.

Darío was the consummate modernist poet and the great reinventor of Hispanic American poetry, though his "modernism" was of a different sort than Martí's and ultimately had a greater impact. Darío's was flowery and in a sense old-fashioned, yet when he wrote about New York, his verse acquired a bold, Martí-esque, downright modern style. Take "The Great Cosmopolis," for example:

> *That gigantic wonder*
> *Where everything shines and rings*
> *In an oppressive atmosphere*
> *With its conquests of steel*
> *With its struggles for money*
> *Without knowing that therein lies*
> *The whole root of sorrow.*[7]

Darío's third and final visit to New York occurred in the winter of 1913–14, on the eve of the First World War. He came with the hope of earning great amounts of money by lecturing about pacifism. Among his hoped-for patrons was philanthropist Archer Milton Huntington, president and founder of the Hispanic Society, who arranged for him to lecture at Columbia University and awarded him a medal that came with a cash award of $500. Despite Huntington's generosity, this amount was nothing compared to what Darío had expected to receive.[8]

Writers continued to visit the city for political reasons. In 1912 playwright and activist Luisa Capetillo arrived in New York to make allies for her cause. The first Puerto Rican woman to wear trousers in public, and originally a reader at *tabaquerías* (tobacco factories), Capetillo wrote plays as well as newspaper articles championing the union movement. Her stay in the city was a short one, whereas the Colombian Alirio Díaz Guerra, who had supported revolutionary forces in Colombia and had been forced into exile in 1895, opted for New York and remained there until his death thirty years later. Upon arriving, Díaz Guerra sold pharmaceuticals to earn a living while writing poetry as well; his first collection was published in 1901 by the Hispano-

American Press. It was followed by a large number of works over the following years, most of them lost, as is his novel, *May*. But in 1914 York Printing Company published his *Lucas Guevara*,[9] arguably the first novel of Hispanic immigration, in which he writes about the experience of moving to New York. The protagonist, recently arrived from "Santa Catarina," which could be any Latin American city, is victimized by city folk, falls into the clutches of urban vice, and eventually commits suicide. New York is Babylon and Santa Catarina is Eden; New York is the kernel of corruption, while Santa Catarina, though poor and backward, is the kingdom of purity and innocence. Kanellos argues that the novel "initiates the ethos and structure that will be repeated" in many Hispanic immigration novels to come.[10]

During the Mexican Revolution, after Victoriano Huerta fell in 1914, José Juan Tablada also arrived as an exile, but he was "fleeing from himself as well as Mexico," as Octavio Paz has argued, and in any event did not occupy himself further with Mexican political affairs. Tablada's decades in New York were fruitful. He wrote poems, essays, and articles, working with Hispanic American presses and, less frequently, New York publishers. Tablada was a cultural connector of sorts, but the literary source of the aesthetic he brought to Spanish-language poetry was not New York but rather Japan and France: from the former, the haiku, and from the latter, the calligram. Tablada also channeled Hispanic American culture into New York, where he wrote about everything from pre-Columbian art to Latin American musicians,

Salvador Dalí, José Moreno Villa, Luis Buñuel, Federico García Lorca, and María Vargas Vila, n.d. Photographer unknown. Fundación García Lorca.

writers, and artists of his era (from Orozco to Covarrubias). In 1921, he opened a bookstore, Libreria de Los Latinos, José Juan Tablada & Co., Exporters, Book Importers, that sold books in Spanish and French (though not very successfully) at 118 East Twenty-eighth Street. Tablada also wrote poetry in English, but it was never published. In Tablada's New York diaries he writes: "When all is said and done, a Mexican bandit is much better than a Wall Street bandit."[11] Tablada had been assigned a post in the Mexican Consulate in New York; upon his death in 1945, the job was handed to Octavio Paz, the future Nobel laureate, who that year came to New York, where he would write some of his masterpieces.

In 1919, the newspaper *La Prensa* initiated a poetry prize based on traditional *juegos florales* ("floral games"), poetry contests that rewarded flowers as prizes. The jury was composed of the Spaniard Federico de Onís, professor of Spanish literature at Columbia University; Pedro Henríquez Ureña, the most prominent Dominican intellectual in the first half of the twentieth century;[12] Orestes Ferrara, a Neapolitan who was famous for fighting in Cuba's war of independence and later became the Cuban ambassador to the United States; and the North American Hispanist Thomas Walsh. The awards ceremony took place on May 5 in Carnegie Hall. The first prize went to a Colombian, José Méndez Rivera. Second place went to F. M. Cesteros, a Dominican poet. A young Puerto Rican named Luis Muñoz Marín, who later became the first democratically elected governor of Puerto Rico, received honorable mention for his poem "I am your flute":

> *Tree, I am your flute.*
> *When the rain stops making music on your leaves,*
> *When a bird soars down in search of sunshine,*
> *You, alone in your shadow, silent shadow,*
> *Give yourself over to the tragedy of silence.*[13]

Salomón de la Selva at age sixteen, New York, ca. 1909. Photographer unknown. Courtesy of Emilio Quintana.

The Nicaraguan Salomón de la Selva, who had served as Rubén Darío's interpreter in his 1914 visit, had arrived in the United States as a teen in 1906, on a grant from the president of his country. In New York he became friends with a group of young poets, notably Edna St. Vincent Millay, with whom he had an affair (immortalized in her poem "Adiós"). He published his first book of poetry, *Tropical Town and Other Poems*, in 1918. Written in English, it was well received by critics; *Forum* magazine named it one of the year's best poetry collections. In London the following year, de la Selva published *A Soldier Sings*, drawing on his experience as a volunteer soldier in World War I. Soon thereafter he moved to Paris, where he began writing his poems in Spanish, incorporating the colloquialism of the English-language poets he had encountered in New York into the Latin American vanguard. It is, in fact, through de la Selva, and not Martí, that the North American poetry of that era left its mark on Latin America. His first book in Spanish was finally published in 1947 in Mexico, where he had gone to live after returning to Nicaragua.

Some writers came to the city for strictly personal reasons. Such was the case with the future Nobel laureate Juan Ramón Jímenez, who spent a few months in New York in 1916. It was a very successful visit: He had come in pursuit of his beloved, Zenobia Camprubí, and in that short time he married her at St. Stephen's Church and wrote *Diary of a Newlywed Poet*.

José Moreno Villa also came for sentimental reasons, but he was unsuccessful in his pursuits. He arrived in New York in 1921 to meet the family of his Jewish fiancée, called "Jacinta the Redhead" in one of his books of poems devoted to their affair. He returned to Spain without her, but with a new book he had written, *Trials in New York*, which his friends referred to as the "Diary of a Newly Single Poet." Years later, he wrote, "There's no doubt that my adventure in New York effected an enormous change in my poetry, just as the rebellion and civil war [in Spain] did. It brought about an ease, or better said, a confidence that my poetry never had, as well as compo-

Federico García Lorca at Columbia University, 1929.
Photographer unknown. Fundación García Lorca.

sure and rigor that I hope are permanent."[14] Moreno Villa lived out his republican exile
in Mexico.

In 1928, the Mexican poet Gilberto Owen, a unique literary personality, arrived
to work at his country's consulate. He wrote a screenplay for his friend Emilio Amero
that has much in common with the screenplay García Lorca later wrote for the same
director. As Guillermo Sheridan has argued, it is possible that in fact they collaborated on the latter.[15]

García Lorca, who traveled from Spain to New York in 1929 to learn English
at Columbia University, didn't even stay for a year and never learned English. In the
city his work became imbued with contemporary avant-gardism, most probably due
to his contact with Spanish-speaking poets, among them Owen, who had a similar
impact on Octavio Paz and other Mexican poets.

Earlier, in 1927, the celebrated Chilean poet Vicente Huidobro, a millionaire

and star of the avant-garde (he was friends with Picasso, Tristan Tzara, Erik Satie, Jean Cocteau, André Breton, and Joan Miró), had arrived in the city. After winning a $10,000 prize from the League for Better Pictures for a screenplay he wrote, he had come to produce the movie with Romanian director Mime Mtzu. Composer Edgar Varèse, who in 1921 had premiered *Offrandes*, a cantata based on the texts of Huidobro and Tablada, introduced Huidobro to Charlie Chaplin, Douglas Fairbanks, and Gloria Swanson. While in New York, Huidobro wrote the epic poem "Ode to Lindbergh."

In 1928 the Argentinian Victoria Ocampo came to New York to make her mark with her sister, the short story writer and poet Silvina Ocampo. The sisters, who came from an aristocratic and wealthy family, visited the Vanderbilts at their mansion on Fifth Avenue shortly before it was demolished to make way for the Bergdorf Goodman store. During her stay in New York Victoria met novelist and social critic Waldo Frank, whose friendship and advice proved vital in founding the magazine *Sur* (which published Borges, Bioy Casares, and José Bianco, among others) in 1931, and the Sur publishing house two years later.

At the end of April 1928, José Eustacio Rivera arrived in New York and rented an apartment on West Seventy-third Street. Author of one of the classics of Hispanic American literature, *The Vortex*, set in a rubber-tree jungle, he founded Editorial Andes, a publishing house for which he had high economic expectations, being certain New York could serve as a distribution hub to the rest of the Americas and the world. He also planned to have his novel translated into English and adapted for a film. But soon after launching his publishing house, Rivera was struck with a mysterious ill-

Julia de Burgos, n.d. Photographer and publisher unknown.

ness, was hospitalized for three days, and died. (According to Tablada, he died from a poison dart the jungle had aimed at him from afar.) His body was shipped back on the United Fruit Company's *Xixaloe* to Colombia, where it lay in state.

José de Diego, champion of the Antillean Union, also died in New York, in 1921, while reciting a poem. The Chilean Nobel laureate Gabriela Mistral died in the city too, in 1957, from cancer. In 1930 she had spent a year in New York at the invitation of Barnard College, and in the 1950s she moved to the city to run the consulate and to be near her companion, Doris Dana.

Our final writer, who also died in New York, was probably Puerto Rico's most important woman poet, Julia de Burgos. She visited New York periodically beginning in 1940, and settled there in 1945. Julia de Burgos was an author in search of her own identity as a woman poet, as can be clearly seen in her most famous poem, addressed to herself:

> To Julia de Burgos
> *Already people whisper that I'm your enemy*
> *because in verse I give you to the world.*
> *They lie, Julia de Burgos, they lie. They lie, Julia de Burgos.*
> *The one that rises in my verse is not your voice: it's mine.*
> *You're only the clothing: the essence, though, is me;*
> *and the deepest chasm yawns between the two.*[16]

Suffering from an unhappy love affair, the grief of living apart from her beloved Puerto Rico, and alcoholism, she spent her days wandering the streets of East Harlem, bottle in hand. Her health steadily deteriorated, and in 1953, having contracted pneumonia, she collapsed on a city street and was taken to a hospital, where she died at age thirty-nine. Because she had no identification and no one came to claim her remains, she was buried by the city in a communal grave as "Jane Doe."[17] Eventually identified, de Burgos's remains were transported to Puerto Rico, where she was properly buried with the highest honors. One of her last poems, "Farewell from Welfare Island," was written in English. It was indeed her farewell. But Julia de Burgos's work also represented a rebirth. By the end of the Second World War, New York had become an entirely different place for Hispanic American authors, especially those who chose to stay. In time, a new literary movement would arise from the Puerto Rican community: Nuyorican poetry. Since many of the poets were bilingual, language was neither a barrier nor crucial to their identity, as it had been for their predecessors. The Nuyoricans are the heirs to all those traditions: the Spanish, the Latin American, the African, the American. But that's another story.

NOTES

1. Matías Montes Huidobro, ed., *El Laúd del Desterrado* (Houston: Arte Público Press, 1995), 3.

2. Vicente Quirarte, "Benito Juárez and New York City," *The Brooklyn Rail*, December 2006–January 2007, http://www.brooklynrail.org/2006/12/express/benito-jua.

3. José Martí, *Nuestra América* (Barcelona: Linkgua Ediciones, 2008), 168.

4. Dionisio Cañas, *El poeta y la ciudad: Nueva York y los escritores hispanos* (Madrid: Cátedra, 1994).

5. José María Vargas Vila, preface to *Obras completas* (Medellín, Colombia, 1900), 11, http://www.scribd.com/doc/6702291/COLOMBIA-Vargas-Vila-Jose-Maria-La-Simiente.

6. Rodrigo J. Lazo, "Los Filibusteros: Cuban Writers in the United States and the Deterritorialized Print Culture," *American Literary History* 15, no. 1 (spring 2003): 87–106.

7. Rubén Darío, *Cuarenta y cinco poemas* (Caracas: Biblioteca Ayacucho, 1994), 105.

8. In one night alone during a previous visit to the city, Darío spent $300 in a Times Square brothel. Legend has it that the Peruvian-born Colombian Juan Arana Torrol traversed the city begging for change to help the poet, who was being held hostage at the whorehouse, to pay his debt and be liberated. See José Joaquín Jiménez, "Juan Arana Torrol, Enviado Celestial," *El Tiempo* (Bogotá), April 27, 1935, Biblioteca Luis Ángel Arango, http://www.lablaa.org/blaavirtual/historia/cronicasximenez/25.htm.

9. Nicolás Kanellos et al., eds., *Herencia: The Anthology of Hispanic Literature of the United States* (New York: Oxford University Press, 2002), 348.

10. Nicolás Kanellos, *Hispanic Literature of the United States: A Comprehensive Reference* (Santa Barbara, CA: Greenwood Press, 2003), 194.

11. José Juan Tablada, *Obras IV: Diario (1900–1944)*, ed. Guillermo Sheridan (Mexico City: Nueva Biblioteca Mexicana, UNAM, 1992), 163.

12. Borges wrote of Ureña: "Not a day passes without my remembering him." Ureña had spent part of his early life in New York and returned to live there between 1915 and 1916.

13. Luis Muñoz Marín, "Yo soy tu flauta" (1919), Fundación Luis Muñoz Marín, http://www.munoz-marin.org/pags_nuevas_folder/discursos_folder/lista_pensamientos_ab.html.

14. José Moreno Villa, *Vida en claro* (Mexico City: Fondo de Cultura Económica, 1976), 206.

15. Guillermo Sheridan, "Gilberto Owen y Federico García Lorca viajan a la luna," *Vuelta* 259, May 1988:16–22.

16. Julia de Burgos, "To Julia de Burgos," trans. Roberto Márquez, in *Puerto Rican Poetry: An Anthology from Aboriginal to Contemporary Times* (Amherst: University of Massachusetts Press, 2007), 222–23.

17. It was said that in order to fit her body into the coffin provided by the city, her legs had to be amputated.

PAINTERS, POLITICS, AND PASTRIES:

How New York Became a Cultural Crossroads of the Americas, 1848–99

KATHERINE E. MANTHORNE

NEW YORK'S WINDOWS ON LATIN AMERICA: ART, COMMERCE, POPULAR CULTURE

When Frederic Church's *Heart of the Andes* went on view on April 28, 1859, at the Tenth Street Studio Building in New York City, it created an unprecedented sensation. The large-scale canvas (5 by 10 feet) was framed in a walnut structure designed to resemble a window casement, creating the illusion of a vista onto the South American landscape. The artist had twice explored Ecuador and Colombia, in 1853 and 1857, giving him an authority that was not lost on the crowds who lined up to pay their 25-cent admission charge (approximately $6.75 in today's currency) and to study the details of the picture as outlined in one of two written pamphlets available for an additional sum at the door. Visitors were advised to bring opera glasses to observe closely Church's detailed treatment of flora and fauna, and then to step back to appreciate the grand sweep of the mountain chain that included the mighty Chimborazo. It was, as one viewer put it, "the complete condensation of South America" on exhibition from morning to night (when there was artificial illumination) for all to see, right in Lower Manhattan.[1] By the time the picture appeared at the Metropolitan Sanitary Fair in 1864, portraits of Presidents Washington, Adams, and Jefferson hung above the picture, visually claiming the Andes for the United States in a gesture of imperialism.[2]

While Church's picture went on national tour and to Britain,[3] New Yorkers could have had numerous other encounters with things Latin American in the course of their daily lives. Along the city's waterways, ships from the Caribbean were a common site, carrying the coffee, chocolate, and especially sugar that were becoming indispensable to a good table. In the early nineteenth century, the Havemeyer family's sugar operation on Vandam Street consisted of a small building and five employees. Soon thereafter, New York merchants, led by Moses Taylor, began to funnel vast quantities of Caribbean sugar into the city. Simultaneously, refinery technology

Frederic Edwin Church (1826–1900). *Heart of the Andes*, 1859. Oil on canvas. 66⅛ x 119¼ in. (168 x 302.9 cm). The Metropolitan Museum of Art, New York, Bequest of Margaret E. Dows 09.95. Image copyright © The Metropolitan Museum of Art / Art Resource, NY.

INGENIO BUENA-VISTA
Propriedad del Sōr. D. Justo G Cantero

improved dramatically. The combination proved irresistible to the Havemeyers. In 1858 Frederick C. Havemeyer secured a substantial waterfront property across the East River in Williamsburg and erected a state-of-the-art plant serviced by its own docks and warehouses. By 1860 the Havemeyers and their thirteen competitors were producing half the nation's supply, and Brooklyn was officially the greatest sugar-refining center in the world.[4]

Readily available sugar permanently changed American eating habits. Once a luxury of the rich, sweets became indispensable to middle- and working-class tables, as suggested in some of Rubens Peale's still life paintings or those of his brother, Raphaelle Peale, where cupcakes and other pastries look good enough to eat. These dietary preferences are evident in books like Catharine Beecher's *The Domestic Receipt Book* (1846, first edition), which includes abundant descriptions of tea cakes and pies, and separate discussions of plain and rich cakes. Born into a distinguished family that included sister Harriet Beecher Stowe and brother Henry Ward Beecher, Catharine single-handedly established home economics as a discipline. Her emphasis on sweets and pastries can therefore be taken as a measure of sugar's importance to the American culinary arts.

The Havemeyer complex on the Brooklyn side of the East River was a reminder of the growing importance of Latin America to New York. So too was their fabulous collection of French and especially Impressionist pictures, which Louisine Havemeyer had acquired using the enormous profits her husband had amassed via the Sugar Trust. She bequeathed key works by Monet and Degas alongside those of her friend and advisor Mary Cassatt to the Metropolitan Museum of Art, where they hang

THE OLD PRISON, (*Das alte Gefängnis*) C? of ROSE S? N. YORK.

today. Another major art collection born of these sweet fortunes—riches made from trade between New York and Latin America—was more immediately available in the home of Robert L. Stuart, which included Church's *Cayambe*. The two-by-three-foot canvas epitomizes Church's grasp of Prussian naturalist Alexander von Humboldt's world view. Cayambe's peak straddles the equator, a natural marker in its own right. The artist painted a small ruin at its base that symbolizes the pre-Columbian civilizations that inhabited the Andes long before Europeans ever set foot there, and unites the multiple strands of the picture's global agenda. First, it references Humboldt, who in his illustrated atlas *Vues des Cordilleras* interspersed landscape views and ancient artifacts, thereby visually associating environments with the civilizations they foster. Second, it connects to the picture's owner, Robert L. Stuart, who was the first president of the American Museum of Natural History, a major collector of American art, and owner of sugar refineries with trade interests in Latin America. Third, it alludes to the artist himself, who stood on this very spot to sketch the scene, collected ancient artifacts, and bequeathed his Aztec reliefs to the Metropolitan Museum of Art in the hope of promoting awareness of American antiquities. *Cayambe* embodies a trans-American identity, "painted to order" for a patron of hemispheric business interests.[5]

Church's travels, like the Caribbean business interests of Havemeyer and Stuart, depended on shipping. And New York shippers depended on moving ocean vessels, men, and goods in the shortest time and safest manner possible. Prior to the opening of the Panama Canal in 1914 this meant sailing around Cape Horn at the tip of South America, or traveling via the Atlantic to Panama by sea, crossing the isthmus by land, and then catching another steamer on the Pacific side. Church followed

Raphaelle Peale (1774–1825). *Still Life with Cake*, 1818. Oil on wood. 10¾ x 15¼ in. (27.3 x 38.7 cm). The Metropolitan Museum of Art, New York, Maria DeWitt Jesup Fund. Image copyright © The Metropolitan Museum of Art / Art Resource, NY.

this second route. Not surprisingly, the notion of an interoceanic canal was on the minds of many, and before the French began construction in Panama, other sites in Central America were under consideration. Some explorations were led by government-sponsored expeditions, others by private individuals hungry for adventure and profit.

Among the most colorful of the private explorers was Irish revolutionary Thomas Meagher, whose expedition led to another publicly exhibited picture of the region contemporary with Church's. Exiled from Ireland to Tasmania, he had escaped and headed for New York, where he studied law and was admitted to the New York Bar. In the United States Court he defended those involved in the Nicaraguan filibusters (from the Spanish *filibustero*, meaning pirate or buccaneer), unauthorized military expeditions made into the country to foment revolution and take it over for private gain. As a result of these efforts, he conceived the idea of his own expedition to Central America—and looked up Ramón Páez.

Accompanying his father, José Antonio Páez, a trusted general of Simon Bolívar and the flamboyant first president of Venezuela, Ramón Páez had arrived in New York in 1850 to live out his years in exile. Educated in Britain, Páez was fluent in English, which must have been a great asset as he and his father were assimilated into the life of the city. When Páez was not aiding his father in planning armed interventions in Venezuela, he was engaged in his own pursuits: writing travel accounts and textbooks, painting and illustrating, studying natural history, and practicing diplomacy. For those eager for information on Spanish America, Páez was their man: a tireless educator and promoter.[6] In 1858 he traveled to Costa Rica with Meagher, who was engaged to write a series of articles on the region for *Harper's Monthly*, while Páez drew the landscape and local people. In 1859, simultaneously with the publication of the magazine articles, Ramón collaborated with the artist Joseph Kyle on a panorama of Costa Rica that was shown in the city.[7] Inspired as a visual artist by his cousin Carmelo Fernandez, an artist on the state-sponsored expedition to Colombia in the 1850s, Páez developed an eye for the varied landscape of Venezuela, from the pampas to the mountains to the tropical rivers. This he combined with a special pride in the customs and history of his country, as seen in pictures such as *La Toma de las Flecheras*.

Páez had purchased the painting *Orchids and Hummingbirds* by Martin Heade, who had made several journeys to Brazil, Central America, and Jamaica. Of all the New York–based artist-travelers to Latin America, though, it was probably Church whose friendship Páez most valued. Throughout the 1860s and 1870s the two men were in close contact, acquiring pictures from one another and exchanging information on the equinoctial regions that were so close to their hearts.[8] Páez likely played an advisory role when Church was painting *Heart of the Andes*, for his native Venezuela borders the region Church depicted and shares a geographical similarity. Páez's daughter Catalina went on to translate several important literary works from Spanish into

English, emblematic of the Páez family's efforts to bridge the Anglo-Hispanic worlds. As a final testimony to the country that had welcomed them, Páez bequeathed his father's sword to the Smithsonian Institution in Washington, D.C., a symbol of the wars of independence fought in both his native land and his adopted country.

U.S.-MEXICAN WAR, 1846–48

But we are getting ahead of ourselves. Our story properly begins in the summer of 1848 with the Treaty of Guadalupe Hidalgo, which concluded the U.S.-Mexican War, established the Texas border at the Rio Grande, and provided for the purchase of a huge tract of land encompassing present-day California and Nevada, and parts of Arizona, New Mexico, Colorado, and Utah. It fulfilled the dreams of President Polk, whose one term in the White House (1845–49) effected a near doubling of America's boundaries.[9] A copy of the treaty, signed by Mexican officials, arrived in Washington, D.C., rather conveniently by courier on the Fourth of July, during celebrations for the laying of the cornerstone for the Washington Monument. In New York's City Hall a few days later, on July 10, the Sacred Music Society sang an ode by George Pope Morris at a huge mass funeral for the fallen Mexican War heroes.[10] That moment marked the beginning of a distinct rapprochement between New Yorkers and Latin Americans. The city became a jumping-off point for revolutions, the birthplace of global financial schemes, a trysting spot for hemispheric love affairs, and, most interestingly, a crossroad of cultures, based on the mixing of painters, writers, and their patrons from across the Americas. Latino or Hispanic New York is often assumed to be a phenomenon of

Martin Johnson Heade (1819–1904). *Cattleya
Orchid with Two Hummingbirds,* ca. 1880. Oil on
canvas. 16 x 21 in. (40.6 x 53.3 cm). Collection
of The Newark Museum (65.118). The Newark
Museum / Art Resource, NY.

the twentieth century. We discover, however, that visitors from Mexico all the way to Patagonia exerted a strong presence in the city from early on and laid the nineteenth-century roots for Nueva York.

MEXICO IN NEW YORK, 1864–67

Between 1864 and 1867, Mexico endured occupation by the French invasion led by Emperor Maximilian of Hapsburg. During those highly charged years, many illustrious Mexicans moved to New York City, which they regarded as a safe haven in spite of the Civil War raging between the American North and South. Their numbers were sufficient to establish a Mexican Club (inaugurated in October 1864), which functioned as a political forum, working behind the scenes to restore Republicanism in Mexico. The most famous among them was the highly visible Margarita Maza de Juárez, wife of the constitutionally elected president, Benito Juárez. The Mexican government had sent the Juárez family out of the country as the French forces gained momentum. A plaque marks their 1864–66 residence at the current 208 East Thirteenth Street in the East Village, next door to the future home of the anarchist and political activist Emma Goldman.[11]

Antonio López de Santa Anna, the five-time president of Mexico and the nemesis of Juárez, also sought asylum in New York in 1866. Although cautioned to "remember the Alamo," most New Yorkers did not seem to hold it against "the old gentleman" that he had once laid waste to the Alamo Mission in San Antonio de Béxar (modern-day Texas) with his take-no-prisoners policy. Led to believe that the United States government backed him in his desire to return to power, he arrived in New York and set up household in an expensive home in Elizabethport, New Jersey, from which he issued his Elizabethport Manifesto of June 5, 1866. Forced to downsize when he realized that no support was forthcoming, he moved to Staten Island and employed Thomas Adams, a local secretary, to assist him in his affairs. Inquiring about the tropical vegetable that Santa Anna chewed regularly, Adams learned it was chicle, the elastic sap of the sapodilla tree. Legend has it that the young secretary then added sweetening to it and created Adams NY Gum #1. Santa Anna, in the meantime, received a pardon and returned to Mexico penniless. But he left New Yorkers and their countrymen with chewing gum ever since.[12]

1870S: EXPANDING HORIZONS AND CROSS-FERTILIZATIONS IN RECONSTRUCTION-ERA NEW YORK

During the post–Civil War years, New Yorkers could experience numerous facets of Latin American life, from the fine arts to a broad sampling of popular culture. In 1872, before the cowboy had been enshrined as a symbol of the Western frontier, New Yorkers could observe his Mexican counterpart in performances that anticipated Buffalo Bill's

Wild West Show. The *New York Times* reported in 1872: "An exhibition of the well-known skill of Mexican vaqueros in the art of driving and lassoing the half-wild cattle of their country was recently given in the Capitoline Grounds, in Brooklyn, by a troop of these men who had been brought east by an enterprising showman."[13] Two years later, the exhibition *Mexican Curiosities. Antiquities from Palenque and Ecuador* was previewed by a *New York Times* reporter in anticipation of its public display:

> *Mr. José Ortiz de Tapia . . . arrived in this city a short time ago from Mexico, bringing with him a large and valuable collection of antiquities, obtained principally from the ruins of the ancient City of Palenque, in the state of Chiapas southern Mexico. Yesterday a Times reporter was favored with a private view of the collection, which, so soon as it can be properly arranged and the objects classified, will be opened to public inspection. It will be a rare treat to the archaeologists and lovers of curiosities, as there are some of the objects which are supposed to be 20,000 years old.*[14]

"The American girl" was becoming a staple of American novels by Henry James and others. The stories told of the daughters of the nouveaux riches, who were sent on tours of the Continent to find culturally refined if financially strapped European husbands. In a trans-American variation of these tales, the wedding of the only daughter of De Souza Cabral of Brazil, "the great diamond king of South America," to George Arthur Throckmorton of Kentucky was recounted in successive articles.[15] The chronicling of the opulence and excesses of every dimension of the wedding—from the invitations and decoration of the palatial Cabral home to the bride's dress—confirmed the wildest imaginings of South American riches and the possibilities for union between the two continents.

Colombians also entered the mix. Poet, diplomat, and translator Rafael Pombo took a room in a Gramercy Park boardinghouse, where he joined numerous other Spanish-speaking bachelors. He frequented Lower Broadway and Printing House Square, the nerve center of the booming publishing business. He wrote extensively for the New York press during his long-term stay, including contributions to the *Guía de los Estados Unidos para viajeros españoles* (Guide for Spanish Travelers to the United States), in which he praised the democratization of its print culture but bemoaned the lack of interest in the fine arts.[16] Little wonder then that when he met the internationally celebrated Mexican painter Felipe Santiago Gutiérrez in New York, he convinced him to travel to Colombia and establish an art academy in Bogotá.[17] In 1874 another future Colombian painter, Epifanio Garay, traveled to New York City to study voice at the Academy of Music, then located on Fourteenth Street and Irving Place.[18] His father's death in 1877 forced his return home to Bogotá, but in the intervening three years he pursued not only operatic singing but also the visual arts.

GILDED AGE NEW YORK

"In a beautiful house on Fifth Avenue, New York, lives Donna Francisca Apaucio vel [sic] Vescuciadiayo de Quesaltenango Barrios, who is a very wealthy woman. Her husband was President of Guatemala, and was killed while attempting to secure the union of the five Central American Republics, in April, 1885." So began one press notice on Mrs. Barrios, who along with her eleven children and entourage of household servants became a fixture of Gilded Age New York. Her name appeared alongside those of well-known women such as Mrs. William Astor and the "Witch of Wall Street," Hetty Green. It was her romantic past that fascinated New Yorkers, especially the "love at first sight" that took her from the bosom of her old aristocratic family to the presidential palace of the social and political upstart Justo Rufino Barrios. William Eleroy Curtis elaborated on the circumstances in a *Cosmopolitan* profile:

> While he was making a journey through the country soon after his election to the Presidency, he saw in a convent a very beautiful girl. It was love at first sight. Inquiring the name and residence of her parents, he wrote to them saying that he would like to make the daughter his wife as soon as she was old enough to be married, which he thought would be in about two years. In the mean time he desired her to be educated in French and English.[19]

That training in English proved useful in Mrs. Barrios's later life in exile, enabling her to participate fully in the life of New York City. Unfettered by language barriers that would have confined her—as it did many émigrés—to the company of the Spanish-speaking community, she was able to attend concerts, art exhibitions, and salons and mix with a cross section of society from around the city and the globe.

Mrs. Barrios likely found her way to the home of Juan J. Peoli, which became a meeting place for social and cultural leaders of both North and South America in residence in New York. Cuban revolutionary José Martí, upon his arrival in the city on January 3, 1880, headed there and made contacts that led to his career as a journalist as well as to his meeting with Carmita Miyares, his future lover and political collaborator. Born in New York of Venezuelan parents, Peoli was praised by his contemporaries as "a singularly good type of a New-Yorker."[20] At a young age he moved with his parents to Havana and began art studies at the Royal Academy of San Alejandro. Early proficiency won him a scholarship to Rome, where he lived for eight years, except for time spent in Paris and Madrid. At the end of his fellowship he returned to Cuba, where he headed the art school in Matanzas, the location of his 1,400-acre sugar plantation. In the early 1860s he returned with his family to New York, where he gathered a circle of artists and writers and welcomed any visitor passing through the city with an interest in things American to join them. His embrace of the two Americas is embodied in the pair of portraits that hung in his sitting room in later

years: his depictions of notorious American Civil War General Dan Sickles at one end of the room and of Venezuelan general and one-time president José Antonio Páez at the other.[21] Ramón Páez must have found some measure of comfort after the death of his father during his visits with the Peolis, casting his eyes upon the full-length portrait. On those visits he also functioned as unofficial South American ambassador, advising on the much-debated canal that would eventually be constructed in Panama, among other trans-American matters.

FROM MEXICAN WAR TO SPANISH-AMERICAN WAR: EMERGING CARIBBEAN EMPIRE

In 1890 Colombian artist Ricardo Acevedo Bernal made a necessary stop in New York when his funds ran out on the way to Paris. Perhaps he, too, found his way to the home of the Peolis, who could have put him in touch with William Merritt Chase, with whom he is said to have studied. We do know that Acevedo Bernal remained in New York for about five years, doing decorative work for the Swedish artist Normann (or Norhmann). Perhaps at night or on weekends he took classes at the Art Students League or elsewhere in the city where Chase taught. He painted a range of subjects— landscapes, patriotic events, religious subjects—but was most noted for his portraits of the high society and leaders of Bogotá, such as his portrait of Rafael Reyes. His expressive brushwork and touches of pastel colors reflect the Impressionist influence of his time in Europe and in the United States, under Chase's tutelage, whether as an official student or a viewer of his acclaimed work.[22]

Rafael Reyes Prieto (1849–1921; president of Colombia 1904–09), January 16, 1913. Photographer unknown. Library of Congress Prints and Photographs Division, Washington, DC.

Around mid-century Frederic Church had established the role of the artist-traveler as a conveyor of visual information about Latin America. Many viewers studied his canvases as geography lessons in paint; some considered the natural resources they depicted; others meditated on the god who had created these Eden-like places; and all came to realize that there was a vast and still little-known continent just to the south. By the end of the nineteenth century, Church had substituted his adventurous Andean expeditions with winters in Mexico, now accessible by train. By then rheumatism prevented him from wielding the brush as he once had. Now younger artists created their visions of tropical America for the next generation.

Conrad Wise Chapman was not only one of the first U.S.-born artists of consequence to live and paint extensively in Mexico, but also a link between the two national schools. He was the son of leading painter and illustrator John Gadsby Chapman, author of the *American Drawing Book*. In the days when all educated Americans possessed some skill in drawing, Chapman became a household name. Born in Washington, D.C., in 1842, he moved to Rome with his family when he was a child. He was just beginning to paint professionally when the Civil War broke out, and he returned to the United States to serve with the Confederacy as both soldier and artist. Like many former Confederates, after the war he settled in Mexico, where he was much taken with the local mountain scenery. Chapman painted numerous views of the Valley of Mexico, demonstrating a predilection for landscape painting that may have been encouraged by a friend from his days in Rome, Eugenio Landesio, a professor of landscape at the Academy of San Carlos. Through him he undoubtedly became acquainted with José Maria Velasco, who went on to head the Mexican landscape school. (Having learned Italian as a child, Chapman soon learned to speak Spanish in Mexico, which would have facilitated communication with local artists and patrons, an ability that few of his fellow American artists possessed.)

Chapman lived in Mexico, with brief interruptions, for four decades and rendered its scenery many times, including a mural, *The Valley of Mexico* (1866–67), which is known through an old photograph but whose current location is unrecorded. This sweeping vista moves from a pastoral foreground to the distinctive peaks of Popocatepetl and Ixtacihuatl marking the horizon. Like other renderings he made of the revered valley, the mural moves beyond the merely topographical to demonstrate a deep emotional connection with the country.[23] Chapman sold his work on both sides of the border (among his patrons was Elihu Root, then U.S. Secretary of War) and exhibited in the annuals at New York's National Academy of Design and at the commercial galleries beginning to appear around the city. His pictures kept the image of Mexico vivid for New York audiences, who paid renewed attention to their southern neighbors in the 1880s and 1890s with the rise of tourism and trade with Mexico and the Caribbean. One of the last works Chapman painted before leaving Mexico for good was a self-portrait in which he demonstrated a penetrating psychological realism. It is inscribed to the poet Auguste Genin, a Frenchman from Mexico City who was the artist's friend and supporter throughout his later career. Even more immediate in style is the sketch for the finished work, which shows Chapman with a long beard and a penetrating gaze, paying homage to Mexican artist-seers from Velasco to the modernist Dr. Atl while placing himself within that tradition.

The U.S.-Mexican War (1846–48) was America's first military incursion into Latin America. When the Treaty of Guadalupe Hidalgo was signed, New Yorkers gathered at City Hall to honor the brave men who had fought and died. General William Worth, who served in Mexico, has the unique distinction of being buried beneath the monument erected in his honor, located near the northwest corner of Madison Square. By the century's end the country was once more engaged in combat in the Western Hemisphere, in the Spanish-American War, during which the American forces took both Cuba and Puerto Rico in a matter of weeks. Again, Madison Square was the site where the citizens of Manhattan mounted a massive homecoming to pay tribute to the war's greatest hero, Admiral George Dewey, commemorated by a giant triumphal arch erected by the artistic community. In egalitarian spirit, New York also feted the Spanish admiral Pascual Cervera, whose forces had recently been defeated at Santiago de Cuba. The many dinners held in their honor (Dewey came to bemoan all the occasions he had to attend) featured fabulous desserts, all dependent on the sugar plantations the United States had just waged naval battle to control. In the fifty years between these two wars, Latin Americans from throughout the hemisphere had arrived and helped shape the life of the city. Perhaps some of them were among the celebrants who took to the streets to mark the country's emergence as an imperial power in the Caribbean, with New York its de facto capital, leading the city on its way to becoming Nueva York.

Frederic Edwin Church (1826–1900). *Cotopaxi*,
1855. Oil on canvas. 28 x 42 in. (71.1 x 106.7 cm).
Smithsonian American Art Museum / Art Resource, NY.

Conrad Wise Chapman (1842–1910). *View of Monterrey from Bishop's Palace*, 1901. Oil on wood. 6¼ x 13¼ in. (15.9 x 33.7 cm). Valentine Richmond History Center, V.46.117.2.

Conrad Wise Chapman (1842–1910). *Self-Portrait*, 1908. Oil on paper. 10 x 5 in. (25.4 x 12.7 cm). Private collection.

NOTES

1. See my *Tropical Renaissance: North Americans Exploring Latin America, 1839–1879* (Washington, DC: Smithsonian Institution Press, 1989), for a discussion of this phenomenon.

2. Kevin J. Avery, *Church's Great Picture: The Heart of the Andes* (New York: Metropolitan Museum of Art, 1993).

3. For a thorough summary of the events surrounding the picture's exhibition, see John K. Howat, *Frederic Church* (New Haven, CT: Yale University Press, 2005), 83–90. It had opened at Lyric Hall on April 27, but moved the following day to the Tenth Street Building due to complaints about poor viewing conditions.

4. See Edwin G. Burrows and Mike Wallace, *Gotham: A History of New York City to 1898* (New York: Oxford University Press, 1999), 660–61, for background.

5.. Manthorne, *Tropical Renaissance*, 101–3.

6. R. B. Cunningham Graham, *José Antonio Páez* (Port Washington, NY: Kennikat Press, 1970; reprint of 1st ed., 1929), provides background.

7. Thomas Francis Meagher, "Holidays in Cost Rica," *Harper's New Monthly Magazine* 20 (December 1859, January 1860, and February 1860): 18–38, 145–64, and 304–25, respectively.

8. Letter quoted in Manthorne, *Tropical Renaissance*, 17.

9. See Walter R. Borneman, *Polk: The Man Who Transformed the Presidency and America* (New York: Random House, 2008), for a recent reevaluation.

10. Vera Brodsky Lawrence, *Strong on Music: The New York Music Scene in the Days of George Templeton Strong* (Chicago: University of Chicago Press, 1988), vol. 1, 533. Morris wrote the words; the composer of the music is unidentified.

11. For a useful summary of these events, see Vicente Quirarte, "Benito Juárez and New York City," *The Brooklyn Rail*, December 2006–January 2007, http://www.brooklynrail.org/2006/12/express/benito-jua.

12. Will Fowler, *Santa Anna of Mexico* (Lincoln: University of Nebraska Press, 2007), provides a fine biographical overview of his career.

13. "The Art of Cattle Driving. Scenes at Communipaw—Texan Steers and Mexican Vaqueros," *New York Times*, November 12, 1872, 1.

14. "Mexican Curiosities. Antiquities from Palenque and Ecuador," *New York Times*, April 4, 1874, 3.

15. See, for example, "Letter from Richard Scudder," *New York Times*, November 10, 1874.

16. Kirsten Silva Greusz, *Ambassadors of Culture: The Transamerican Origins of Latino Writing* (Princeton, NJ: Princeton University Press, 2002), 163–76.

17. Maya Jimenez, "Colombian Painters in Paris, 1850–1899" (PhD diss., Graduate Center, City University of New York, scheduled for defense 2010), 29.

18. Ibid., 49. The Academy of Music was founded in 1854, and the building was demolished in 1926.

19. William Eleroy Curtis, "Wealthy Women of America," *The Cosmopolitan* 7 (October 1889): 594–95.

20. "A Noteworthy Collection: Prints, Drawings, Water Colors, and Oils Amassed by John J. Peoli," *New York Times*, May 4, 1894, 4.

21. *Exhibition of Paintings by the Late J.J. Peoli* (New York: American Art Galleries, 1894) contains biographical information.

22. Jimenez, "Colombian Painters in Paris," 55–56. Registration records have yet to be located to document this connection firmly.

23. The most complete source to date is Ben L. Bassham, *Conrad Wise Chapman: Artist & Soldier of the Confederacy* (Kent, OH: Kent State University Press, 1998), from which biographical details are gleaned. The mural is illustrated and discussed on pp. 209–13.

BLAME IT ON WASHINGTON IRVING:

New York's Discovery of the Art and Architecture of Spain

RICHARD L. KAGAN

In the summer of 1890, the City of New York inaugurated a new Madison Square Garden, the second one known by that name. The first, at the corner of Madison Avenue and Twenty-ninth Street, proved too small, and the Garden's owners, following a design competition, opted to replace it with a new, more sumptuous arena designed by Stanford White, one of the city's most prominent architects and a partner in the architecture firm McKim, Mead & White. Built in the Italian Renaissance style, the new Garden's main building housed a ten-thousand-seat amphitheater, at the time one of the largest in the world. What was particularly striking about the new building was its brightly illuminated tower, which, at 304 feet, was exceeded in height only by the New York World Building on Park Row.

Even more remarkable was the Garden tower's unusual design. The first skyscrapers in New York and other cities were typically constructed in a neoclassical idiom, either Roman or Greek. White wanted something different—an unusual crowd-pleaser. He consequently modeled the tower on Seville's Giralda, a minaret dating from the twelfth century, an era during which that southern Spanish city was part of al-Andalus, or Muslim Spain. Miraculously, the Giralda survived Seville's conquest by Christian forces in 1248, and later served as the bell tower of the hulking Gothic cathedral constructed on the site of the mosque. In the sixteenth century the Giralda was "Christianized" to the extent that it acquired a spire of Renaissance design topped by the statue of an angel known as the Giraldillo, symbolizing the triumph of Christianity over Islam. Otherwise the Giralda, with its intricate, interlaced brickwork, impressed most visitors to Seville as a striking reminder of Spain's Muslim past. Presumably, the Garden's Giralda-like tower evoked similar memories, although White, having incorporated what he called his "snuggery" on one of the tower's upper floors, brazenly replaced the statue of the angel with one of a naked Diana, Roman goddess of the hunt.

Not surprisingly, this Diana elicited considerable comment in the New York

Madison Square Garden, New York, n.d.
Photographer unknown. Gelatin silver print.
New-York Historical Society (PR 020).

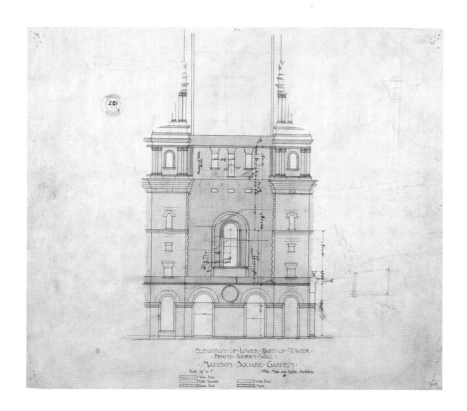

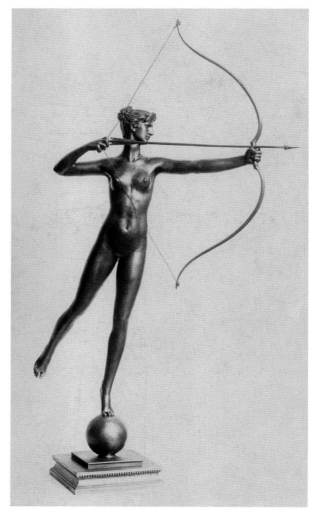

McKim, Mead & White Studio. *Madison Square Garden, Elevation of Lower Part of the Tower Behind Screen Wall*, n.d. Ink, wash, and graphite on linen. New-York Historical Society, McKim, Mead & White Collection.

Diana of the Tower by Augustus Saint-Gaudens, n.d. Photograph by Louis H. Dreyer. Gelatin silver print. New-York Historical Society, McKim, Mead & White Collection

press. But so too did White's decision to replicate the Giralda in New York. Why he did so remains something of a mystery. White had no direct personal connection with Spain, although he had a number of close friends and acquaintances who did. However, according to an article commenting on the tower's design, White was profoundly interested in Spanish architecture and decorative art. The architect undoubtedly was familiar with any one of a number of published drawings of the Giralda, notably those that appeared in the 1885 issue of *The American Architect*. The Giralda also was in keeping with the so-called neo-Moorish style of architecture that initially made its appearance in New York in the design of the Temple Emanu-El on Fifth Avenue, and subsequently in the Casino Theatre at Broadway and Thirty-ninth Street, a building said to resemble Spanish Saracenic architecture. As for White's tower, critics were hard pressed to classify its design. One labeled it somewhat erroneously as baroque, others referred to it as Spanish, but all seemed to agree with the critic who lauded the Garden as the most beautiful building in New York.[1]

Neither the Garden nor its tower was destined to last; both were demolished in 1925. During its time, however, this landmark both reflected and was partially responsible for what can be described as New York's protracted love affair with Spanish art and design. White's tower, for example, inspired yet another Giralda that served as the focal point of Dreamland, a Coney Island amusement park that opened in 1903; it inspired as well the facade of the Manhattan Municipal Building, also designed by McKim, Mead & White and completed in 1908. The Giralda also was referenced in any number of Spanish-style buildings, most spectacularly the string of luxury apartment blocks—each named after a different Spanish city—erected on Central Park South in 1895.

Yet architecture alone proved insufficient to satisfy the city's enchantment with the arts and culture of Spain. In 1890, a few months before the inauguration of the Garden's Giralda, La Carmencita, a glamorous gypsy dancer also known as the "Pearl of Seville," became a local celebrity after a private performance in the studio of the artist William Merritt Chase. La Carmencita's audience on that occasion was small but select, and included Stanford White, a notorious womanizer whose interest in the performer is likely to have involved more than a desire to learn about flamenco music and dance. Whether La Carmencita ever visited White's infamous snuggery remains unknown, but at the very least White managed to express his passion for Spanish culture by purchasing several portraits by Spanish Old Masters and subsequently according them pride of place in his sumptuous Gramercy Park home. White, it was said, favored Spanish paintings because of their "strong decorative qualities," a factor that, starting in the 1890s, possibly inspired other wealthy New York art lovers to purchase paintings attributed to El Greco, Velázquez, Goya, and other artists connected to what was then known as the "Spanish School" of art. Another factor that influenced these acquisitions was the perceived connection between the Spanish Old Masters and such "modern" painters as Manet and the Impressionists. Harry and Louisine Havemeyer were among the first major New York collectors to recognize this connection, but they were quickly joined by the likes of Henry Clay Frick, Benjamin Altman, and Philip Lehman, all of whom spent lavishly in a practically cut-throat competition to acquire choice pieces of Spanish art. This interest in Spanish art reached a climax in 1908 when thousands of New Yorkers swarmed up Broadway to Audubon Terrace to view the treasures housed in the newly opened museum of the Hispanic Society. Brainchild of Archer Milton Huntington, this museum was the first ever to be exclusively devoted to the arts and handicrafts of Spain.

Gotham's "discovery" of Spanish art and design was by no means unique. It paralleled similar trends in California, Florida, and other portions of the United States that once belonged to Spain's sprawling empire in the New World. The 1890s, for example, marked the development of the so-called Mission style of architecture in

Dreamland, Coney Island, New York. Postcard,
n.d. New-York Historical Society (PR 054).

Municipal Building, ca. 1914. Photograph by
James S. Hall. Gelatin silver print from a glass
plate negative. New-York Historical Society,
George P. Hall & Son Photograph Collection.

Southern California and in 1896 Los Angeles inaugurated La Fiesta, a celebration meant to highlight that city's connections with the cultures of both Mexico and Spain. But these were connections that New York lacked, for historically, the city had few direct ties with Spain. Moreover, in contrast to Los Angeles, with its growing Hispanic population, the number of Spanish (let alone Mexican and other Hispanic) immigrants living in New York at the end of the nineteenth century was minuscule, especially when compared to its rapidly growing population of Chinese, Irish, Italians, and Eastern Europeans. Prejudices connected to the Black Legend—the primarily but not exclusively Protestant tradition of anti-Spanish sentiment that began in the sixteenth century—further complicated New York's relationship with the arts and culture of Spain. These prejudices, far stronger in the eastern United States than in the west, taught generations of schoolchildren that Spain was a land of "bigoted Catholics" prone to "the practice of every vice."[2] As for the country's intellectual achievements, the 1817 anonymously written essay "Trait of Spanish Character" summed up the prevailing opinion that "as a nation, the Spaniards are at present a full century behind every other nation in Europe in the arts of life, the refinements of society, and enlightened views of civil polity; and almost a millennium, in modes of education, and intellectual culture. It may be questioned whether they have taken a step in the right road of learning since the days of the Cid."[3]

The impact of such ideas on the way New Yorkers viewed Spanish culture cannot be underestimated. They help to explain why, for example, Samuel Osgood, a distinguished man of letters (and member of the New-York Historical Society) who visited Madrid's Prado museum in 1854 felt obliged to comment on the "imperfect nature" of Spanish sacred art. Traces of the Black Legend also can be found in the writings of Kate Field, a *New York Herald* editor who, following her visit to Spain in 1864, described the Escorial monastery, one of the country's proudest monuments, as a "hideous burlesque."[4] As for the cathedral and churches in Toledo, Field's only comment was that the "stones" of the old city "told stories of bloodshed and violence."[5] Similar prejudices influenced the manner in which both critics and collectors viewed Spain's artistic achievements. There were exceptions, of course, among them William H. Aspinwall, a New York merchant who, beginning in the 1860s, assembled a small collection of paintings attributed to Murillo, Velázquez, and other Spanish artists. Otherwise, most collectors seemed to agree with the influential New England art collector and critic James Jackson Jarves, whose *Art Thoughts*, first published in 1874, had the following to say about Spanish art:

> We need not look for the poetical or imaginative in Spanish art; seldom for very
> refined treatment, and never for any intellectual elevation above the actual
> life out of which it drew its restricted stock-motives. What could be expected of

painting in a country where masked inquisitors visited every studio and either destroyed or daubed over any details that did not accord with their fanatical scruples. . . . There are admirable points in Spanish painting, but it is not a school of popular value or interest. Besides its two chief names [Velázquez and Murillo] it has no reputation beyond its own locality. The fixed purpose of its priest-ridden work was to stultify the human intellect and make life a burden instead of a blessing.[6]

In view of the weight of such ideas, what was underlying both White's decision to replicate the Giralda in New York and the city's newfound penchant for Spanish culture and art?

The answer begins with another New Yorker: Washington Irving, the Old Knickerbocker, whose *Tales of the Alhambra*, first published in 1832, was instrumental in changing the way New Yorkers—and most Americans—viewed Spain. This change did not occur overnight, given the strength of the Black Legend and attendant prejudices. At the end of the century anti-Spanish sentiment also bubbled up in such popular newspapers as the *New York World* in the run-up to the Spanish-American War in 1898.

Despite such challenges, Irving's Spain won the day. The Spain of the Black Legend was somber, dark, and despotic; his was lighthearted, sunny, filled with song and romance. Irving's Spain was irresistibly picturesque, bristling with crumbling ruins, colorful gypsies, dashing bullfighters, and dark-eyed women whose beauty their mantillas could do little to hide. Irving also equated Spain with Andalusia, the southern part of the country whose Islamic monuments, especially Granada's Alhambra and the Giralda in Seville, fired his romantic imagination and miraculously transported him back to the era of al-Andalus. Largely for this reason Irving "orientalized" Spain; as he put it, "The country, the habits, the very looks of the people, have something of the Arabian character."[7]

John Sartrain (1808–1897). *Washington Irving* (1783–1859). Engraving for *Ededic* magazine. New-York Historical Society (PR 052).

Irving's *hispanofilia* set him apart from most of his contemporaries, but it also helped to create the image of a country that many New Yorkers were keen to learn more about. Irving's influence, for example, can be found in the writings of other New Yorkers who visited the country and reported on what they saw. One was Alexander Slidell Mackenzie, a young naval officer whose works *A Year in Spain: By a Young American* (1829) and *Spain Revisited* (1836) both represented Spain in a positive light. Mackenzie also was the first American writer to provide a detailed description of the Prado, a museum that opened to the public in 1819 and was soon touted as the finest gallery of paintings in the world. This sentiment melded well with Mackenzie's description of the museum, but what he especially liked were its heated galleries, comfortable chairs and benches, and "order and stillness."[8]

Whether it was the Prado or the picturesque that provided the lure, it was not long before a number of intrepid New Yorkers traveled to Spain to experience its pleasures first hand. Among the first to do so was the prominent millionaire John Jacob Astor, whose name appears in the Prado's 1845 visitors' register. Another was the editor and poet William Cullen Bryant (for whom New York's Bryant Park is named), who traveled the length and breadth of Spain in 1857 and recorded his reactions in a series of letters published in the *New York Evening Post*. Influenced by Irving's romantic vision of the country, Bryant saw Spain as "a curious old place, with many picturesque and interesting peculiarities," among them its decidedly "oriental" character. As for the Prado, Bryant wrote that he was "intoxicated by the spectacle " of its collections and especially pleased to have discovered there the "works of the Spanish masters" whose full merit, he wrote, "cannot be known to those who have never visited Spain."[9]

Bryant's invitation received an enthusiastic response. During the following decade, and despite the upheavals of America's Civil War—or just possibly because of them—the number of New Yorkers visiting the Prado increased steadily. What began as a trickle soon became a steady stream. During the late nineteenth century—an era of peace and growing prosperity for both Spain and the United States—the number of Americans visiting not only the Prado but other parts of the country continued to rise. In the meanwhile, stay-at-homes could satisfy their curiosity through a variety of publications that invariably presented Spain as an accessible "other": backward, yet charming and quaint. *Harper's Weekly* and the *Century* magazine, for example, enticed readers with such articles as "Spain, Her Ways, Her Women, and Her Wines" and "Madrid: From Noon to Midnight." Travel books did the same. Noteworthy among these offerings were such titles as *Gazpacho: or, Summer Months in Spain* (1851), *Spanish Vistas* (1883), and *Spain: Land of the Castanet* (1896), the last of which, following its publication in New York in 1896, prompted one irate Spanish reviewer to suggest that the book's title was the equivalent of calling the United States "the land of bacon." (Cultural stereotyping, it seems, can easily go both ways.)

But this last book is also interesting as it came from the pen of H. C. Chatfield-Taylor, a Chicago-based author who had previously served as honorary chairman of the Spanish pavilion erected at his city's World's Columbian Exposition in 1893. Visited by thousands of Americans from all parts of the country, this important gathering featured as one of its central themes Spain's long-standing relationship with the United States, and showcased statues of Columbus, a replica of the La Rábida monastery where he supposedly formulated his plans to go to China by sailing westward, and reproductions of his three caravels. Overall, the fair offered a wholly favorable impression of both Spain and its culture that subsequently served as something of an antidote against the torrent of anti-Spanish criticism that surfaced before and during

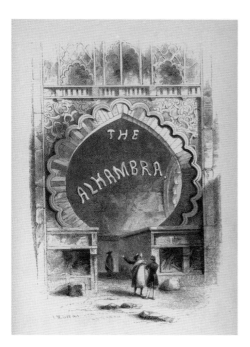

Frontispiece for Washington Irving, *The Alhambra*, author's revised edition, with illustrations by Felix O. C. Darle. New York: George P. Putnam, 1851. Fales Collection, New York University Libraries.

the war of 1898. So too did the Pan-American Exposition held at Buffalo in 1901. Organized around yet another outsized and brilliantly illuminated replica of the Giralda, this fair offered New Yorkers a sympathetic view of Hispanic culture in both the Old World and the New.

From this perspective, New York's discovery of the art and architecture of Spain was only one facet of a broader cultural phenomenon—call it the "Spanish craze"—that swept across the United States at the dawn of the twentieth century. As the craze developed, however, the city was more than a simple bystander; to the degree that it was among the first to integrate the culture and traditions of Spain (and Spanish America) into its own, it was actually a pacesetter. Starting in the 1860s, a growing number of New York–based artists, partly inspired by Irving's romantic portrayal of the country, had journeyed to Spain in search of picturesque subjects. One of the first was Samuel Colman, who was already a leading member of the Hudson River School when he visited the Prado and then Andalusia during the summer of 1860, sketchbook in hand. Colman soon transformed his sketches into a series of paintings featuring the Alhambra, the Giralda, and other equally pleasing subjects, all of which met with critical acclaim when they were initially placed on display in 1864.

Colman never returned to Spain, but in his capacity as director of New York's National Academy of Design, he undoubtedly inspired other artists to visit the coun-

try and, most significantly, to paint what they saw. To be sure, inspiration also came
from other sources, especially from France and the Spanish-themed pictures of
Édouard Manet. Eager to learn more about Velázquez, Manet first visited the Prado
in 1865, and was quickly followed by Thomas Eakins, Mary Cassatt, John Singer
Sargent, and other American artists based in Paris. The naturalness, apparent simplicity, and individuality of Velázquez's style offered these artists an escape from the
confines of the Beaux-Arts tradition in which they were trained. For this same reason
Velázquez held out a special appeal for a contingent of New York artists who belonged
to the Art Students League, an organization founded in 1875 to encourage artists to
embrace the newer methods of painting associated with Manet and other contemporary European painters whose work was judged both modern and new. J. Alden Weir,

Samuel Colman (1832–1920). *The Hill of the Alhambra*, 1865. Oil on canvas. 47½ x 72½ in. (120.7 x 184.2 cm). The Metropolitan Museum of Art, New York. Gift of Mrs. Oswald C. Hering, in memory of her husband, 1968 (68.19). Image copyright © The Metropolitan Museum of Art / Art Resource, NY.

Frank Duveneck, Robert Blum, and Childe Hassam all made a point of visiting the
Prado, although their interest in Spain, like that of Colman before them, principally
was derived from their search for subjects deemed picturesque.

Another of the New York artists who "discovered" Spain during this era was
William Merritt Chase. In 1881, during his first trip to Spain, Chase executed a series
of drawings—later published in *The Century Magazine*—that latched onto water sell-
ers, gypsies, and similar picturesque themes. But Chase also went to Spain to study
Velázquez, and did so by visiting the Prado to make copies of several of his most
famous works. It was then, it seems, that Chase fell in love with Velázquez, an artist
he would soon characterize as "the greatest painter that ever lived," and one whose
influence upon Chase's own manner of painting was profound. Over the years Chase
returned to the Prado again and again, and starting in the 1890s he led groups of art
students there so that they would also have the opportunity "to revel in Velázquez . . .
not forgetting Greco, Goya, and a few more," including both Sorolla and Zuloaga, two
contemporary Spanish artists whose talents he was among the first to promote.[10]
Small wonder then that Chase's Tenth Street Studio, decorated with his copies of
Velázquez's work, served as the stage where La Carmencita first danced in New
York. More importantly, the studio served as a mecca for other New Yorkers eager to
study and learn about the art and culture of a people Chase described as the epitome
of hospitality itself.

Chase, in this sense, served as Spain's greatest champion in New York, and
through lectures, interviews, and especially his own Velázquez-inspired paintings, he
arguably did as much as anyone else to help the city overcome its old prejudices about

Diego Rodríguez de Silva y Velázquez (1599–1660). *Don Gaspar de Guzmán, Count-Duke of Olivares*, ca. 1625–26. Oil on canvas. 87⅜ x 54¼ in. (222 x 137 cm). Hispanic Society of America, New York.

Spain and its art. Chase, however, was not alone. His enthusiasm for the arts of Spain proved infectious, first for Stanford White, and later for two of the city's prominent art critics, Royal Cortissoz and Charles Caffin, both of whom, starting around 1900, touted the "modernity," the expressiveness, the individuality, and the importance of Spanish Old Master art.

What followed was the artistic equivalent of the Klondike Gold Rush that swept the country in 1897, directed toward the acquisition of an El Greco, a Velázquez, a Goya, or some other choice example of Spanish art, for those who could afford it. Already in 1898, this particular frenzy led to the suggestion that following its victory in the war over Spain, the United States should demand, in the form of an indemnity, the contents of the Prado in lieu of Cuba and Puerto Rico. This suggestion went nowhere, but the city's—and America's—seemingly unquenchable thirst for Spanish art continued to grow.

The principal loser in this particular frenzy was, of course, Spain itself. Many Spaniards reacted with dismay as they watched some of their country's finest art treasures spirited out of the country via a complicated network of unscrupulous anti-quarians and dealers, whose activities await further detailed study. The clear winner, on the other hand, was New York, which in the course of a decade could lay claim to what was arguably the finest assemblage of Spanish paintings in America. Most of these paintings were acquired by wealthy private collectors such as the Havemeyers or Frick. The *Times*, however, regarded these acquisitions as a permanent addition to the cultural patrimony of the city itself. Moreover, the newspaper on occasion went further with such headlines as "America Secures an El Greco," a sure sign that its editors viewed the acquisition of important art treasures as an act of patriotism that would ultimately redound to the benefit of the city, and ultimately, the nation as a whole.

But what about those New Yorkers who would never set foot in the Havemeyers' picture gallery or Henry Clay Frick's sitting room? What opportunities did they ever have to see the Spanish pictures whose arrival the *Times* deemed headline news? Under the rubric the "Spanish School," the 1903 catalogue of the city's Metropolitan Museum of Art listed only a dozen or so pictures, all of which had entered the collection through private bequest. In 1905, in keeping with the city's growing interest in El Greco, the museum's trustees authorized the purchase of an *Adoration* by him, although it is worth noting that in 1906 they rejected Harry Havemeyer's suggestion that they purchase this same artist's *Assumption of the Virgin*, a spectacular work that went instead to Chicago's Art Institute.

As the Met hesitated, other institutions, public and private, helped to satisfy the city's interest in Spanish art. In 1905, for example, the Ehrich Galleries on West Thirty-third Street organized a public exhibition devoted exclusively to what the *Times* headlined as "Old Paintings from Spain." Together with works attributed to

El Greco (1541–1614). *Portrait of a Cardinal, Probably Cardinal Don Fernando Niño de Guevara (1541–1609)*, ca. 1600. Oil on canvas. 67¼ x 42½ in. (170.8 x 108 cm). The Metropolitan Museum of Art, New York, H. O. Havemeyer Collection, Bequest of Mrs. H. O. Havemeyer, 1929 (29.100.5). Image copyright © The Metropolitan Museum of Art / Art Resource, NY.

El Greco, Murillo, Ribera, and Zurbarán, this exhibition also featured works by lesser-known artists such as the Velázquez disciple (and son-in-law) Juan Martínez del Mazo. The opening of the Hispanic Society's museum in 1908 brought other Spanish paintings, including several works by Goya, as well as Velázquez's portrait of the Count Duke of Olivares, together with a host of Spanish books and handicrafts. In 1912, the prestigious Knoedler Gallery organized a special charity exhibition of works by El Greco and Goya that ordinarily hung in the Havemeyers' private gallery. In its coverage of this exhibition, the *Times* referred to both the "recent popularity" of works by El Greco and the fact that the "increasing vogue" for Spanish painting meant that the cost of works by such artists as Goya had risen by almost 300 percent.[11] Spanish art, in other words, remained in demand, and the fact that Knoedler devoted a second charity exhibition to works by El Greco and Goya indicates that the "increasing vogue" had yet to run its course.[12]

More needs to be written about the character of this "vogue," about the architects who built in the Spanish idiom, the collectors and dealers who brought Spanish paintings and handicrafts to New York, and the designers who furnished homes and offices in what one critic labeled the "simplicity" and "absence of meaningless applied decoration and ornament" associated with the "Spanish style." All this awaits further inquiry. But for those seeking a short answer for why this particular vogue first arrived in New York, the response is simple: Blame it on Washington Irving.

NOTES

1. See, for example, Marianna Griswald Van Rennselaer, "Madison Square Garden," *Century Magazine* 47, no. 5 (March 1894): 732–47.

2. Jedidiah Morse, *The American Universal Geography*, 2 vols., 3rd ed. (Boston: Isaiah Thomas and Ebenezer T. Andrews, 1796), 2:297.

3. Anonymous, "Trait of Spanish Character," *North American Review* 5 (1817): 54.

4. Kate Field, *Ten Days in Spain* (Boston: James R. Osgood, 1875), 168.

5. Ibid., 179.

6. James Jackson Jarves, *Art Thoughts: The Experiences and Observations of an American Amateur in Europe* (New York: Hurd and Houghton, 1871), 75.

7. Washington Irving, *The Alhambra* (New York: G. P. Putnam, 1851), 15.

8. A. Slidell (Mackenzie), *Spain Revisited*, 2 vols. (New York: Harper & Brothers, 1836), 1:196.

9. Letter, "To the *Evening Post*," dated Madrid, November 1, 1857, in *The Letters of William Cullen Bryant*, ed. William Cullen Bryant II and Thomas G. Voss (New York: Fordham University Press), 3:485.

10. For these remarks, see the article "Get Together, Says Mr. Chase to Fellow-Artists," *New York Times*, May 21, 1905.

11. "El Greco and Goya Paintings for View," *New York Times*, March 29, 1912, 12.

12. Note that in 1915 Knoedler's sponsored yet another loan exhibition of works by El Greco and Goya, and in its coverage of the show the *Times* again noted how "in recent years the fame of El Greco and Goya has grown with astonishing rapidity." See "Art Notes. Loan Exhibition of Paintings by El Greco and Goya at Knoedler's," *New York Times*, January 13, 1915.

ART WORLDS OF NUEVA YORK

EDWARD J. SULLIVAN

Throughout the nineteenth and twentieth centuries and into the present, New York City has served as a magnet for visual artists from the Iberian peninsula and Latin America. They have come from all parts of the Spanish- and Portuguese-speaking world to study in art schools and academies, to show their work in the museums and galleries of Manhattan, and in many cases to assimilate themselves into the larger New York art world. Some have arrived as major international figures, celebrated by their patrons and the public alike, while others have come as students and returned to their countries after their stays. Still others have come to New York City seeking freedom of expression in times of political or social stress. Art in New York has benefited greatly from the presence of this wide spectrum of artists, and it is no exaggeration to say that this art-conscious (if not art-obsessed) city would be a much poorer cultural force without the continuing contributions of artists from Spain, Latin America, and the Caribbean.

The following essay is a broad-brush examination—by necessity a very partial view—of some of the artists from Spain and Latin America who were influential within the New York cultural imagination from the nineteenth century until the 1940s. This discussion of the Hispanization of New York City cultural life includes not only the artists themselves but also the patrons who purchased their works and the institutions that displayed them.

SPANISH ART AND ARTISTS (CA. 1860–1945) AND NEW YORK CITY

The affinity between the city and the Spanish-speaking world began as early as the 1830s, when New Yorkers began to show an intense interest in the romantic views of Spain presented in the writings of Washington Irving (as Richard Kagan discusses in his essay in this volume). Fine art's role in this story began when American artists began to travel to Spain and Latin America. Romantic landscapists such as Frederic Edwin Church, who painted well-known views of the Ecuadorian volcanoes Cayambé and Mount Chimborazo in 1857, and other members of the Hudson River School made journeys to Latin America, stimulated in part by the writings of the German naturalist and artist Alexander von Humboldt, one of the first foreigners to be admitted to the virtually closed Spanish colonies of the New World. (Katherine Manthorne, one of this book's essayists, has written about this phenomenon and its meanings.[1])

Rufino Tamayo (1899–1991). *New York from My Terrace*, 1937. Private collection. Photo: Mary-Anne Martin Fine Art, New York. © D.R. Rufino Tamayo / Herederos / México / 2010, Fundación Olga y Rufino Tamayo, A.C.

no 2
Morning

3. Valle de Chillo   Beautiful Church house   Cayambe from hill of 72
Temple del Sol
June 24th 57

The glazed tiled domes of the   The Horizon to the East was a line of
Churches glitter as if wet. Shadow   snow generally, lying on the summits
very very dark (green)   of the lower mountains and páramos

Opposite, top: Frederic Edwin Church (1826–1900). *Cayambé, Morning, from the Temple of the Sun, Quito, Ecuador, June 24, 1857*. Graphite, brush, and white gouache on tan wove paper. 6⅞ x 10⁹⁄₁₆ in. (17.5 x 26.8 cm). Cooper-Hewitt, National Design Museum, New York, Gift of Louis P. Church, 1917-4-738. Cooper-Hewitt, National Design Museum, Smithsonian Institution / Art Resource, NY.

Opposite, bottom: Frederic Edwin Church (1826–1900). *Study of Mount Chimborazo, Ecuador*, 1857. Brush and oil paint, traces of graphite on paperboard. 13³⁄₁₆ x 20⁹⁄₁₆ in. (34.4 x 52.2 cm). Cooper-Hewitt, National Design Museum, New York, Gift of Louis P. Church, 1917-4-1296-b. Cooper-Hewitt, National Design Museum, Smithsonian Institution / Art Resource, NY.

Above: William Merritt Chase (1849–1916). *Sunny Spain*, 1882. Oil on canvas. 19 x 28¾ in. (48.3 x 73 cm). Collection of Arthur and Lois Stainman.

For the most part, North American artists did not begin visiting Spain until after the American Civil War. New York artist Samuel Colman, however, went even earlier. Inspired by Irving's writings, he left Manhattan in 1860 bound for Andalusia, the southern region of Spain that was to figure heavily in the "picturesque" visions of the Iberian peninsula created by his and subsequent generations of American painters who fell under the spell of decaying Moorish buildings, gypsy dancers, and beggar children. John Singer Sargent's famous work *El Jaleo (Gypsy Dance)*, painted in 1882 for the Boston collector Isabella Stewart Gardner, is a latter-day example of this genre. Equally romantic are many of the Spanish landscapes and figure studies done around the same time in Spain by William Merritt Chase. Nonetheless, as the art historian M. Elizabeth Boone has pointed out in her important study of American artists in Spain from 1860 to 1914, Chase's work also began to incorporate a more realistic approach to a country that, by the 1880s, was modernizing at a surprisingly rapid rate.[2]

Diego Rodríguez de Silva y Velázquez (1599–1660). *Portrait of Philip IV*, 1623–24. Oil on canvas. 24⅜ x 19¼ in. (61.9 x 48.9 cm). Meadows Museum, Southern Methodist University, Dallas, Alger H. Meadows Collections, MM. 67.23.

By the mid-nineteenth century, many New York art collectors as well as other culturally oriented individuals were also traveling to Spain, familiarizing themselves with the riches of the Museo del Prado. The artist who had the greatest impact on the visual imaginations of Americans at the time was Diego Velázquez, court painter to King Philip IV and creator of one of the most famous group portraits in the Western tradition, *Las Meninas* (The Maids of Honor) (1656). American travelers also studied many of the architectural treasures in the southern region of Andalusia, the former Islamic territory known as al-Andalus, as well as what remained (after earlier nineteenth-century wars and plunder) of the Renaissance and Baroque paintings and sculptures in the churches, convents, and monasteries throughout the country.

Spanish art exerted a strong pull on the imaginations of many wealthy art patrons, as Kagan describes in his essay. While it is true that the mostly Protestant, conservative art collectors in the United States were generally more attracted to secular Dutch and Flemish works of art (which form the bulk of the Old Master collections of several American museums), the Spaniards El Greco, Velázquez, and especially Goya were nonetheless very appealing to many. Henry Osborne Havemeyer and his wife, Louisine, whose fortune came from the Caribbean sugar trade, were great admirers of some of the classic Spanish artists, and they eventually acquired some sixteen Goya paintings. Only four of these, however, are now considered originals; even the authenticity of *Majas on a Balcony*, the best known of them, has been questioned. Long considered one of Goya's most beautiful, lyrical pieces, this work, now in the Metropolitan Museum of Art, is related in subject to the famous painting *Two Women at a Window* (in Washington's National Gallery of Art) by the seventeenth-century master Bartolomé Esteban Murillo. The Havemeyer painting may well have influenced, in turn, Édouard Manet's 1868 *The Balcony* (at the Musée d'Orsay in Paris). Despite its current designation as "attributed to" Goya, the work has been a favorite ever since the family donated it to the Met.

Some of the modern Spanish artists who were most influential in New York in the late nineteenth and early twentieth centuries either did not go to Manhattan at all or spent only brief periods there. The Catalan Mariano Fortuny y Marsal never came to the U.S., but he was lionized for his glittering, light-filled paintings, which were collected avidly by wealthy New Yorkers, Philadelphians, and others, and provided immense pleasure to audiences and inspiration to American artists. Fortuny, from the northeastern Spanish city of Reus, spent his relatively brief life in Spain, Paris, Morocco, and Italy; his son Mariano would later became a well-known painter and designer of fabrics in Venice. The elder Fortuny's work was seen as a bridge between the grand generation of the Spanish Baroque (Velázquez and others) and modern forms of outdoor painting. Some of his most characteristic pieces, such as the 1867 *Arab Fantasy*, are reminiscent of works by other nineteenth-century Orientalists such as the Frenchman Jean-Léon Gérome.

Francisco de Goya y Lucientes (1746–1828). *Majas on a Balcony*. Oil on canvas, 76¾ x 49½ in. (194.9 x 125.7 cm). The Metropolitan Museum of Art, New York, H. O. Havemeyer Collection, Bequest of Mrs. H. O. Havemeyer, 1929 (29.100.10). Image copyright © The Metropolitan Museum of Art / Art Resource, NY.

Mariano Fortuny y Marsal (1838–1874). *Arab Fantasy*, 1867. Oil on canvas. 20½ x 26⅜ in. (52.1 x 67 cm). Walters Art Gallery, Baltimore.

Fortuny had spent considerable time in Morocco, first sent there by the city government of Barcelona to document the Spanish-Moroccan War of 1860. Many of his best-known works depict highly romanticized (and, in a number of instances, convincingly realistic) scenes of the harems, festivals, and street life of Tangier, Tetuan, Ceuta, and elsewhere. Battles between Spaniards and Moroccans were also part of his repertoire in the early 1860s. Orientalism meant something quite different for a Spanish audience at the time than it did for viewers from other parts of Europe. Located very close to Morocco, Spain had been under partial Muslim rule from 711 to 1492, when cities like Granada and Seville were grand centers of Islamic civilization. Nineteenth-century evocations of the Islamic past by Spanish artists (or architects, as a neo-Moorish building style was also in vogue at this time) represented a mixture of nostalgia and an attempt to depict one of the three "civilizations" (also including Christian and Jewish) that Spanish intellectuals of the period looked to as the cornerstones of their national identity. Whether or not such subtleties were apparent to Fortuny's foreign collectors and followers is difficult to say, but his

Moorish themes found a receptive audience among New Yorkers and other post–Civil War Americans interested in investigating people and places outside their immediate frame of visual, racial, and historical reference. Many Americans themselves became Orientalists of a sort: Church installed his great collection of art and exotica in his neo-Moorish palace called Olana above the Hudson River in Columbia County, New York.

Fortuny's most famous painting in an American collection (in the Corcoran Gallery of Art, Washington, D.C.) is the 1874 *Choice of the Model*, one of his many eighteenth-century costume pieces. For Fortuny and many of his contemporaries the eighteenth century was as removed from banal reality, and almost as "exotic," as the Islamic world. It provided a stage for creating images of people clothed in delicate lace, shimmering satins, and elaborate hats. *Choice of the Model* had belonged to one of Fortuny's major American collectors, William Hood Stewart, an American expatriate in Paris. The year after Stewart's death in 1897, his art collection sold at auction at Chickering Hall (normally a concert venue) on Fifth Avenue and Eighteenth Street for record prices. The most expensive work was, in fact, a Fortuny (*Court of Justice in the Alhambra*), which sold for $13,000 to Harry Payne Whitney, who, according to a *New York Times* article, outbid Henry Clay Frick.[3] Nine years before the Stewart sale, the Metropolitan already had acquired a Fortuny, *Portrait of Madame Gaye*, a gift of the collector Alfred Corning Clark, the Singer Sewing Machine Company heir, art collector, and father of Sterling and Stephen Clark, who also went on to become great European painting collectors.

Fortuny was an artistic hero to a generation of American artists who made their homes in New York.[4] In June 1884, American painters William Merritt Chase and Robert F. Blum, both Manhattan residents, began a two-week sea voyage to Europe. They passed the time each evening with masquerades and parties, one of which was a dinner given in honor of Fortuny, who had died ten years earlier. The menu was hand-painted by Blum and included his own signature, inspired by that of Fortuny. The after-dinner speeches were all about Fortuny's artistic achievements and how important they were for the celebrants. While toasting the deceased artist, the Americans surely hoped they would return to New York as famous as their Catalan hero.[5]

Robert Blum was born in Cincinnati and came to New York in 1878. Best known as an illustrator, he worked for a variety of journals in Manhattan, including the monthly Catalan newspaper *La Llumanera de Nova York*, published between 1874 and 1881. In Manhattan, Blum became friendly with an entire circle of artists who were devotees of Fortuny's work, including Harry Humphrey Moore, who had studied with Fortuny for several years in the 1860s in Spain and later in Rome, where the Catalan artist spent a good deal of his mature life.[6] When Moore returned to his native New York, he set up an elaborate studio on Fourteenth Street filled with

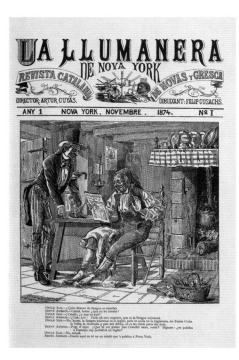

Front page of *La Llumanera de Nova York*, no. 1 (November 1874). General Research Division, New York Public Library, Astor, Lenox and Tilden Foundations.

Robert Frederick Blum (1857–1903). *Venetian Lacemakers*, 1887. Oil on canvas. 30⅛ x 41¼ in. (76.5 x 104.8 cm). Cincinnati Museum of Art, Gift of Elizabeth S. Potter.

objects he had purchased in North Africa, where he had gone following Fortuny's example, and proudly displayed the prized palette and brushes given to him by Fortuny himself. Both Moore and Blum, as well as many other New York artists, imitated and borrowed themes from Fortuny in their works in oil and watercolor, as seen in Blum's evocative *Venetian Lacemakers* (1887). Here he shows a special affinity for Fortuny's many romantic views of Venice, a subject also well developed by Sargent, another admirer of the Catalan artist.

One of the most direct homages to the Spanish Old Masters was by William Merritt Chase in his painting *The Infanta (My Little Daughter Helen Velázquez Posing as an Infanta)* (1899). The work is based on Velázquez's *Las Meninas*, which the artist studied in the Prado, often in the company of his students who regularly accompanied him on trips to Spain. Chase's more informal works, however, also bear the imprint of his fascination with modern Spanish painting, including the works of Fortuny. His *Open Air Breakfast* (ca. 1888) depicts a family scene reminiscent of a famous 1874 work by Fortuny, *The Artist's Children in the Japanese Salon*, in the Prado. It sparkles with light and displays the artist's seemingly effortless use of

William Merritt Chase (1849–1916). *The Infanta (My Little Daughter Helen Velázquez Posing as an Infanta)*, 1899. Oil on canvas. 32 x 24 in. (81.3 x 61 cm). Private collection.

the quickly applied brushstroke to suggest spontaneity and freshness. These impressionist effects are ultimately derived from Chase's interest in Fortuny's achievement.

Fortuny died at the very young age of thirty-six, having never traveled to the United States. Although many of his fellow-artist admirers and collectors in New York did not meet him, they did have the opportunity to become acquainted with his son-in-law, the portraitist and genre painter Raimundo de Madrazo y Garreta. Madrazo was a member of an artistic dynasty in Spain that included his father, the painter Federico, and grandfather, José, a student of Ingres; both men also served as director of the Prado. Raimundo spent considerable time in New York and became enormously popular among the members of Manhattan high society.[7] His paintings

William Merritt Chase (1849–1916). *The Open Air Breakfast*, ca. 1888. Oil on canvas. 38 x 57 in. (96.5 x 144.8 cm). Toledo Museum of Art.

were purchased by prominent families such as the Vanderbilts, and several of them
entered the collection of the Metropolitan Museum in its early days. These include
Girls at a Window (ca. 1875), clearly derived from a composition by Murillo, and given
to the museum by Catherine Lorillard Wolfe along with the rest of her collection in
1887, as well as *Samuel P. Avery* (1876), depicting the well-known art dealer, who
established the New York Public Library's Print Room in 1900 and whose painting
collection went to the Metropolitan after his death in 1904.

The Spanish-American War of 1898 (treated in detail by several of the writers
in this book) was a calamitous event for Spain as it represented the end of its dominion in the New World. With the Treaty of Paris ending the war, Spain's last two colonies on this side of the Atlantic, Cuba and Puerto Rico, passed into American hands
politically and economically. But the war also had the effect of awakening a much

Archer Milton Huntington (1870–1955), 1909.
Photographer unknown. Hispanic Society of
America, New York.

Frederick Brosen (b. 1954). *Audubon Terrace*,
1998. Watercolor on heavy watercolor paper.
43 x 29 in. (109.2 x 73.7 cm). New-York Historical
Society, Partial Gift of Mr. and Mrs. John J. Roche
and the 20th Century Acquisition Fund (2001.304).

larger interest in Spain and Spanish culture than had existed before in the United
States. James Fernández eloquently describes the rise of Spanish immigration into
New York in the early 1900s and the establishment on West Fourteenth Street and
other parts of the city of a veritable "Little Spain," with a dynamic life of commercial
and cultural institutions. For the visual arts, this increased interest reached a cre-
scendo in 1908, when the museum of the Hispanic Society of America opened its
doors in a series of elaborate neoclassical buildings on Audubon Terrace, at 155th
Street and Broadway.[8] Archer Milton Huntington, the heir to a railroad fortune and
a great admirer and student of Spanish history, language, and art, was the guiding
force behind the creation of this important center for the display and study of Spanish,
Portuguese, and Latin American art. The society continues to be the premier collection of Spanish art, antiquities, and manuscripts outside of Spain.

Huntington (who later married the sculptor Anna Hyatt, responsible for the
monumental image of El Cid opposite the society's main door) was an ardent admirer
of modern Spanish art and sought to make his museum into a nexus for interaction
between the most up-to-date Spanish visual expressions and the New York City public. He succeeded in a very big way when the enormous retrospective exhibition of
the work of Joaquín Sorolla y Bastida, which opened in February 1909, became the

best-attended exhibition in any New York museum until that time. With some 168,000 visitors, the show (which later traveled to Buffalo and Boston) made Sorolla virtually a household name in the United States. Although his huge body of work has many facets, it is generally seen as a continuation of the romanticizing tradition in Spanish art, conveying a positive view of the country's landscapes and its forms of everyday life. Sorolla's work was one of two sides of the artistic coin at the turn of the twentieth century, with the other side belonging to younger contemporaries, such as Ignacio Zuloaga and José Gutiérrez Solana, who concentrated on the darker realities of a nation defeated by the Spanish-American War and struggling to modernize in keeping with its northern neighbors on the European continent.

Born in Valencia in 1863 and trained in Madrid and Rome at the Spanish Academy, Sorolla is noted for literally hundreds of paintings and sketches he made of the warm, sunny landscapes of Andalusia and Valencia as well as the central plains and mountains of Castile. Recent research by Spanish and American art historians has pointed out his affinities with such pan-European trends as realism, Symbolism, and Impressionism.[9] Many of Sorolla's works before 1900 recall themes of melancholy, pain, and alienation not unlike the subjects treated by some of his contemporaries, such as Vincent van Gogh in his images of poor Dutch peasants or Edvard Munch in his depictions of illness or drug addiction. One of the last of Sorolla's naturalist paintings was very familiar to generations of New Yorkers: *Sad Inheritance* (1899), a monumental canvas showing a priest caring for a group of orphan boys afflicted with a variety of debilitating diseases. The artist had seen such a group of naked, indigent children on a Valencian beach and, touched by the pitiful sight, started to sketch what would become this dramatic tableau. Sorolla gave the first of these sketches to Chase and another to Sargent.

Sad Inheritance was exhibited at the Universal Exposition in Paris (1900) and the National Exhibition in Madrid (1901), winning medals of honor in both. It was acquired in 1904 by New York industrialist John E. Berwind, who had large stock holdings in the San Juan Hotels Corporation and the South Porto Rico Sugar Company. Berwind donated it to the Sunday School of the Episcopal Church of the Ascension at Fifth Avenue and Tenth Street, where it hung for many years in a side chapel, a beautiful complement to the grand mural painting by John LaFarge over the main altar. For decades the church was a virtual pilgrimage site for New York artists and other Americans from farther afield in the thrall of Spanish painting, all eager to study Sorolla's masterpiece. (The church sold the picture at a Christie's auction in 1981 to the Caja de Ahorros de Valencia, Castellón y Alicante, in whose collection it remains today.)

Sorolla's 1909 Hispanic Society exhibition was a "complete triumph in American high society, and . . . [represented] the conquest of a new clientele that

Joaquín Sorolla y Bastida (1863–1923). *Sad Inheritance*, **1899. Oil on canvas. 82¾ x 112¼ in. (210 x 285 cm). Private collection, Valencia, Spain. SCALA / Art Resource, NY.**

Joaquín Sorolla y Bastida (1863–1923). *Grand Army Plaza, New York, Seen from a Window of the Savoy Hotel*, 1911. Gouache on cardboard. 17½ x 8½ in. (44.5 x 21.7 cm). Hispanic Society of America, New York.

would elevate him to the highest echelons of international fame."[10] He made his first trip to New York for the opening and returned in 1911. Sorolla made a number of sketches of New York City street scenes, including views of Grand Army Plaza as seen from the Savoy Hotel (now the site of the General Motors Building) at Fifth Avenue and Fifty-ninth Street, where the artist stayed during his 1909 and 1911 visits.[11] They serve as informal testimonies to his identification with the city where he made many new friends and met clients whose portraits he painted with enthusiasm. One of the most beautiful of these is his 1911 portrait of Louis Comfort Tiffany, who posed for Sorolla as a working artist in the garden of his Oyster Bay, Long Island, estate. Tiffany had purchased a number of the Spaniard's paintings for Laurelton Hall (built in 1904), but this portrait had pride of place. Perhaps the apogee of Sorolla's portrait career in the United States came when he depicted President William Howard Taft in a portrait painted in the White House (it is now in the Taft Museum in Cincinnati).

Joaquín Sorolla y Bastida (1863–1923). *Louis
Comfort Tiffany* (1849–1933), 1911. Oil on canvas.
59¼ x 88¾ in. (150.5 x 225.5 cm). Hispanic
Society of America, New York, Donated by Mrs.
Francis M. Weld (née Julia DeForest Tiffany).

Huntington maintained his friendship with Sorolla, and during a 1910 visit to Paris, where the artist often traveled with his family from their home in Madrid, they began a discussion about a series of decorative panels for the library of the Hispanic Society. The result was a brilliant group of large-scale paintings, *Visions of Spain* (also known as *Provinces of Spain*), which Sorolla executed between 1912 and 1919. Working at times with photographs, but more often doing small gouaches on site throughout the country, Sorolla produced a unique body of work that sought not to "report" on the customs and costumes of Spain, but rather to create a series of impressions of the immense variety of regional differences. *Valencia*, a panel from 1916 that was ultimately installed in 1926 (and recently restored and exhibited throughout Spain in 2008–09), is a sun-drenched scene of a religious procession on horseback through the orange groves for which the province is so famous.

Ignacio Zuloaga (1870–1945). *Victim of the Fiesta*, 1910. Oil on canvas. 111⅞ x 135½ in. (284.4 x 344.1 cm). Hispanic Society of America, New York.

Sorolla's positive vision of timeless Spanish customs could hardly contrast more dramatically with the work of his younger contemporary Ignacio Zuloaga. The latter's 1910 painting *Victim of the Fiesta*, now in the Hispanic Society's collection, shows a *picador*, one of the members of the *equipo* of a bullfight, mounted on an exhausted and wounded horse walking through a dramatically dark and cloudy Castilian landscape. The *picador* was one of the artist's favorite models, Francisco el Segoviano, and the landscape is similar to those that appear repeatedly in the Basque artist's paintings of a country that itself had been deeply wounded by the 1898 conflict. Many authors have sought to connect Zuloaga's view of Spain with that of the Generation of 1898, a group of writers and philosophers including Antonio Machado, Miguel de Unamuno, Pío Baroja, and José Martínez Ruíz (known as Azorín), whose works ruminated on their country's identity and often demonstrated a marked pessimism regarding its future.[12] The differences between Sorolla's and Zuloaga's views of Spain were very clear to New York audiences who attended both artists' exhibitions at the Hispanic Society in 1909. Although Archer Huntington's plan to present a large show of the two painters together never materialized, Zuloaga's exhibition of thirty-eight paintings opened in April 1909, just a few months after that of his older contemporary. The public was fascinated by his work, and Zuloaga's fame, which had already been considerable in Europe, was consolidated in Manhattan and, later, throughout the United States. Although Zuloaga did not come to New York for this opening, he did attend another opening, in January 1925, of a series of New York shows of his work at the Reinhardt Gallery.

Priscilla E. Muller, Curator Emerita of the museum at the Hispanic Society and an authority on the work of both Sorolla and Zuloaga and their relationships with their American contemporaries, points out that the Manhattan painters who knew his work well and were closest in spirit to Zuloaga were members of the Ashcan School, especially Robert Henri, who had seen the Spaniard's paintings in Paris in the late 1890s. Henri and his colleagues depicted genre scenes of New York streets as well as portraits of fashionable members of New York society in a manner reminiscent of Zuloaga's manipulation of thick brushwork in gray and black, which also connected them to the effects achieved in the portraiture of Velázquez and Goya. As a result of his very successful New York shows, Zuloaga received numerous commissions for portraits, all of which he painted in his studio in Spain. Mrs. Bernard Gimbel, the Valencia-born Metropolitan Opera star Lucrezia Bori, and the Polish pianist and patriot Ignace Jan Paderewski were among the famous figures of the day to be portrayed by Zuloaga. The Paderewski portrait was purchased by the Steinway piano company for a record $25,000 and hung in the main recital area of Steinway Hall when it opened it doors at 109–113 West Fifty-seventh Street on October 27, 1925. The portrait (still in situ for all visitors to see) also was used by Steinway and Sons in a series of successful advertising campaigns.[13]

Zuloaga died in 1945, six years after the end of the Spanish Civil War and the triumph in 1939 of the Spanish Falange Party under the leadership of General Francisco Franco. Although hundreds of artists and writers whose political sympathies were deeply antithetical to the nationalist, conservative values espoused by the victorious forces left Spain for Latin America, the United States, the Soviet Union, and elsewhere, Zuloaga remained in Spain and apparently in the good graces of the new political regime. He kept a relatively low profile in the postwar years, but his 1939–40 portrait of Franco in the official Falange uniform, set against a broad Castilian background, is a gauge of his affinities for the dictator and the new political landscape of the country.[14] Zuloaga's political sympathies represented the opposite side of the coin from those of many of the other Spanish artists who helped create the artistic landscape of Nueva York in the 1930s and '40s. Many were political refugees or had come prior to the beginning of the Spanish Civil War, sensing the precarious position in which they would ultimately find themselves in their home country.

In his essay in this book James Fernández discusses the brief but important stay in New York of the Spanish poet and playwright Federico García Lorca from June 1929 to March 1930. Lorca did not come to New York for political purposes, but ostensibly to learn English at Columbia University. The major declaration of his (mostly negative) feelings for the city is found in his poetry anthology *Poet in New York*. Although Lorca paints a picture of solitude and alienation, Fernández makes clear that the poet traveled within a rich cultural world of Spanish writers, artists, and musicians living in Manhattan. A highly creative visual artist as well as a literary giant, Lorca made some of his most compelling drawings in New York, including a self-portrait in which the squiggly, biomorphic lines recall the manner of fellow Spanish artist Joan Miró as well as that of other Surrealist painters and draftsmen.[15] Six years after his stay in New York, Lorca would be murdered in Granada by Falangist soldiers.

Julio de Diego was among the many artists from Spain (a number of whom were associated, sometimes loosely, with the international Surrealist movement) whose careers developed in New York in the 1930s and '40s.[16] Diego settled in New York in 1924 and became well known not only for his paintings but also for his designs for theater and dance productions (such as *The Wild Cat*, starring his wife, the entertainer Gypsy Rose Lee). He was a staunch opponent of Franco, and his 1938 antiwar painting *Homage to the Spanish Republic* (private collection) shows two extremely elongated, expressive figures (in the manner of El Greco) against a Castilian landscape in ruins as a result of the catastrophic hostilities of 1936–39.

Esteban Francés, a refugee in New York from Franco's Spain, was more directly involved with some of the founders of pictorial Surrealism such as the Chilean painter Roberta Matta and Gordon Onslow Ford. Like Diego, Francés, whose bio-morphic forms are reminiscent of paintings by the French Surrealist André Masson, collaborated on theatrical sets for George Balanchine's New York City Ballet as well as others.

Like many of the Spanish artists who came to New York at the time of the Spanish Civil War, Esteban Vicente had produced a substantial body of work before arriving in 1936, yet he destroyed much of it at some time in the later 1940s.[17] A native of the province of Segovia, he had trained in the 1920s at the Royal Academy of Fine Arts in Madrid, where he became a close colleague of many of the cultural figures whose careers would develop outside Spain. Among these was the writer Juan Ramón Jiménez, a member of the Generation of 1898 who spent the Civil War years in Cuba, eventually settled in Puerto Rico, and was, for a brief time, a resident of

Esteban Vicente (1903–2001). *Untitled: Portrait of a Youth, New York City*, ca. 1936. Esteban and Harriet Vicente Foundation, New York. Photo: Dorothy Zeidman.

Esteban Vicente (1903–2001). *Labels*, 1956. Collage. 48⅞ x 35⅜ in. (124.1 x 89.9 cm). Museo de Arte Contemporáneo Esteban Vicente, Segovia.

Manhattan. Vicente also became a good friend of Lorca and of the filmmaker Luis Buñuel, who spent his post–Civil War life in New York, where he worked in the film department of the Museum of Modern Art, and later in Mexico. Vicente's first New York home and studio were on Minetta Lane in Greenwich Village; he spent the next thirty years in downtown Manhattan, including apartments and studios on Bleecker Street, West Tenth Street, and lower Second Avenue. During his early years in New York Vicente mixed a strong streak of social realism with the appealing, realistic style of painting he had developed in Spain. A ca. 1936 painting, *Untitled: Portrait of a Youth, New York City*, is a fine example of this combination of elements in his work. Yet Vicente's fame was established mainly by his abstract paintings and collages from the mid-1940s until his death in 2001 at age ninety-eight. Vicente was the only Spanish-born member of the first-generation New York School of Abstract Expressionism, regularly showing in group exhibitions at galleries that represented such artists as Willem and Elaine de Kooning, Franz Kline, and Jack Tworkov.[18]

One of Vicente's most noteworthy achievements was his teaching. He trained several generations of artists at New York University, Columbia, Princeton, and, most notably, the New York Studio School on Eighth Street, of which he was a founding

member in 1964. In addition, after the end of the Franco era, Vicente, like other exiled artists and writers, renewed his ties to his native country, returning to Segovia and creating the Museo Esteban Vicente de Arte Contemporáneo. Vicente's multifaceted career and his enormous impact on the cultural life of New York City during his long residency there stands as a paradigm for the many important contributions of Spanish artists to the cultural life of Manhattan and the United States throughout the later nineteenth century and into the present.

Spanish artists from Fortuny to Zuloaga were important to their New York counterparts for the links they provided to the grand Spanish pictorial traditions and the lessons they imparted about color and brushwork. Yet they were still "foreign," if not always exotic. From the 1930s on, however, many Spaniards arrived in Manhattan not to stress their differences, but to become part of the city's fast-developing art world; people like Diego, Francés, and Vicente contributed to the larger flow of artistic production. In writings about Vicente's Abstract Expressionist work, references to Spain as his place of origin are relatively rare. It is much more common to encounter discussions of his work that focus simply on his visual production as part of the larger developments in midcentury contemporary art in what critic Jed Perl has called "New Art City."[19] When Meyer Schapiro and Clement Greenberg chose Vicente to participate in the major *Talent 1950* exhibition at Manhattan's Kootz Gallery, they did so for his promise as a young abstract painter, not for his "Spanishness." In the post–World War II period, Spanish artists, as well as their Latin American contemporaries (and American, European, and Asian-born cohorts), formed tightly integrated components of the bourgeoning world of art in Nueva York.

The academic study of Spanish art history is also a part of this story. Since the early 1930s, New York University has been the leading institution in the United States to promote the study of the arts of the Iberian Peninsula. The graduate Institute of Fine Arts at NYU has been the academic home to some of the most renowned scholars in the field, both Spanish and American. The institute's founder and first director, Walter W.S. Cook, was a distinguished Hispanist who had received a doctoral degree in Spanish art history from Harvard, studying with the renowned Spanish medievalist Chandler R. Post in the 1920s. Cook started the university's graduate program in 1932, opening the institute's first venue in a brownstone at the corner of Madison Avenue and Eighty-third Street. It soon moved to 17 East Eightieth Street, and in the 1950s to the former residence of tobacco heir James B. Duke on the corner of Seventy-eighth Street and Fifth Avenue (a building captured in a beautiful photograph by Berenice Abbott). Cook specialized in Spanish medieval art, with a particular interest in Catalan panel painting (the subject of some of his best-known publications). He taught until his retirement in 1953 and was responsible for making the institute a premier venue for art historical research in Manhattan.

Over the years Cook gathered a stellar cast of academics to serve as the institute's corps of professors.

Among these was José López-Rey, who came to NYU at Cook's behest in 1945. A committed anti-Francoist, he had been persona non grata in Spain for a number of years. López-Rey taught courses on many aspects of Spanish Renaissance, Baroque, and eighteenth- and nineteenth-century art. His interest in Goya was intense, and he published numerous articles and books on his work, but it is for his 1963 catalogue raisonné of the art of Velázquez that López-Rey is best remembered.[20] He taught until the early 1970s, mentoring a number of students who are still active in the field. The noted young scholar Jonathan Brown began to teach at the university in 1973, where he has continued to uphold its strong reputation in the field of Spanish art historical studies.

LATIN AMERICAN ART AND ARTISTS (CA. 1900–45) AND NEW YORK CITY

To approach the subject of artists from Latin America and the (Spanish-speaking) Caribbean in New York and their interaction with U.S. artists, collectors, and arts institutions is a daunting task. Instead of dealing with one country, as in the case of Spain, we must consider the cultural histories of some twenty nations as they were woven into the fabric of the developing New York art world in the early twentieth century. Fortunately, this story has been the subject of many serious monographic studies and museum exhibitions over the past two decades, and a number of Latin American, American, and European scholars have contributed to our understanding of the relationship between Latino artists and the city. El Museo del Barrio's 2009–10 exhibition *Nexus New York: Latin/American Artists in the Modern Metropolis* stands as one of the most distinguished of the enterprises that have investigated this subject for Manhattan audiences. In the show and accompanying catalogue curator Deborah Cullen and a group of notable art historians created a deeply satisfying panorama of Hispanic artists in New York.[21]

Nexus New York was, in fact, the most recent of a number of exhibitions that have examined the impact of the "Nueva York" phenomenon on the visual arts. As early as 1981, Jacqueline Barnitz curated an exhibition of Latin American artists working in the United States before 1950.[22] A 1988 exhibition at the Bronx Museum of the Arts, *The Latin American Spirit: Art and Artists in the United States, 1920–1970*, dealt with the wider theme of the United States as a venue for Latin American creativity.[23] In 2004, another Museo del Barrio exhibition explored the New York–Latin American art relationship in depth, focusing on the collection of the Museum of Modern Art. Since its founding in 1929, the Modern has demonstrated a deep interest in the art of the region, amassing the finest collection of modern Latin American art in this country. In the exhibition, *Latin American and Caribbean Art: MoMA at El Museo*, curators Miriam Basilio, Fatima Bercht, Deborah Cullen, Gary Garrels, and Luis Pérez-Oramas explored the history of the collection and its most outstanding pieces.[24] In addition, many recent monographs and exhibitions have dealt with the careers of specific Latin American artists in New York and the U.S.[25] Thus, the following remarks may serve for scholars as merely a reminder of the more complete work done by others to explain the history and meanings of artists from the Americas in New York; for general readers, these comments summarize a very complex story through a few paradigmatic examples. (Two of the essays in this volume also treat some of the issues related to this chapter of cultural history: Katherine Manthorne discusses the important role of Latin American artists in New York culture in the nineteenth century, while Anna Indych-López focuses on the importance of the New School for Social Research in bringing together key figures from Ecuador, Argentina, Puerto Rico, and Mexico in the 1930s and beyond.)

This history can be framed by considering the careers of a number of key individuals and the institutions that collected and exhibited their works from around 1900 until World War II. Among the earliest well-known figures from Latin America to integrate himself into the worlds of both art and society in Manhattan was the Mexican Marius de Zayas. In the early years of the twentieth century he became influential as an artist of penetrating caricatures of leading American (and interna-

tional) artistic and political figures, publishing in newspapers and popular magazines for several decades. (His work anticipates that of Miguel Covarrubias, another Mexican caricaturist, who worked in Manhattan in the 1920s and 30s.[26]) From 1910 to 1913 the photographer and arts entrepreneur Alfred Stieglitz exhibited the work of de Zayas in his 291 Gallery (at 291 Fifth Avenue) and published it in the magazine of the same name (as well as in his other publication, *Camera Work*), which was produced in luxury editions, meant to stand as works of art in their own right. De Zayas was also a respected art dealer; from 1915 to 1918 he ran his own exhibition space, the Modern Gallery, and from 1918 to 1921, the de Zayas Gallery. It was in the former venue that the Mexican artist and art promoter had the distinction of offering to the New York public their first glimpse of the work of his compatriot Diego Rivera in 1916. The exhibition consisted of a selection of Rivera's Cubist paintings, a style he would abandon by the time he made his first appearance in Manhattan in 1931. (See below for a further discussion of Rivera in New York.)

Few twentieth-century Latin American artists have had such an enormous impact on painting, sculpture, graphic art, and even architecture in South America, Europe, and the United States as Joaquín Torres-García.[27] This peripatetic Uruguayan artist had moved in many artistic circles since coming to maturity in the Art Nouveau environment of turn-of-the-century Barcelona, including those in Madrid, Italy, and

Joaquín Torres-García (1874–1949). *New York Docks*, 1920. Oil and gouache on cardboard. 19¹¹⁄₁₆ x 26 in. (50.2 x 66 cm). Yale University Art Gallery, Gift of Collection Société Anonyme. © 2010 Artists Rights Society (ARS), New York / VEGAP, Madrid.

Diego Rivera (1886–1957). *Agrarian Leader Zapata*, 1931. Fresco. 93¾ x 74 in. (238.1 x 188 cm). The Museum of Modern Art, New York, Abby Aldrich Rockefeller Fund (1631.1940). © 2010 Banco de México Diego Rivera Frida Kahlo Museums Trust, Mexico, D.F. / Artists Rights Society (ARS). Digital Image © The Museum of Modern Art / Licensed by SCALA / Art Resource, NY.

Paris (where he exhibited with the Cercle et Carré group of geometric abstract painters). After 1934 he returned to his native Montevideo, and the last phase of his career there was enormously productive; he also trained generations of students who have continued the spirit of his geometrically based works even to the present. Yet what concerns us most is his New York period, a brief but critical sojourn in Manhattan from 1920 to 1922. Torres had come to New York to find both an appreciative audience and a venue for the production of his wooden toys. These human and animal figures, first produced at the Artist's Toy Makers Company (cofounded by Torres) and after 1924 at the Aladdin Toy Company (located at 20 Wooster Street), were admired for their simplicity and charm not only by children but by members of New York's high society such as Gertrude Vanderbilt Whitney.[28] While in New York, the artist fell under the spell of the speed, verticality, and bourgeoning modernity of the city, and he became friends with artists such as Joseph Stella and Stuart Davis who were kindred spirits in their appreciation of New York's boundless energy. His paintings, drawings (some of which he showed at his Whitney Studio Club show of 1921), and notebook pages attest to his interest in capturing the vigor of New York in a variety of contemporary stylistic modes, including Futurism and Cubism.

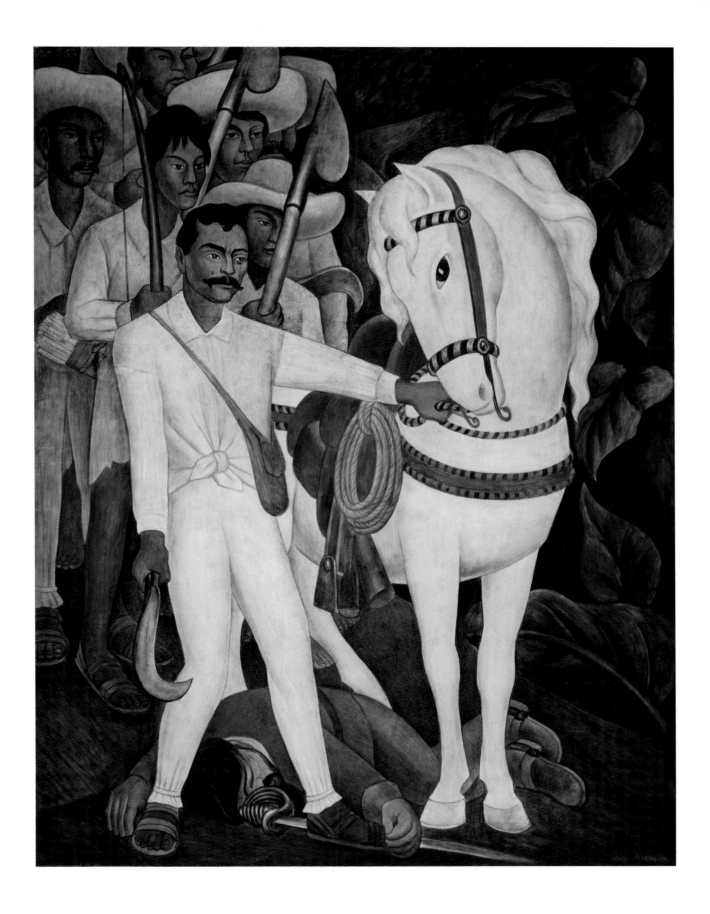

Many of the major Latin American artists in New York in the first half of the twentieth century came to the city having already established substantial careers, not only in their own countries but, in many cases, in Europe as well. New York was not yet the "center" of the art world; Paris is said to have held that distinction until the start of World War II. Nonetheless, many of the best-known artists from Latin America who constituted the first or second generation of modernists—including the Argentinean Emilio Pettoruti, the Brazilian Anita Malfatti, the Chilean Roberto Matta, and the Cubans Amelia Pelaez and Wifredo Lam—had been trained in their home countries as well as in the artistic centers of Italy, Spain, or Germany before their work was seen by New York audiences anxious to absorb as much novelty as possible. But perhaps the most famous Latin American artist to make an immediate success with a large-scale museum show in New York after a successful European career was Diego Rivera.

Rivera's Cubist art was already known in Manhattan thanks to de Zayas, but it was his 1931 solo show at the Museum of Modern Art (then located at 730 Fifth Avenue) that brought him widespread attention in this city. Indeed, the New York public was hungry for more Rivera, as his reputation as a creator of murals on a heroic scale in Mexico City had preceded him with glowing reports in the press. Lithographs made by Rivera in 1932 of his Mexican murals from the 1920s were distributed widely in the United States, assuring him broad fame within a New York and American public.[29] Included in the enormously successful MoMA show (which received more than 57,000 visitors) was a series of portable murals, on a much smaller scale than those he had executed for the enormous public buildings in Mexico City. (The portable murals are now in the collections of MoMA, the Philadelphia Museum of Art, and elsewhere.)

Rivera had been a member of the Mexican Communist Party, and his works often evince a dedication to socially committed themes. Two years after his show at MoMA, these affinities would bring him serious difficulties when he became embroiled in one of the most notorious and well-known New York scandals of the decade. Rivera had been contracted by the Rockefeller family to paint a mural for the main lobby of the new Rockefeller Center's RCA Building. The theme was "man at the crossroads," and a preliminary drawing shows a horizontal scheme of workers in the United States and the Soviet Union (where he had visited in 1927). However, the final mural, completed with the assistance of many other artists, including Ben Shahn, also featured a portrait of Lenin—an element that was unacceptable to the building's developers. The mural was covered and eventually destroyed, to be replaced by a less confrontational series of frescoes by the Spanish artist José María Sert. But Rivera was not daunted by this defeat, and his last work in New York consisted of a series of fresco panels on Socialist themes for the New Workers School, the headquarters of the American Communist Party, at 51 West Fourteenth Street.

Throughout his stay in Manhattan, Rivera was accompanied by Frida Kahlo, often referred to in the press as "Mrs. Diego Rivera." (Kahlo's reputation as a painter and a personality has grown exponentially since that time, and recently she has become even better known than Rivera, judging from the number of books, exhibitions, and a recent film that have focused on her turbulent life.) Rivera and Kahlo lived in Greenwich Village during their Manhattan stay; and while Kahlo did some of her own work (she had only recently begun to make prints and paintings on a more-or-less full-time basis), she also enjoyed popular entertainments, especially the movies. Her interest in film is manifest in one of the few works that directly document her ambivalent reactions to New York City. The 1933 work *My Dress Hangs There* is an indirect self-portrait, in which Kahlo's dress, a traditional garment often worn by women from the southern Mexican Tehuantepec peninsula, hangs between two classical columns (one topped by a large toilet bowl, the other by a bronze trophy). Aerial views of Manhattan appear at the top of the image and a cityscape below, showing Federal Hall, factory buildings, skyscrapers, a church, and a burning New York Stock Exchange. Film star Mae West makes an appearance in a billboard at the left, and large, unruly crowds are suggested by the artist's use of collaged photographs. This quasi-cinematographic montage of glimpses and impressions of Manhattan's chaos and attractions captures the dynamism of the city.[30]

Kahlo did not have a solo show in New York during her lifetime, but three years before she painted *My Dress Hangs There*, another important woman in the history of Mexican modern art did. María Izquierdo had the first solo show of a Mexican woman artist in New York at the Art Center (65 East Fifty-sixth Street). Opening on November 17, 1930, and organized by Mexican arts promoter Frances Flynn Paine, the exhibition featured a selection of portraits and genre scenes by this native of Jalisco and resident of Mexico City, whose work is an amalgam of modernist formal reduction and subject matter drawn from rural and urban proletarian life in Mexico. Izquierdo had also participated in a large-scale exhibition, *Mexican Arts*, which opened at the Metropolitan Museum of Art in October 1930.[31] Featuring pre-Hispanic and modern art as well as a large selection of folk crafts, this was one of many exhibitions of Mexican art in New York and other major American cities throughout the 1930s and '40s. These exhibitions represented not only an effort to show the range of Mexican art but also a gesture toward a neighbor whose friendship was important for political and commercial interests in New York and throughout the United States. The most notable of these exhibitions was organized by the Museum of Modern Art (by then in its permanent home at 11 West Fifty-third Street) in 1940. The show, *20 Centuries of Mexican Art*, featured work from all periods of Mexico's history (some of it for sale, a not uncommon practice in MoMA exhibitions at the time). The catalogue included essays by prominent experts on Mexican art, including a discussion

Miguel Covarrubias (1904–1957). *Twenty Centuries of Mexican Art at the Museum of Modern Art*, 1940. Watercolor. 15⅜ x 22½ in. (39.1 x 57.2 cm). Yale University Art Gallery, Gift of Sra. Rosa R. de Covarrubias.

of modern art by artist Miguel Covarrubias, who also did a famous illustration that portrayed the glittering crowd of attendees from the highest ranks of Manhattan society at the opening reception. Virtually all of the most important Mexican modern artists were in the show, including those who had made a large impact on the New York scene in the 1930s. Among them were Rivera, José Clemente Orozco, and David Alfaro Siqueiros, *los tres grandes* ("the three great ones") of the Mexican mural movement, which had inspired the American mural "renaissance" that produced so many Depression-era WPA murals in the public buildings of New York and across the country.

Orozco was a longtime resident of Manhattan, and many of his works from the late 1920s and early '30s—such as *The Subway* (1928)—depict New York City scenes. For the 1940 MoMA show he executed a mural entitled *Dive Bomber and Tank*, its subject evoking the terror and destruction of World War II, which was then raging in Europe. As he created the mural on site in the museum, visitors were able to see the famous artist at work on his semi-abstract composition. Orozco's other major New York project was his earlier frescoes for The New School (discussed by Anna Indych-López in this volume); he also was responsible for an impressive cycle of paintings for the Baker Library at Dartmouth College in Hanover, New Hampshire. Siqueiros, the youngest of the three *grandes*, spent less time and did fewer works in Manhattan than his fellow muralists. Nonetheless, his activities at the Experimental Workshop at 5 West Fourteenth Street from 1936 to 1938 were crucial for the development of art in New York City in later decades. Founded by the artist, the workshop was dedicated to creating anti-Fascist and anticapitalist imagery (on parade floats and banners, for example) to be used at public events such as rallies and workers' demonstrations. Siqueiros also used the workshop as a platform for his students to experiment with the use of industrial paints and nontraditional techniques. The young Jackson Pollock, who studied at the workshop, was profoundly affected by Siqueiros's use of unorthodox materials and seemingly random methods of applying paint to a variety of surfaces.[32]

In 1937, the Mexican painter Rufino Tamayo painted *New York from My Terrace*, a scene that depicts the artist looking out over the landscape of Manhattan. His wife, Olga, with her back to Tamayo, also surveys the rooftops of the Upper East Side, where they lived. That same year Tamayo, who had begun visiting New York in 1926 (and would live there full time from 1936 to 1949), had his first exhibition at the prestigious Julian Levy Gallery at 602 Madison Avenue at the corner of Fifty-seventh Street, an important venue for contemporary art (especially the European Surrealists). A native of the southern Mexican state of Oaxaca, Tamayo had studied in Mexico City. In 1933, he executed a mural for the National School of Music that was notably lacking in political content, putting the painter in direct opposition to his more socially committed older contemporaries. Throughout his career he espoused the virtues of what he called "universalism," attempting to divorce his art from the

many stereotypes that Mexican painting had accrued, especially to audiences abroad.

By the mid-1930s, Tamayo was deeply immersed in the Manhattan art world. He had exhibitions at the Art Center and the Weyhe Gallery, an important venue that supported many Latin American artists, especially printmakers. Beginning in 1938, Tamayo also served as professor of art at the Dalton School on East Eighty-ninth Street. Some of his pupils, most notably Helen Frankenthaler, went on to distinguished careers of their own. New York also offered Tamayo the opportunity to see the most advanced contemporary art, and he was especially impressed by Picasso's *Guernica*, which he saw at the Valentine Gallery at 45 West Forty-fourth Street, in an exhibition that opened in January 1939 and was organized by the American Artists' Congress to aid victims of the Spanish Civil War. Tamayo's experience of Picasso's antiwar masterpiece had a significant impact on much of his later work, and he absorbed the Spaniard's use of strong diagonal lines and highly expressive figures. Although Tamayo was in Manhattan during World War II (spending most of his summers in Mexico), the terrible events of the period touched him deeply. In their depictions of agonized beasts (influenced in part by Picasso's work), Tamayo's series of figures engulfed in flames and, especially, his images of wild dogs, birds, and other

José Clemente Orozco working on the fresco *Dive Bomber and Tank*, in preparation for the exhibition *Twenty Centuries of Mexican Art* at the Museum of Modern Art, New York, June 1940. The Museum of Modern Art, New York. Digital Image © The Museum of Modern Art / Licensed by SCALA / Art Resource, NY.

creatures convey his reactions to the horrors he read about in New York newspapers and saw in the newsreels at Manhattan movie theaters.

New York audiences (and artists) were able to view a great deal of Mexican painting in the 1930s and '40s. This art had an enormous impact on the development of American painters, both realist and abstract, as pointed out by many historians of the period. But its presence in the city also provided a stimulus for New Yorkers to travel south of the border to see Mexico and absorb some of the "picturesque" scenery and "exotic" types that artists like Rivera depicted in their canvases (although the majority of Mexicans in New York had no interest in displaying the touristic side of their homeland).[33] Milton Avery, one of the great mid-century New York painters whose own work straddles the line between realism, abstraction, and colorism, was an admirer of Tamayo (they both showed at the Valentine Gallery), and it may have been partly his influence that compelled Avery to visit Mexico with his family in the

Rufino Tamayo (1899–1991). *Strawberry Ice Cream*, 1938. Oil on canvas. 44 x 59 in. (111.8 x 149.9 cm). Private collection, New York. © D.R. Rufino Tamayo / Herederos / México / 2010, Fundación Olga y Rufino Tamayo, A.C. Photo: Mary-Anne Martin Fine Art, New York.

summer of 1946, when they spent six weeks in San Miguel de Allende. The visit resulted in a series of exquisite oils and watercolors based on the many sketches Avery did on site.[34]

Mexico was not, of course, the only spot in Latin America visited by tourists and artists alike in the years preceding and during World War II. Cuba was even closer to the United States, and Americans (including legions of New Yorkers) flocked to Havana on the many boats and daily flights that serviced the Cuban capital. While many American visitors were attracted to gambling and other pleasures afforded them in the hotels and nightclubs of Havana, some of the more culturally minded New Yorkers were drawn there by having seen one of a series of Latin American art exhibitions organized during the 1940s by MoMA's director, Alfred Barr, and his colleague Lincoln Kirstein, a Latin American art advisor to the museum who became more famous as the founder of what would become the New York City Ballet.[35] The exhibition *Modern Cuban Painters* opened at MoMA in April 1944, the result of a collaboration between Havana-based dealer María Luisa Gómez Mena (who owned the Galería del Prado), arts promoter José Gómez Sicre, and Barr. The exhibition featured members of the first and second generations of Cuban vanguard painters, some of them showing their work for the first time in New York. Among the most outstanding artists in the exhibition was Amelia Peláez, the creator of jewel-like still lifes and figure studies whose forms were partly derived from the characteristic iron grillwork

Rufino Tamayo (1899–1991). *Animals*, 1941. Oil
on canvas. 30⅛ x 40 in. (76.5 x 101.6 cm). The
Museum of Modern Art, New York, Inter-American
Fund. © D.R. Rufino Tamayo / Herederos /
México / 2010, Fundación Olga y Rufino Tamayo,
A.C. Digital Image © The Museum of Modern Art /
Licensed by SCALA / Art Resource, NY.

and stained glass windows of Havana's nineteenth- and early twentieth-century domestic architecture. Peláez had studied in Paris with the Russian avant-garde painter and stage designer Alexandra Exter, and had also spent several months in 1924 at the Art Students League in New York. Several key works by Peláez remained at the Modern, purchased from the selection in *Modern Cuban Painters*.

Modern Cuban Painters was only one in a series of important Latin American exhibitions organized during the 1940s by MoMA. Others included *Portinari of Brazil* in 1940 and, three years later, the exhibition *Brazil Builds*, which documented both traditional and modern architecture through the photographs of G. E. Kidder Smith. This exhibition generated a catalogue that has been used for decades by architects and architecture students in Brazil as a textbook for the country's built environment.[36] The most complete showing of the museum's Latin American holdings also came in 1943 with *The Latin American Collection of the Museum of Modern Art*, curated by Lincoln Kirstein. This exhibition displayed some 267 works, many of which had been purchased by MoMA through the Inter-American Fund, established in 1942 and anonymously endowed by Nelson Rockefeller, who had served as president of the museum's board of trustees from 1939 to 1941.[37] The range of work in the exhibition was startling, from the indigenist paintings of Peruvian José Sabogal to the Surrealist canvases of Chilean Roberto Matta, one of many émigré Surrealists in Manhattan (where he lived from 1939 to 1947).[38] Mexico and Argentina were the two nations best represented in the MoMA show. One of the members of the Argentine contingent, Emilio Pettoruti, was well known to museumgoing New Yorkers, many of whom had seen his solo show the same year at the National Academy of Design (with a catalogue written by Metropolitan Museum director Francis Henry Taylor). Pettoruti, a native of La Plata and director of its regional museum, had spent considerable time in Italy as a young artist and absorbed the lessons of both Futurism and Cubism.[39] The 1934 *Verdigris Goblet* (purchased in April 1943 for MoMA by Barr) is part of a series the artist painted in the 1930s, in which cups are suspended in unspecified space and seen from a variety of angles.

During the later 1930s and into the war years of the '40s Latin American art held a place of honor in the museum as well as in other exhibition venues in Manhattan. These included the Riverside Museum, which was in operation from 1939 to 1971 at Riverside Drive and 103rd Street and organized many significant exhibitions of artists from the Americas, especially in 1939–40, when the shows were meant to complement the national pavilions of Latin American countries at the New York World's Fair.[40] The Good Neighbor policy had a marked effect on the way New York (and U.S.) audiences perceived work from south of the border. The country had a vested interest in promoting the display and acquisition of art from the Americas, and many exhibitions of the time received some amount of government sponsorship.

Amelia Peláez del Casal (1896–1968). *Still Life in Red*, 1938. Oil on canvas. 27¼ x 33½ in. (69.3 x 85.1 cm). The Museum of Modern Art, New York, Inter-American Fund. © Copyright. Digital Image © The Museum of Modern Art / Licensed by SCALA / Art Resource, NY.

Although many Latin American artists (especially those in New York) were as interested as their colleagues from elsewhere in following stylistic trends of the time, their art was still seen by many for its "picturesque" or "exotic" potential for mass audiences. After World War II, much of the art from 1900 to 1945 was put away in museum storerooms and not exhibited or studied again until the late 1980s, when a Latin American art "boom" initiated by New York auction houses was reflected in an increased number of exhibitions and scholarly writings. Nonetheless, during the postwar period, scores of Latin American and Caribbean artists flocked to New York in ever-increasing numbers. (Some highly distinguished Puerto Rican artists, such as Rafael Tufiño, were actually born in New York.) They came to identify themselves not as "Latin Americans" but rather, like their Spanish counterparts, as simply part of the powerful flow of the New York art world. They have played, and continue to play, enormously vibrant roles in the creation of Latino Manhattan.

NOTES

1. Katherine Manthorne, *Tropical Renaissance: North American Artists Exploring Latin America, 1839–1879* (Washington, DC: Smithsonian Institution Press, 1989).

2. M. Elizabeth Boone, *Vistas de España: American Views of Art and Life in Spain, 1860–1914* (New Haven, CT: Yale University Press, 2007). See also the exhibition catalogue by Suzanne L. Stratton, *Spain, Espagne, Spanien: Foreign Artists Discover Spain, 1800–1900* (New York: Spanish Institute, 1993). On larger issues related to Hispanism in the United States, see Richard L. Kagan, ed., *Spain in America: The Origins of Hispanism in the United States* (Urbana: University of Illinois Press, 2002).

3. "The Stewart Picture Sale: First Night's Auction of the Famous Collection Brings Over $133,000—The Prices Realized," *New York Times*, February 4, 1898, http://query.nytimes.com/gst/abstract.html (accessed November 19, 2009).

4. See Mercè Doñate, Cristina Mendoza, and Francesc M. Quílez i Corella, *Fortuny (1838–1874)* (Barcelona: Museu Nacional d'Art de Catalunya, 2003).

5. Ronald Pisano, *William Merritt Chase 1849–1916: Leading Spirit in American Art* (Seattle: Henry Art Gallery, University of Washington, 1983), 6. See also Edward J. Sullivan, "Fortuny in America: His Collectors and Disciples," in *Fortuny: 1838–1874* (Barcelona: Fundació Caixa de Pensions, 1989), 99–117.

6. Moore traveled in Spain in 1869–70 with fellow American artist Thomas Eakins. See Boone, *Vistas de España*, chapter 3, 61–87.

7. For a contemporary appreciation of Madrazo's fame in the late nineteenth century, see David Hannay, "Madrazo: The Spanish Painter," *The Magazine of Art* (London, Paris, and New York), 7 (1884): 10–14.

8. *History of The Hispanic Society of America, Museum and Library* (New York: Hispanic Society of America, 1954).

9. See Edmund Peel, ed., *The Painter Joaquín Sorolla* (San Diego: San Diego Museum of Art, 1989); Blanca Pons Sorolla, *Joaquín Sorolla* (London: Philip Wilson Publishers, 2005); and the most recent catalogue of his work, José Luis Díez and Javier Baron, *Joaquín Sorolla 1863–1923* (Madrid: Museo Nacional del Prado, 2009). The latter is available in a Spanish and an English edition. The most complete account of the relationship between Sorolla and the Hispanic Society is Priscilla E. Muller and Marcus B. Burke, *Sorolla: The Hispanic Society* (New York: Hispanic Society of America, 2004).

10. Díez and Baron, *Joaquín Sorolla*, 419.

11. I am grateful to Priscilla E. Muller for confirming the information about Sorolla's lodging during his 1909 and 1911 stays in New York in her email correspondence to the author of December 9, 2009.

12. Some of the more recent literature on Zuloaga includes *Ignacio Zuloaga in America 1909–1925* (with an essay by Suzanne L. Stratton) (New York: Spanish Institute, 1989); *Sorolla. Zuloaga. Dos visions para un cambio de siglo* (Madrid: Fundación Cultural Mapfre Vida, 1998); and Dena Crosson, "Ignacio Zuloaga and the Problem of Spain" (PhD diss., University of Maryland, 2009).

13. Theodore E. Steinway, *People and Pianos: A Pictorial History of Steinway and Sons* (New York: Steinway and Sons, 1953, reprinted 2005).

14. See Miriam Basilio, "Genealogies for a New State: Painting and Propaganda in Franco's Spain, 1936–1940," *Discourse* 24, no. 3 (fall 2002): 86. See also Basilio, *Visual Propaganda, Exhibitions and the Spanish Civil War* (forthcoming).

15. On Lorca's drawings, see Christopher Maurer, *Line of Light and Shadow: The Drawings of Federico García Lorca* (Durham, NC: Duke University Press, 1991).

16. On Diego and other Spaniards from the period, see the catalogue for the exhibition *El nexo español: Spanish Artists in New York, 1930–1960* (New York: Instituto Cervantes, 2009).

17. On Vicente, see Elizabeth Frank, *Esteban Vicente* (New York: Hudson Hills Press, 1995).

18. See the forthcoming exhibition at the Grey Art Gallery, New York University (2011), *Concrete Improvisations: Collages and Sculpture by Esteban Vicente*.

19. Jed Perl, *New Art City* (New York: Alfred A. Knopf, 2005). Perl discusses Vicente on pp. 53, 459, and 476, never mentioning his place of birth.

20. José López-Rey, *Velázquez: A Catalogue Raisonné of His Œuvre* (London: Faber and Faber, 1963).

21. Deborah Cullen, ed., *Nexus New York: Latin/American Artists in the Modern Metropolis* (New York: El Museo del Barrio and New Haven, CT: Yale University Press, 2009). This catalogue contains a wealth of material, from essays by leading scholars to a useful timeline of artistic and political events as well as biographies of dozens of significant Latin American artists and the North American colleagues with whom they interacted in New York.

22. Jacqueline Barnitz, *Latin American Artists in New York Before 1950* (New York: Godwin-Ternbach Museum, Queens College, 1981).

23. Luis R. Cancel et al., eds., *The Latin American Spirit: Art and Artists in the United States, 1920–1970* (New York: Bronx Museum of the Arts and Harry N. Abrams, 1988).

24. Miriam Basilio et al., eds., *Latin American and Caribbean Art: MoMA at El Museo* (New York: El Museo del Barrio and the Museum of Modern Art, 2004).

25. See, for example, Renato González Mello and Diane Miliotes, eds., *José Clemente Orozco in the United States, 1927–1934* (Hanover, NH: Hood Museum of Art, 2002); Michele Greet, *Beyond National Identity: Pictorial Indigenism as a Modernist Strategy in Andean Art, 1920–1960* (University Park: Penn State University Press, 2009); and Anna Indych-López, *Muralism without Walls: Rivera, Orozco, and Siqueiros in the United States, 1927–1940* (Pittsburgh: University of Pittsburgh Press, 2009).

26. On de Zayas, see Douglas Hyland, *Marius de Zayas: Conjurer of Souls* (Lawrence: Spencer Art Museum, University of Kansas, 1981), as well as the recent edition of de Zayas's own text, *How, When and Why Modern Art Came to New York*, ed. Francis Naumann (Cambridge, MA: MIT Press, 1998)

27. On Torres-García, his followers, and his international impact, see Mari Carmen Ramírez, ed., *El Taller Torres-García: The School of the South and its Legacy* (Austin: University of Texas Press, 1992), and Mario Gradowczyk, *Torres García: Utopia y transgresión* (Montevideo: Museo Torres García, 2007).

28. The most recent study of Torres-García's toys and sculptures in wood is Mari Carmen Ramírez, ed., *Joaquín Torres-García: Constructing Abstraction with Wood* (Houston: Menil Collection and New Haven, CT: Yale University Press, 2009).

29. See Indych-López, *Muralism*.

30. Within the enormous body of literature dedicated to Kahlo, the most complete discussion in English of the paintings is Hayden Herrera, *Frida Kahlo: The Paintings* (New York: HarperCollins, 1991).

31. On Izquierdo, see *María Izquierdo 1902-1955* (Chicago: Mexican Fine Arts Center Museum, 1996); Elizabeth Ferrer, *The True Poetry: The Art of María Izquierdo* (New York: Americas Society, 1997); and James Oles et al., *Un arte nuevo: el aporte de María Izquierdo* (A New Art: The Contribution of María Izquierdo) (Mexico City: Colección Blaisten, Universidad Nacional Autónoma de México, 2008).

32. On the activities of the workshop within the larger panorama of Siqueiros's activities in the 1930s, see the exhibition catalogue *Siqueiros: Portrait of a Decade* (Santa Barbara, CA: Santa Barbara Museum of Art, 1997).

33. This phenomenon is discussed extensively by James Oles in his book *South of the Border: Mexico in the American Imagination, 1917-1947* (Washington, DC: Smithsonian Institution Press, 1993).

34. See Edward J. Sullivan, "Milton Avery in Mexico," in *Avery in Mexico* (Scottsdale, AZ: Riva Yares Gallery, 2009).

35. On Kirstein's interest in Latin American art, see Martin Duberman, *The Worlds of Lincoln Kirstein* (New York: Alfred A. Knopf, 2007).

36. Philip L. Goodwin, *Brazil Builds: Architecture New and Old 1652-1942* (New York: Museum of Modern Art, 1943).

37. See the essay by Miriam Basilio, "Reflecting on a History of Collecting and Exhibiting Work by Artists from Latin America," in *Latin American and Caribbean Art: MoMA at El Museo*, 52-68.

38. On émigré Surrealists (including Latin Americans) and their impact on art in New York in the 1940s, see Martica Sawin, *Surrealism in Exile and the Beginning of the New York School* (Cambridge, MA: MIT Press, 1995).

39. On Pettoruti, see Edward J. Sullivan and Nelly Perazzo, *Emilio Pettoruti (1892-1971)* (Buenos Aires: Fundación Pettoruti, 2004).

40. I am grateful to Susanna Temkin, a graduate student at NYU's Institute of Fine Arts, for detailed information on the Riverside Museum in her unpublished paper "A Pan-American Art Exhibit for the *World of Tomorrow*: The 1939 and 1940 Latin American Art Exhibitions at the Riverside Museum."

THE DISCOVERY OF SPAIN IN NEW YORK, CIRCA 1930

JAMES D. FERNÁNDEZ

"GREAT NATIONS IN THE LITTLE"

"There is a Spanish-speaking colony of size in New York. It is like Spain itself, with rivalries of old provinces still lingering. It is like all the Spanish-speaking world in the two hemispheres, great nations lying here in the little, keeping separate at home, yet mingling in common interests. Here are not Chelsea, nor old Peter Stuyvesant's farm, but Estremadura and Leon: half across the town, Argentina lies next to Castile and Uruguay is near by, with Cuba in the offing." A vivid portrait of a vibrant and diverse community of some thirty thousand "Spanish" in New York City, "half of them from Spain," emerges from this March, 23, 1924, *New York Times* article.[1]

In that same year, Konrad Bercovici devoted to the Spanish section of Gotham an entire chapter of *Around the World in New York*, a book built on the conceit that one could trot around the globe simply by taking a stroll in the city. "I walked through the Rumanian section, a corner of the Austro-Polish section, the Austrian, touched on the German section, edged the French one, and then arrived into Spain. Which only means that I went from Fourth Street to Eighth Street on foot, then walked along Second Avenue to Twenty-third Street, and followed Twenty-third Street to Seventh Avenue, the edge of the Spanish district. It extends from there southward to Abingdon Square and encompasses all that lies between Seventh and Eighth Avenues."[2]

Both of these texts use the term "Spanish" as a synonym for "Spanish-speaking," although they go on to recognize the international diversity of New York's "Spanish" residents—Spaniards, Cubans, Puerto Ricans, Mexicans, Chileans, and others. The texts illustrate how, in New York in the 1920s, significant numbers of people from diverse regions of Spain lived alongside Spanish speakers from other parts of the world, and how those different subnational and national groups would occasionally emphasize their differences, and at times would make common cause. Bercovici refers mainly to the Spanish enclave in the West Village/Chelsea section of Manhattan, while the *Times* article mentions other sites scattered around the city: for example, near

Galician immigrants, Lower East Side, ca. 1920.
Photographer unknown. Courtesy of Dolores
Sánchez and Manuel Alonso.

The Spanish Influence Upon Winter Fashions
Anticipated by The Wanamaker Store

For many weeks we had heard rumors in Paris that some of the couturiers had turned to Spain for new inspirations. It seemed logical, as frequently Parisian fashion artists have been guided by current events.

Last Spring when His Royal Highness, the Prince of Wales—made a long sojourn in the French Basque country there was a renewed interest in that exquisite and colorful land—and when thinking of it one does not stop at the frontier for immediately there looms in the imagination the lovely Basque country of Spain.

Then this Summer that exquisite and fascinating Spanish artist, *Raquel Meller*, has had a great success in Paris. When seeing and hearing her one cannot refrain from thinking of colorful Spain.

So We Went to Spain

Our own Fashion representatives went to Spain—to the source of this new inspiration—to get original documents of art that could be reproduced so that Wanamaker Spanish-inspired fashions might be authentic, and EXCLUSIVE—and more beautiful.

The important galleries, museums and palaces of Spain were visited. Then we searched for embroideries, unusual colorings and even costumes of the glorious past. We hurried with them to Paris, where we found beautiful materials with which to interpret the fashions for which Spain had furnished the inspiration.

And then these treasure trunks of old romance were hurried to New York—and immediately upon their arrival several of our best tailors and dressmakers collaborated with us so that we might first present the

Spanish-inspired Fashions for the Winter Season

The collection includes dresses, wraps and suits for women; also frocks for Miss 14 to 20—also negligees.

P. S.—Recent cables from our Paris House confirmed the early rumors—some of the leading couturiers have sounded the Spanish note in their Winter fashions.

Gray Fashion Salons, Second Floor, Old Building

Advertisement for Wanamaker Department Store, *New York Times*, September 9, 1924.

the East River piers at the foot of the Brooklyn Bridge (around Roosevelt, Cherry, and Catherine streets), and "here and there in unexpected corners of Manhattan and Brooklyn . . . where the pimento is a staple or where women's hands deftly pat-pat-pat as they flip tortillas into their pancake shape."[3]

Both texts make reference to, and in some ways enact, what Richard Kagan has called the "Spanish craze": a remarkable appetite for all things Spanish in New York and, indeed, throughout the United States in the first two decades of the twentieth century. The craze ranged from the country's novelists, like Vicente Blasco Ibáñez, to its painters, like Joaquín Sorolla or Ignacio Zuloaga, who had been featured in New York's first blockbuster museum shows at Archer M. Huntington's newly inaugurated Hispanic Society of America (1909); from its playwrights, like Jacinto Benavente, to its femmes fatales, like Raquel Meller, the sultry *diseuse* who took the city by storm in 1926. Bercovici explicitly relates this Spanish craze to the mindset of the city's Spanish residents: "a few years ago, when all America seemed to be at the feet of Señor Blasco Ibáñez, there was a great revival of interest in everything Spanish in this city. . . . It made the Spaniards of New York raise their heads with pride. It redeemed them from the position to which they had sunk after the Spanish-American War."[4]

Taken together, these two contemporaneous texts investigate a number of issues of great interest to anyone attempting to reconstruct the contours and textures of the history of Spaniards in New York. Both texts illustrate how, in the decades immediately following a war between Spain and the United States, Spain and things Spanish had somewhat surprisingly become all the rage among non-Hispanic New Yorkers. And the texts powerfully convey a simple but often overlooked fact: by the early 1920s, there was a sizable colony of Spaniards in New York. "Here are its own churches and organized life and its functions, and it makes its way and grows into an important part of the American commercial scheme," the *New York Times* declared.[5]

The period between 1898 and 1936 constitutes the apex of Spanish New York, in great measure because of the unique confluence of three related currents: the presence in the city of a commercial, professional, and academic elite from Spain, well positioned to contribute to, and benefit from, both the burgeoning presence of Hispanics in the city and the ever-stronger links between the United States and Spanish-speaking America; the presence in the city—for the first and only time in its history—of a critical mass of working-class immigrants from Spain, many of whom had reimmigrated from Latin America to New York and would live and work in New York alongside other Latinos; and the keen appetite among certain sectors of the city's non-Hispanic population for things Spanish or Hispanic.

THE BEGINNING OF THE END

"Spaniards in the Americas." For many people, the phrase might conjure up images of the deeds or misdeeds, the exploitations or exploits, of the conquistadores, explorers, and missionaries who, in the sixteenth and seventeenth centuries, carried out the conquest and colonization of the New World on behalf of the Spanish crown. The phrase "Spaniards in the U.S.," moreover, is likely to evoke the portion of that same imperial story that took place on territory that would eventually become part of the United States, in the West, Southwest, and Southeast of the country: the explorations, for example, of Ponce de León, Hernando de Soto, Alvar Núñez Cabeza de Vaca, or Pedro Menéndez Avilés. The first presence of Spaniards in the Americas—and in what today is the United States—is, of course, bound up with the establishment and early enterprises of the Spanish empire. And the notions and stereotypes that make up the U.S. imagination about Spaniards can, for the most part, be traced to the early imperial period. A *New York Times* reporter, commenting on the dance culture of the city's Spaniards in the 1920s, could not help but quip: "Cortez learns to fox-trot."[6]

But in many ways, it was actually the dissolution of the Spanish empire that most strongly influenced the scale of the presence of Spaniards in the Americas, South, Central, and North. Mass immigration of Spaniards to the Americas was largely a postimperial phenomenon, and did not really take off until the last decades of the nineteenth century and the beginning of the twentieth—the decades that straddle Spain's definitive loss of empire in 1898.

Accordingly, for most of the nineteenth century, the Spanish presence in the U.S. was primarily limited to small groups of representatives of trading firms or shipping concerns, import-export merchants, or the occasional independent entrepreneur, almost always related to the circuits and commodities of the Latin American trade. The violence and political unrest generated by the Latin American wars of independence in the first decades of the nineteenth century would force some Spaniards to relocate from Latin America to different spots in the United States. It has been estimated, for example, that three quarters of Mexico's Spaniards left that country between 1827 and 1834. Most of them went to New Orleans.

But it was the final unraveling of Spain's stronghold over Cuba and Puerto Rico (1868–98), its last colonies in the Americas, that would generate the most significant surge in the influx of Spaniards (and, of course, Cubans and Puerto Ricans), who relocated from the Antilles to the U.S. Political strife and labor unrest in Cuba, for example, were among the things that led the Spaniard Vicente Martínez Ybor to move his cigar business from Cuba to Key West in 1869 and to establish in 1885, in partnership with another Spaniard, Ignacio Haya, a vast cigar-making center in Tampa, Florida. New York's first Spanish mutual aid society, La Sociedad Benéfica Española, would be established in 1868 by the city's small and well-to-do Spanish colony, initially to aid the many Spaniards who were arriving to the city in flight from the violence of what would eventually become known as the Ten Years War in Cuba (1868–78).

Martínez Ybor was supportive of the Cuban independence movement, but during these final three decades of empire, most of the leaders of the New York Spanish colony would defend Spanish sovereignty in Cuba and Puerto Rico, just as they would attempt to promote a positive image of Spain and of Spain's history—and future—in the Americas. Such efforts can be seen clearly in the Iberian-language press of New York at the time, such as *El Cronista*, founded in 1866 and directed by the unabashed apologist for slavery Ferrer de Couto; *La Llumanera de Nova York* (1874–81), a Catalán-language monthly edited by Arturo Cuyás, a fierce defender of Spanish rule in Cuba; and *Las Novedades* (founded in 1876), whose editor, Enrique Muñiz, a former collaborator of Ferrer de Couto, promoted a more liberal defense of Spain's rights over Cuba. Even an enlightened, republican Spanish New York paper like *El Progreso*, founded in 1884 by Ramón Verea, defended the legitimacy of Spanish rule in Cuba, though, for pragmatic reasons, the paper advocated the sale of the island to the United States. It is interesting to note that all four of these pillars of New York's late nineteenth-century Spanish colony—Ferrer de Couto, Arturo Cuyás, Enrique Muñiz, and Ramón Verea—had come to New York after stints in Cuba, as did the businessman and inventor José Francisco Navarro and the sugar baron Manuel Rionda, arguably the wealthiest members of the colony at the time.

The major cultural initiatives of New York's Spanish colony during this period—such as the attempts to celebrate the figure of Cervantes as the epitome of a unified Spanish/Hispanic civilization, or to secure for Spain a major role in the celebrations of the fourth centennial of Columbus's first voyage (1892)—can be seen in this same light. Ana Varela Lago has demonstrated how virtually all the attempts of New York's Spaniards at identity formation and image promotion were both spurred and stymied by the Cuban lobby, who, with support from the Hearst press, tapped into the long-standing imagery of the Black Legend of Spain as part of their campaign to gain popular support in the U.S. for their independence movement. More than any other issue, the "Cuban question" would strongly condition the projects and lives of most Spaniards living in the United States during the final third of the nineteenth century.[7]

Few Americans—and few Spaniards, for that matter—are aware of a jarring fact: during the half-century from 1880 to 1930, more Spaniards emigrated to the Americas than in the almost four hundred years between Columbus's first voyage in 1492 and 1880. Thus, one could add up all the Spaniards who had crossed the Atlantic during almost the entire period of the empire (1492–1880), and that total would not approach the number of Spaniards who left Iberian shores for the Americas in the last two decades of the nineteenth century and the first three of the twentieth.

For a complex set of reasons worthy of careful analysis, Spain's participation in the vast demographic revolution that reshaped both Europe and the Americas in this period has gone largely unacknowledged and unexplored. From a conventional nationalist standpoint, this is a largely "unheroic" immigration, not easily assimilated into the predominant national mythologies of Spain or the Latin American republics. Even though most of the immigrants in this massive wave were bound for the Spanish-speaking Americas, a significant number of them would end up in the United States, often after stints in Argentina, Cuba, Mexico, or Puerto Rico. But in the context of the immigration history of the U.S., these Spaniards would constitute a drop in the proverbial bucket. They have become, in many ways, invisible immigrants.

Be that as it may, the presence of hundreds of thousands of mobile and enterprising Spanish immigrants in Latin America, and the strengthening of the commercial, cultural, and transportation links between that part of the world and New York, together contributed significantly to the considerable reimmigration of Spaniards to the U.S. via Latin America—particularly Cuba and Puerto Rico—that took place in the late nineteenth and early twentieth centuries. New York's strong links to three key components of the Antillean economies—shipping, sugar, and tobacco—must certainly have been a factor in shaping this process of reimmigration.

Direct immigration from Spain to the United States also became part of the picture around the turn of the century. During the first two decades of the twentieth century, several waves of recruitment-driven mass immigration developed directly from Spain to the U.S. Thousands of Basques passed through New York en route to the western states where there was a need for shepherds; thousands of *asturianos* came through Gotham on their way to prearranged jobs at coal mines or zinc plants in West Virginia or Pennsylvania; and thousands of *santanderinos* stopped over in the city on their way to work the granite quarries and stone sheds of northern Vermont. This direct immigration probably reached its high point during World War I, when Spaniards could find employment in any number of heavy industries whose workforce had been decimated by the draft at the very time that increased industrial output was most needed. Places like Akron, Ohio; Lackawanna (Buffalo), New York; and Bridgeport, Connecticut, were not uncommon destinations for Spanish workers passing through immigration control at Ellis Island between 1915 and 1922.

A good number of these thousands of potential transients, like Valentín Aguirre, probably ended up staying in New York. Aguirre arrived in New York in 1895 like so many Basques, planning to look for work in the West. But he liked what he saw in the city and ended up staying, eventually marrying another Basque immigrant and establishing a boardinghouse, restaurant, and employment and travel agency, as well as a niche for himself and his family as the New York greeter and placer of Basque immigrants in the U.S. Undoubtedly thousands of other Spaniards came to the city with

Consuelo Suárez and Carmen Alonso, Wallkill, New York, ca. 1935. Photographer unknown. Courtesy of Dolores Sánchez and Manuel Alonso.

Suárez emigrated directly to New York from Cuadroveña, in eastern Asturias, in 1920. One of her first jobs was as a live-in maid/nanny. Alonso (the author's grandmother) emigrated to New York from Sardéu, in eastern Astruias, the same year, and also worked as a maid/nanny for a Mexican family in Brooklyn. The women met their Asturian-born husbands in New York; both men were cigar makers who came to New York via Havana and Tampa.

Las Musas cigar store, Flatbush Avenue, Brooklyn, ca. 1915. Photographer unknown. Courtesy of Dolores Sánchez and Manuel Alonso.

The store was owned by the Suárez family, who had come to New York from Asturias, via Cuba.

the intention of staying, attracted, in many cases, by informal regional networks and employment opportunities in the tobacco and sugar businesses, construction, the needle trades, shipping and dock work, or, particularly in the case of women, in private homes as domestics. By the 1930s, certain diffuse patterns were discernible in the New York employment choices of Spaniards from different regions of the peninsula: *asturianos* and *gallegos* were strongly represented in the cigar and sugar trade; *gallegos* and Basques in shipping, heavy construction, and the operation of high-pressure machinery (boilers, steam turbines, and so on); and *valencianos* in the silk business. There is also some evidence that the more well-to-do Spanish-speaking families in New York—both Spanish and Latin American—preferred Spanish-born domestic help.

Thus, throughout the first half of the nineteenth century, the beginning of the end of the Spanish empire in the Americas, coupled with the concomitant thickening and strengthening of the ties between the U.S. and the Spanish-speaking Americas, would account for the presence in New York of a small colony of Spaniards. The final phase of the end of the empire—the end of the end—and its immediate aftermath coincided with and fomented an unprecedented episode of mass migration of Spaniards to the Americas. The U.S. in general, and New York in particular, received a modest but significant number of the protagonists of this process, either as reimmigrants from points in the Spanish-speaking Americas, or direct immigrants, often recruited for specific forms of labor. The *New York Times* article from 1924 took note of the existence of two of the many immigrant associations being established in the city in the early decades of the century as a result of this process: the Sociedad Vasco Americana and Sada y sus Contornos, a group from a town just outside La Coruña.

The end of empire had a number of additional effects that would strongly influence the history of Spanish Nueva York. The end of Spanish rule in what would be called the "American hemisphere" eliminated the idea that Spain was somehow a threat to hemispheric security. It could be argued that the removal of this "threat factor" helped clear the way for a renewed "Spanish craze" in the U.S. It is almost as if once Spain had been expelled as a political player from the hemisphere, and once the U.S. had begun to imagine itself as the seat of a new kind of benign and enlightened empire, certain Spanish cultural forms—which before may have seemed backward or decadent—could be reinscribed or reappropriated as exotic or picturesque or even stately. The stage was set for Bercovici and the *New York Times* reporter to discover the charm and dignity of Spain on the streets of New York.

WHAT FEDERICO GARCÍA LORCA SAW IN NUEVA YORK

From June 1929 to March 1930, the great Spanish poet and playwright Federico García Lorca visited New York. The main tangible legacy of that trip is a book of poems, *Poeta en Nueva York*, whose very title seems to name an almost ontological out-of-placeness. For in the capitalist and utilitarian wasteland that was García Lorca's Nueva York, there was seemingly no room for poets and poetry—or, for that matter, Spaniards.

García Lorca's Nueva York presents a strange, desolate, almost postapocalyptic landscape, and the singular, lonely, and out-of-place *poeta* of the title comes across like an Old Testament denouncer of the violence and emptiness of the fallen city. In a troubled and troubling representation, García Lorca seems to find the city's only sign of authentic life in its African American community. This was a community with which he, as a poet, identified, and which he aligned with a primitivist, junglelike nature of monkeys and serpents, zebras and crocodiles: a telluric community that somehow seemed to predate and to have survived the apocalypse of numbers and right angles that was modern New York.

To be fair, *Poeta en Nueva York* is a brilliant work of experimental poetry, not a sociological treatise; it would make little sense on ethnographic grounds to find fault with García Lorca's choice of subject matter or his sources of inspiration. Scholars and biographers have attributed Lorca's peculiar and dismal view of New York in these poems to a combination of factors that are personal (he came to New York in flight from a series of profound personal crises); historical (he witnessed the stock market crash and the deprivations of the Great Depression); and poetic (in the wake of the extraordinary success of his neo-traditional *Romancero gitano*, he was searching for a nonromantic and stridently vanguardist poetic voice). Notably, however, what is arguably the best-known book written about New York by a Spaniard is probably the work that most completely effaces the city's Hispanic presence; ironically, it was a book written precisely at a time when others (like Bercovici and the unnamed chronicler of the *New York Times*) were struck by the booming presence of Spaniards and Spanish speakers in the city. The naive reader of *Poeta en Nueva York* might be forgiven for thinking that García Lorca had been the first and only Spaniard ever to set foot in the city, and that the poet's time in New York was spent in painful and alienated isolation.

Nonetheless, García Lorca's letters from New York, and the painstaking research of his main biographer, Ian Gibson, allow us to piece together quite another story.[8] When Federico disembarked from the SS *Olympic* on June 25, 1929, a group of distinguished Spaniards was there on the docks to greet him. If we were to trace on an atlas the trajectories that brought these men to that pier, we would see a recognizable, if dense, web of imperial and postimperial sojourns, with an already thoroughly Spanish/Hispanic Nueva York as the principal knot.

Among the people on the docks awaiting García Lorca was León Felipe. Born in the province of Zamora, Spain, in 1884, this pharmacist, actor, fugitive, poet, and adventurer had traveled to Mexico in the summer of 1923 with the intention of making his way to New York. While in Mexico, he met Berta Gamboa, who had a job as a Spanish teacher in New York and was, at the time, vacationing in her native Mexico. León Felipe accompanied Gamboa back to New York in the fall of 1923, and soon after, the couple married in Brooklyn. Felipe taught at New York's Berlitz School until he met Professor Federico de Onís of Columbia University, who convinced him to enroll in graduate school. After completing his studies at Columbia, he went on to teach at Cornell and to translate Walt Whitman and Waldo Frank.

Also on the White Star Line piers to greet García Lorca was Angel del Río. Born in Soria in 1900, del Río became a professor of Spanish at Columbia in 1926, after a stint at the University of Puerto Rico, where he had met and married the young Puerto Rican writer, critic, and Vassar alumna Amelia Agostini. Del Río, a distinguished scholar, later became a respected interpreter of the Hispanic world for an "Anglo" audience, and vice versa. Also part of the welcoming committee was an old friend of García Lorca's: the printer, graphic designer, and painter Gabriel García Maroto, who was born in Ciudad Real in 1889 and had moved to Mexico in 1927 with his Mexican wife, Amelia Narezo. Before coming to New York in 1929, García Maroto was an early critic of Diego Rivera and Mexican muralism. In a letter to his family, García Lorca would describe the effusive surprise encounter of these two old friends: "You'll never guess who was there! Maroto, who wildly hugged and even kissed me! He's just arrived from México and is making good money as a painter and graphic designer."[9]

José Camprubí, the owner of *La Prensa*, New York's most important Spanish-language daily, also was there on the docks. Camprubí was born in Ponce, Puerto Rico, in 1879, the son of a Spanish engineer who at the time was working for the Spanish colonial government, supervising the construction of the Ponce-Coamo road. Camprubí was educated at the Jesuit School in Barcelona, the Hotchkiss School in Connecticut, and Harvard University, where he studied civil engineering. After a series of positions as an engineer in the United States and abroad, Camprubí purchased *La Prensa*, a struggling weekly publication, in 1918. He converted the newspaper to a daily, and by 1929, when García Lorca arrived in New York, the paper was thriving, having become the newspaper of record for the city's burgeoning Spanish-speaking community.

The head of this unofficial welcoming committee was Federico de Onís. A descendant of Luis de Onís, the Spanish foreign minister who oversaw the sale of Florida to the United States, Federico was born near Salamanca in 1885. A disciple of Miguel de Unamuno, de Onís had been tapped in 1916 by Columbia University president Nicholas Murray Butler (on the advice of Unamuno via Archer Huntington) to head up Columbia's newly formed Department of Hispanic Studies and the university's Spanish Institute in the United States. With Europe occupied in World War I, and with the Panama Canal just recently opened for business, the old pan-American dream of North-South hemispheric unity had reached a new pitch of intensity in the U.S. The result was an unprecedented boom in interest in the Spanish language and in the Spanish-speaking world. High school and college enrollments in Spanish classes skyrocketed. Although the engine of this boom was the prospect of hemispheric unity, for a complex set of reasons, Spain and Spanish literature and culture came to occupy a remarkably prominent place in the high school and college Spanish curricula.[10] Spain had produced a young generation of brilliant linguists, historians, and philologists who were well positioned to lead the creation and expansion of Spanish departments in the United States. By 1929, Federico de Onís was at the helm of the flagship enterprise of American Hispanism at Columbia University.

There were three Spanish men of culture—Felipe, del Río, and García Maroto—who had traveled to Spanish America, married Spanish-American women, and converged on Nueva York in large part because of the opportunities generated by the remarkable Hispanic cultural effervescence that was brewing in that city. There was also the Puerto Rican–born son of a Spanish colonial official who now for over a decade had owned the most important daily newspaper of the city's Spanish-speaking community, and the descendant of a Spanish imperial official who was heading up the establishment and professionalization of Hispanic studies in New York and, in many ways, throughout the United States. As teachers, translators, publishers, and/or interpreters of cultural difference, and as Spaniards with extensive experience in

Spanish America, these men were perfectly positioned to operate as intermediaries in the Spanish/Hispanic boom in the city.

In many ways, and pace the *vox clamantis in deserto* pose of *Poeta en Nueva York*, Federico García Lorca and the distinguished members of his dockside entourage were both promoters and beneficiaries of the intense Hispanophile climate of 1920s New York. During his relatively short stay in the city, García Lorca attended concerts by guitarist Andrés Segovia and pianist José Iturbe; dance performances by La Argentina and Argentinita; and lectures by Dámaso Alonso and Ignacio Sánchez Mejías. Lorca himself, a charismatic and talented musician, gave impromptu piano and guitar performances of traditional Spanish music at many parties in the city, to great acclaim, according to his own immodest reports to his family.

In New York, moreover, García Lorca seemed constantly to "run into" or re-encounter friends he had made in Spain, like the young British stockbroker Colin Hackforth-Jones and the journalist and Hispanist Mildred Adams, both of whom García Lorca had befriended in Granada some years before. Adams and her family became assiduous companions of and hosts to García Lorca in New York; Mildred even threw a party to introduce the Spanish visitor to her American friends, where, he reported to his parents, "a rather good pianist played music by Albéniz and Falla, and the girls wore *mantones de Manila* [the bright shawls worn by Andalusian women, particularly flamenco dancers]. In the dining room—Oh, divine surprise!— there were bottles of sherry and Fundador brandy."[11] (García Lorca was no fan of Prohibition.) Another of García Lorca's closest New York friends was Henry Herschel Brickell, a literary critic and publisher who also had been to Granada, where, according to Ian Gibson, he practically stalked the great composer Manuel de Falla, hoping to catch a glimpse of the maestro. Brickell and his wife threw a party for García Lorca on his Saint's Day (July 18) and also organized a Spanish-themed Christmas Eve party in his honor. Before heading off to midnight mass, the guests made wishes while lighting candles set out on a kind of altar made of Talavera tiles. Many of García Lorca's "New York" friends had made the Washington Irving pilgrimage to Granada; they collected Manila shawls and Talavera ceramics; in the midst of Prohibition, they had stashes of Spanish sherry and brandy; and they invited or employed musicians to play Spanish contemporary classical music at their soirees. These were not random run-of-the-mill New Yorkers; they seem more like the veritable priests and priestesses of New York's Spanish craze.

In an oscillation somewhat emblematic of García Lorca's entire stay in New York, on both Thanksgiving Day and Christmas Eve of 1929, the poet ate among his Spanish hosts at Columbia, and then rushed off to dessert and postprandial festivities with his well-to-do American friends the Brickells. Of these American friends García Lorca wrote to his parents: "they are very wealthy and influential, and in their house

I've met people with high-profiles in art and literature and finance. . . . In their house I had an even better time [than with the Spaniards], because it's a different society and I feel like a foreigner."[12] García Lorca was undoubtedly a prodigiously talented, charming, and charismatic man, but surely his entrée into the drawing rooms of New York also had something to do with the Spanish craze that gripped the city and generated unprecedented interest in, and curiosity about, Spain and Spaniards. Be that as it may, the fact that in New York this Spanish poet and playwright could, in the space of a few hours, enjoy both domestic intimacy among a sizable group of compatriots and the adoring attention of Hispanophile New Yorkers who must have seen him as something of an exotic native informant tells us a great deal not only about the makeup of García Lorca but also about the fabric of the city in the late 1920s.

Even during his two summer escapes from the city into the American "wilderness," García Lorca never fully left the orbit of Hispanophilia. He traveled to Eden Mills, Vermont, to visit a young friend he had met previously in Madrid's Residencia de Estudiantes: the budding writer, translator, and Spanish teacher Philip Cummings. In Vermont, their primary activity seems to have been the English translation of García Lorca's first book of poems. From there, García Lorca traveled to the Catskills in the mid-Hudson Valley, where he visited Angel del Río and Amelia Agostini in their rented cabin in Bushnellsville, and then Federico de Onís in his house near Newburgh, on the Hudson. In Newburgh, García Lorca helped de Onís with the preparation of his vast *Antología de la poesía española e hispanoamericana (1883–1932)*, published in 1934. One of the goals of García Lorca's parentally sponsored trip to New York was to learn English, and in his letters he frequently updated his parents with exaggerated reports of his progress in that language. However, judging from García Lorca's itinerary, even in 1929, as now, it was quite possible to live in Spanish, from Vermont to New York.

WHAT GARCÍA LORCA COULD HAVE SEEN IN NEW YORK

Lorca's voice would not have been the only Spanish-speaking one echoing through the meadows and apple orchards of the mid-Hudson Valley in the summer of 1929. The mid-to late 1920s saw the establishment in that precise area of a number of Spanish-owned farms and rural boardinghouses catering to the growing Spanish and Spanish-speaking population seeking fresh food and fresh air during the stifling summer months. The first of these villas had been established by *tampeños*: *asturianos* who had become cigar makers in Cuba and/or Tampa who then reemigrated to New York. While several of these original "Spanish villas" were just a few miles from where García Lorca visited Onís, no mention of them is made in García Lorca's extant correspondence.

When one considers the remarkable Spanish/Hispanic boom in New York reaching its apex right around the time of García Lorca's visit, it is interesting to consider

Advertisement for Villa Rodriguez, ca. 1929.

Villa Rodriguez was a mid-Hudson Valley "resort" for Spaniards established in the late 1920s by the Asturian Alejandro Rodriguez.

what the writer from Granada did *not* say in his poems or his letters to his friends and family. For example, his letters home contained several reflections on the various religious services he attended while in New York (Jewish, Russian Orthodox, African American Protestant, etc.), and almost every one of these reflections concluded with a reaffirmation of the superiority of Spanish Catholicism. He explicitly told his family that "the religious question" was very important in New York, and he went out of his way to describe scenes of Catholic New York. And yet Spain's role in building the city's first Catholic church, St. Peter's, on Barclay Street in 1785, went unmentioned, as did the existence of two relatively new churches built specifically to serve the city's growing Spanish/Hispanic colony: Our Lady of Guadalupe on West Fourteenth Street (1902) and Our Lady of Hope, built on property adjacent to Huntington's Hispanic Society of America at Audubon Terrace (1912). There was one interesting and rare case in which the poet perceived a connection between Iberian history and current-day New York: in his account to his family of his visit to the Sephardic congregation at Shearith Israel, he remarked how some of the names and faces in the temple reminded him of friends and neighbors back in Granada, concluding, "In Granada, we are almost all Jews."[13]

García Lorca's silence on certain issues is intriguing. In his book *La ciudad automática*, Julio Camba, a Spanish journalist and humorist who visited the city in 1929, playfully remarked: "From 110th St. to 116th St., between Fifth and Eighth Avenues, you could say that we are in Spain. A somewhat black Spain for sure, but a true Spain nonetheless, based on language, character, and people's general attitude toward life. . . . It is a poor neighborhood, inhabited mainly by people of color."[14] Given García Lorca's avowed interest in Harlem, and in the Afro-Antillean culture he celebrated during his trip to Cuba, the absence of references to the city's burgeoning Puerto Rican community, particularly in East Harlem, is another somewhat puzzling omission.

The years leading up to García Lorca's stay in New York coincided with a number of major events in the city's growing Spanish working-class immigrant community. In 1922, the Basque immigrants Valentín Aguirre and Benita Orbe opened Jai Alai, a restaurant adjacent to their hotel, the Santa Lucía, which had been in operation since 1910 on the corner of Bank and Bleecker streets in the West Village. In 1924, a Cuban impresario inaugurated a Spanish-language *varietés* theater in East Harlem called the Teatro San José (later known as the Teatro Latino), of which Julio Camba would write in 1931: "In the San José Theater, the audience laughs not only at the Galicians, Catalanes and *baturros* with their respective accents. Next to them on the stage are the *jíbaro* from the Antilles, the *pelado* from Mexico, and the *atorrante* from Argentina."[15] In 1925, Benito Collada, a native of Asturias, Spain, opened El Chico, a major Spanish restaurant and nightclub on Sheridan Square in Greenwich Village. In 1927, a Galician immigrant opened the restaurant El Faro on Horatio

Street, a business still in operation in 2010. In 1928, the Centro Vasco-Americano inaugurated their own building at 48 Cherry Street by the East River docks, in the heart of the city's oldest Spanish neighborhood. In 1929, a group of Spanish immigrants, probably anarchists, bought a seventeen-acre plot of land on the south shore of Staten Island and created the Spanish Naturopath Society—a cooperative bungalow community aimed at providing its members a place to enjoy fresh air and relaxation during the stifling New York summer months. And in that same year, Carmen Barañano and Jesús Moneo inaugurated a Spanish grocery store on Fourteenth Street, Casa Moneo, that would be a fixture of the city's *colonia* well into the 1980s.

Although none of this effervescence seems to have been recorded or mentioned by García Lorca, in one letter to his family, he does write of a meal taken at a Spanish restaurant that may well have been El Faro: "Yesterday I ate with two famous Spanish women, La Argentina [Antonia Mercé Luque], and Lucrecia Bori [Lucrecia Borja González de Rianebo] . . . . They are both delightful. They invited me and it was just the three of us eating at a small restaurant near the Hudson River. We drank Anís del Mono, and they were enthusiastic and pleased; but I noticed that we were being served a counterfeit liqueur —'Anís del Topo'. When I told my hosts at the end of the meal, they made such a scene, I was afraid they were going to assault the owner, who was a very funny and sly gallego."[16] This minor anecdote involving an immigrant from Galicia serving a doubly illicit anise (both counterfeit and bootleg) to these three authentic performers of Spanishness offers a rare glimpse of García Lorca's contact with working-class Spanish immigrants in New York.

One can only speculate why García Lorca seems not to have taken much notice of the bubbling world of Spanish working-class immigrants in New York or of the remarkable pan-Hispanic cultural effervescence that was brewing on the streets and in the barrios of the city in the late 1920s. Perhaps, since he traveled in different circles, he had little occasion to come across these people and phenomena; perhaps he did not find what he saw to be all that noteworthy. Or perhaps, like many figures of the cultural elite of his generation, Federico García Lorca was not disposed to perceive the interest, value, and "authenticity" of cultural forms produced by and for working-class immigrants in what he saw as a strange and rootless city. Then again, perhaps this is far too much significance to be distilled from a single bottle of counterfeit and bootleg anise.

IMMIGRANTS TO EXILES

The 1920s and early 1930s constituted the apex of Spanish New York. Although the anti-immigration legislation of 1922 had virtually slammed the door shut on the legal immigration of Spaniards to the U.S., by then there was already a critical mass of Spaniards living in the city. The tribulations of the Depression in some ways worked to strengthen the community of immigrants in New York, who were forced to organize a remarkably dense web of associations in order to survive. Many enterprising Spanish-born immigrants—most of whom had spent time in Cuba or Puerto Rico—would establish businesses that would thrive, thanks in large measure to the patronage of the even larger and quickly expanding Puerto Rican population of the city. Such is the case, for example, with Prudencio Unanue's Goya foods, established in Lower Manhattan in 1936; or Bustelo's Coffee Roasting Company, founded in East Harlem around 1930; or Joseph Victori's Spanish food and wine import company, with headquarters on Pearl Street. All three of these firms still existed in 2010.

If during García Lorca's time in New York it seemed like Spain's cultural elites in the city could have little to do with the Spanish immigrant community, all of that would change dramatically on July 18, 1936. The outbreak of the Spanish Civil War would bring to the fore the vast network of working-class organizations that had been woven during the Depression. These organizations almost unanimously supported the republic, and they banded together to form a national umbrella organization, the Sociedades Hispanas Confederadas, to coordinate fundraising efforts on behalf of the republic. For the duration of the war, hardly a week would go by without several major dances, rallies, performances, or soccer matches being organized as fundraisers by these *sociedades*.

As in Spain, the Spanish intelligentsia in New York for the most part supported the legally elected government of the Second Republic and opposed the coup led by General Francisco Franco. The group of Spaniards that greeted García Lorca in 1929 is representative in this regard: León Felipe and Gabriel García Maroto returned to Spain during the war to help mobilize artists and writers on behalf of the republic; de Onís and del Río also cautiously supported the republic; and Camprubí's *La Prensa*, though circumspect, also sided with the Loyalists. Fernando de los Ríos, who had made the crossing to New York with García Lorca on the SS *Olympic* in June 1929, was appointed the republic's ambassador to the United States, and would routinely call upon and meet with the city's Spanish immigrant *colonia* to garner support for the beleaguered Spanish government. The liberal intellectual elite and the working-class immigrant *colonia* would, for the most part, make common cause during the war.

A number of New York Spaniards, either because they openly supported Franco or were considered insufficiently supportive of the pro-republican effort, were labeled Fascists and subjected to picketing and boycotts throughout the war. These were mostly members of the *colonia*'s business elite, including, for example, the food and wine entrepreneurs Moneo, Victori, and Bustelo as well as Benito Collada, the owner of El Chico, the nightclub in Greenwich Village. Two distinguished Spanish musicians who were in New York at the time, Andrés Segovia and José Iturbe, were also blacklisted by the city's Loyalists, as was Dr. Ramón Castroviejo, the eminent

CLUB OBRERO ESPAÑOL, New York City.
ATENEO HISPANO, Brooklyn, N.Y.
COMITE SOLIDARIDAD, New York City.
BURO HISPANO DEL PARTIDO COMUNISTA, New York City.
COMITE ANTIFASCISTA ESPAÑOL, Elizabeth, N.J.
CIRCULO DE TRABAJADORES, Brooklyn, N.Y.
CENTRO ANDALUZ, Brooklyn, N.Y.
GRUPO DE HELEN, Helen, W.Va.
COMITE PRO DEMOCRACIA, Niagara Falls, N.Y.
GRUPO AMIGOS DE AZAÑA, N.Y.
COMITE ESPAÑOL DE AYUDA A ESPAÑA, East St. Louis, Ill.
GRUPO ANTIFASCISTA DEL BRONX, New York City.
COMITE A.F. DE WESTCHESTER, White Plains, N.Y.
FRENTE POPULAR ESPAÑOL DE QUEENS, Astoria, L.I.
COMITE FEMENINO DE W.P. White Plains, N.Y.
ATENEO HISPANO AMERICANO, White Plains, N.Y.
GRUPO ANTIFASCISTA, Glen Cove, N.Y.
AGRUPACION OBRERA HISPANA DEL BRONX, New York City
SOCIEDAD NATURISTA HISPANA, New York City.
COMITE DE AYUDA A ESPAÑA, Lodi, N.J.
CIRCULO VALENCIANO, N.Y. City.
CENTRO MONTAÑES, New York City.
FRENTE POPULAR ESPAÑOL, Philadelphia, Pa.
COMITE PRO DEMOCRACIA ESPAÑOLA, New York City.
COMITE PRO CRUZ ROJA ESPAÑOLA, New York City.
CLUB CORUÑA, New York City.
COMITE ANTIFASCISTA FEMENINO, Brooklyn, N.Y.
MUTUALISTA OBRERA MEXICANA, New York City.
SOCIEDAD ESPAÑOLA DE BENEFICENCIA, New York City.
AGRUPACION SOCIALISTA ESPAÑOLA, New York City.
A. JUVENTUDES ESPAÑOLAS UNIFICADAS DE E.S., New York City.
HISPANOS UNIDOS, Newark, N.J.
COMITE DE LOGAN, Holden W.Va.
GRUPO ESPAÑOL, Raynal, W.Va.
COMITE FEMENINO, Raynal, W.Va.

CLUB ESPAÑOL, Barre, Pa.
FRENTE POPULAR DE FAIRMONT, Carolina, W.Va.
ACCION DEMOCRATICA ESPAÑOLA, Pittsburg, Cal.
THE NEW ENGLAND COMMITTEE FOR DEFENSE OF SPANISH DEMOCRACY, Boston, Mass.
GRUPO ESPAÑOL DE ISLAND PARK.
GRUPO ANTIFASCISTA DE Nemacolin, Pa.
COMITE DEMOCRATICO HISPANO AMERICANO, Galveston, Texas.
LOS CAMARADAS DE LA IDRIA, Idria, Cal.
COMITE PRO AYUDA A ESPAÑA, Wharton, W.Va.
GRUPO ESPAÑOL DE ANSONIA Y SHELTON, Ansonia, Conn.
COMITE PRO AYUDA A ESPAÑA, Bartley, W.Va.
ALIANZA OBRERA HISPANOAMERICANA, New York City.
CLUB CUBANO JULIO A. MELLA, New York City.
ALIANZA OBRERA ESPAÑOLA, New York City.
COMITE FEMENINO DEL C.O.R., New York City.
COMITE ANTIFASCISTA ESPAÑOL, Canton, Ohio.
COMITE CATALA ANTIFEIXISTA, New York City.
COMITE ESPAÑOL, Bethlehem, Pa.
COMITE DE AYUDA A LOS NIÑOS DEL PUEBLO ESPAÑOL, Tampico, Tamaulipas, México.
UNITED COMMITTEE TO AID THE SPANISH PEOPLE, Patterson, N.J.
CENTRO ASTURIANO, N.Y. City.
COMITE DE AYUDA A ESPAÑA, Danbury, Conn.
CLUB PORTUGUES "NOVA AURORA" Mount Vernon, N.Y.
COMITE ESPAÑOL, Staten Island, N.Y.
COM. PORTUGUES PRO DEM. ESP. Summerville, Mass.
GRUPO VASCO, New York City
GRUPO ESPAÑOL, Port Arthur, Tx.
CENTRO GALICIA, New York City.
COMITE ANTIFASCISTA, N.Y.C.
COM. ANTIFASCISTA, Scarsdale, N.Y.
SPANISH AMERICAN WOMEN'S CLUB, Niagara Falls, N.Y.

UNION DE COCINEROS, L89, N.Y.C.
UNION DE TABAQUEROS 273, N.Y.C.
COMITE DE MONTPELIER, Montpelier, Vt.
SPANISH AMERICAN CIT. CLUB, Bayonne, N.J.
COMITE FRENTE POPULAR, Weirton, W.Va.
MUTUALISTA HISPANO AMERICANA, Brooklyn, N.Y.
GRUPO ARTISTICO "TEATRO DEL PUEBLO", Brooklyn, N.Y.
FRENTE POPULAR ESPAÑOL, Winterport, Me.
PLUS ULTRA DEMOCRATIC CLUB, Bayonne, N.J.
CENTRO DE ESTUDIOS SOCIALES, White Plains, N.Y.
COMITE S.H.C. Amsterdam, N.Y.
COMITE DE DAMAS DE A.O.K., New York City.
SPANISH AM. CIT. CLUB "LADIES" Bayonne, N.Y.
AMIGOS DE LA DEMOCRACIA ESPAÑOLA DE NEW YORK.
CENTRO BALEAR, New York City
LOS INCANSABLES, New York
AGRUPACION DEMOCRATICA HIJOS DE GALICIA, Habana Cuba.
LA NACIONAL, Brooklyn, N.Y.
COMITE DEL CENTRO CULTURAL ESPAÑOL, New Britain, Conn.
VANGUARDIA PUERTORRIQUEÑA, Brooklyn, N.Y.
GRUPO DE "LA ASTORLOID" New York City.
COMITE PRO VICTIMAS, Bklyn, N.Y.
AGRUPACION DE ESPAÑOLES, Long Beach
GRUPO ANTORCHA, Brooklyn, N.Y.
FRENTE POPULAR, Brooklyn, N.Y.
CLUB "LA PASIONARIA" N.Y. City
SOCORROS MUTUOS "MUÑOS Y SUS CONTORNOS," Newark, N.J.
COMITE PRO DEMOCRACIA, Jersey City, N.J.
COMITE S.H.C. Schenectady, N.Y.
SEGURA F.C.; Brooklyn, N.Y.
SOCIEDAD DE AYUDA A ESPAÑA, Speller, W.Va.
ORDEN INTERNACIONAL DE
COMITE ANTIFASCISTA, New Kensington, Pa
ORDEN INTERNACIONAL DE

TRABAJADORES (SECCION HISPANA) New York City.
JUVENTUDES ESPAÑOLAS, Brooklyn, N.Y.
GRUPO LEONES DE AYUDA A ESPAÑA, New York City.
COM. FEMENINO, Schenectady, N.Y.
FRENTE POPULAR ANTIFASCISTA GALLEGO, New York City.
AGRUPACION IBERIA, Tarrytown, New York
AGRUPACION "TIERRA", N.Y. City.
AGRUPACION SOCIAL, 19 de JULIO, New York City
ATENEO DE EDUCACION SOCIAL, Newark, N.J.
ACCION LIBERTARIA, Jersey City, New Jersey
GRUPO "ATENEO DE CUENTAL", Newark, N.J.
CULTURA PROLETARIA, N.Y. City.
AGRUPACION LIBERTARIA, Yonkers, N.Y.
GRUPO ACRACIA, Newark, N.J.
CLUB BENEFICO HISPANO, Bronx, N.Y.
COLONIA LATINA DE WILLIAMSBURG, Brooklyn, N.Y.
SPANISH AMERICAN CIT. CLUB, Yonkers, N.Y.
LOS PROGRESISTAS, N.Y. City.
FRENTE POPULAR ANTIFASCISTA, Pittsburgh, Pa.
GRUPO SALMERON, N.Y. City.
LA FRATERNAL, Philadelphia, Pa.
COM. DE DAMAS, Perth Amboy, N.J.
COM. FEMENINO East St. Louis, Ill.
COMITE ESPAÑOL DE SOCORRO, San Louis, Mo.
LA FRATERNAL SECCION ANTIFASCISTA "LISTER" Philadelphia, Pa
ACCION DEMOCRATA ESPAÑOLA, Crockett, Cal.
GRUPO ARTISTICO "MIAJA" N.Y.C.
CALPE AMERICAN RECREATION CLUB, New York City.
CLUB ESPAÑOL DEL PORVENIR, Brooklyn, N.Y.
COMITE FEMENINO DE A. e E. East St. Louis, Ill.
EQUIPMENT COMMITTEE, New York City.
COM. FRENTE POPULAR, Rome, N.Y.

List of Spanish and Hispanic organizations in the United States, published ca. 1936 by the Sociedades Hispanas Confederadas.

The Sociedades Hispanas Confederadas, an umbrella organization whose goal was to coordinate pro-republican activities in the Spanish *colonias* of the United States, published this list during the Spanish Civil War. It provides a sense of the *colonias'* diversity and geographical distribution, and the remarkably large number of associations in the New York area.

ophthalmologist and eye surgeon based at Columbia-Presbyterian Hospital. The stakes of the taut ideological climate of the war years can be gauged by a curious event reported in the *New York Times* and two Spanish-language dailies, *La Prensa* and *La Voz*. When, in the summer of 1938, a Spanish-language cinema in East Harlem announced the premiere of *Morena Clara*, a film featuring the Spanish actress Imperio Argentina, pro-Loyalist New Yorkers picketed the theater because the star was known to be a supporter of Franco. The theater owner argued that the film had been made during the Spanish Republic, but the picketers were not convinced, and the theater was forced to withdraw the film from the program.

Some members of New York's Spanish immigrant community in the 1920s and 1930s dreamed of someday returning to Spain. The establishment of the Second Republic in 1931 had raised the hopes of many; but the outbreak—and especially the outcome—of the war would dash those hopes. The flow would move in the opposite direction. Exactly one month after the start of the war, on August 18, 1936, Federico García Lorca was killed by Fascist sympathizers, his body dumped into an unmarked mass grave near his native Granada. In a cruel twist of fate, the poet's brother and sister, parents and grandparents —the recipients of Federico's buoyant letters from New York—would soon arrive in the city that their son seemed to love and hate, not as ambitious cultural diplomats or hopeful immigrants, but rather, like so many of their compatriots, as devastated exiles. So begins a new chapter of *españoles en Nueva York*.

NOTES

I would like to thank Mike Wallace, Carmen Boullosa, Marci Reaven, Elena Martínez, Ana Varela Lago, Mariana García Arias, and the doctoral students in my "Nueva York" seminar for their support, their work, and their feedback on many of the ideas presented here. I am grateful to the descendants of Spanish immigrants Luz Castaños, Joe Mora, Jim and Anita Yglesias, Lillian Charity, José Fernández, Luz Damron (née Díaz), and Emilia Doyaga for sharing with me their memories and knowledge of Spanish immigrants in New York. I am particularly indebted to Manuel Alonso and Dolores Sánchez for their generosity and for allowing me to view and scan images from their remarkable family archive.

1. "City's Spanish Colony Lives in its Own Little World Here," *New York Times*, March 23, 1924, XX18.

2. Konrad Bercovici, *Around the World in New York* (New York: The Century Company, 1924), 277.

3. "City's Spanish Colony Lives in its Own Little World Here."

4. Bercovici, *Around the World in New York*, 290.

5. "City's Spanish Colony Lives in its Own Little World Here."

6. Ibid.

7. Ana María Varela-Lago's dissertation is the best source of information on and analysis of the links between the Cuban question and Spanish immigrants in the United States in the late nineteenth century. "Conquerors, Immigrants, Exiles: The Spanish Diaspora in the United States (1848–1948)" (PhD diss., University of California, San Diego, 2008).

8. Ian Gibson, *Federico García Lorca: A Life* (New York: Pantheon, 1989).

9. Federico García Lorca, *Epistolario completo* (Madrid: Cátedra, 1997), 615.

10. For an analysis of this crucial moment in the history of Spanish studies and Spanish departments in the U.S., see my essay "'Longfellow's Law': The Place of Latin America and Spain in U.S. Hispanism, circa 1915," in *Spain in America: The Origins of Hispanism in the United States*, ed. Richard L. Kagan (Urbana: University of Illinois Press, 2002).

11. García Lorca, *Epistolario completo*, 633.

12. Ibid., 672.

13. *Poeta en Nueva York* includes a poem titled "Cementerio judío," though the Sephardic connection is not explicitly mentioned in the poem.

14. Julio Camba, *La ciudad automática* (Madrid: Espasa Calpe, 1950), 56

15. Ibid.

16. García Lorca, *Epistolario completo*, 679.

MAKING NUEVA YORK *MODERNA:*

Latin American Art, the International Avant-Gardes, and the New School

ANNA INDYCH-LOPEZ

José Clemente Orozco (1883–1949). *Struggle of the Occident*, 1930–31. Mural. The New School Art Collection, New York. © 2010 Artists Rights Society (ARS), New York / SOMAAP, Mexico City.

A unique form of modernism emerged in post–World War I New York, a combination of urban realism, European avant-garde styles, and an American vernacular, which stimulated cultural ferment and excitement in the already-thriving metropolis. While the city did not become an international axis for modernism until after World War II, New York experienced a great influx of artistic figures and activities during the interwar years that laid critical groundwork for future endeavors. This artistic heyday has been called "New York Modern" by historians William B. Scott and Peter M. Rutkoff, who acknowledge that "as the city became ethnically and racially more diverse between the world wars, so too did its artistic communities."[1] Latin American artists were among those who not only participated in but also played a decisive role in establishing the city as a flourishing center of cultural experimentation and artistic dialogue. However, like many observers who assume that only European exiles and European-influenced U.S. artists comprised the American avant-garde of the early part of the century, Scott and Rutkoff mistakenly state that it was not until the 1980s that Hispanics counted among the ranks of the vanguard.[2]

Key interwar events and groups credited with establishing modernism in the United States include the 1913 Armory Show, New York Dada, and European Surrealists exiled in New York. The heady dialogue between refugee European modernists and U.S. intellectuals created the mutable and fluid ethos of New York modernism, known for its plurality of aesthetic styles. With the goal of establishing a separate and uniquely "American" cultural identity, New York modernists gave a nod to European artists for their formal innovations yet resisted their embrace of abstraction. Included in the recasting and redefinition of modernism were Latin American voices—among others—that contributed to and *made* the aesthetic heterodoxy of New York.

Scores of Latin American artists migrated to and practiced their craft in the United States in the twentieth century. Particularly in the 1960s, New York was a mecca for Latin American artists, prompting a now-famous 1964 exhibition entitled *Magnet: New York* at the Bonino Gallery. But artists from Bolivia, Brazil, Chile, Cuba, Ecuador, Mexico, Peru, and Uruguay had been coming to New York in great numbers for decades prior to that time. To be sure, in the interwar years it was more common for Latin American artists to first make the transatlantic journey to receive their artistic training in European capitals and academies, and later to join the ranks of the historical avant-gardes (i.e., Cubism, Futurism, Surrealism). Many of these artists then came to New York after their European sojourns.

Rather than just trace their presence in the city, however, it is crucial to draw out the ways in which Latin American artists were incorporated into the very fabric of cultural activity in the metropolis and helped to make New York modern. As they brought their own local visions, the artists directly participated in broader debates about the burgeoning modernism in New York's urban sphere, laying critical claim to a host of avant-garde practices and production. This essay demonstrates how vital Latin American artists were to the transformation of New York by focusing on one particular institution, the New School for Social Research (now known as the New School University), a center of avant-garde activity from the late 1920s through the 1950s, including high-profile projects in which Latin American artists occupied central roles. At the New School, artists from Ecuador, Mexico, Cuba, Puerto Rico, Uruguay, Argentina, Colombia, and Spain all contributed to the humanist, progressive, and internationalist mission of the university, which itself had a profound imprint on the character of New York.

The long-held and monolithic perception of Latin American culture as rural, timeless, and picturesque has served to exclude its artists from the international vanguards of the early twentieth century. Some may assume that the impact of Latin Americans in New York can be defined by their cultural markers or differences; indeed, intellectual constructs such as nationalism and indigenism were not only vital to many artists' aesthetic and ideological visions but also historically significant. But the New York scene was not necessarily dictated by the imperatives of nationality or identity. Latin American artists helped to create the cosmopolitan cultural milieu of New York by expanding their locally honed practices with vigorous formal experimentation. In fact, one could argue that the socially engaged modernism that developed in New York was a critical part of the international avant-gardes. Latin American artists in New York were generally from privileged backgrounds; rather than marginalized citizens of the metropolis, they were active members and creators of an evolving modernism. To be sure, poor and disenfranchised immigrants also contributed to the physical and economic makeup of modern New York, but they circulated in different spheres from those under discussion here.

Latin American artists' interest in issues such as nationalism and indigenism

The Mexican delegation to the American Artists'
Congress, New York, 1936. Photographer unknown.
Getty Research Institute.

Left to right: Rufino and Olga Tamayo, David Alfaro
Siqueiros, José Clemente Orozco, Roberto Berdecio,
and Angelica Arenal de Siqueiros.

resulted in socially engaged forms of modernism that highlighted the role of radical
politics, a theme central to this time period and to this story. The 1930s was a high
point in the history of art with a "social viewpoint." While the terms of their political
engagement may have differed, many of the artists associated with the New School
espoused a general humanism and were galvanized by, among other issues, the anti-
Fascist struggle and Popular Front causes. The American Artists' Congress (February
1936), one of the key events of the 1930s, served as a rallying cry for leftist artists,
bringing them together under the banner of anti-Fascism. The Mexican delegation to
the congress included Rufino Tamayo, David Alfaro Siqueiros, José Clemente Orozco,
and Roberto Berdecio. The New School played a critical role at the congress, serving
as one of two main venues and therefore helping to further "social viewpoint" art and
ideologies. It also hosted *War and Fascism*, an exhibition that took place from April
15 to May 6, 1936, and in which Siqueiros participated. In the 1930s, the ideal of
social transformation defined New York's modernism, and the politically engaged
ideologies of Latin American artists such as Siqueiros cemented that utopian mix.

The conjunction of political engagement and modernism also was reflected in
the heterogeneous artistic styles developed in New York. These ran the gamut from
radical experimentation to a socially engaged realism, a kind of alternative modernism

that was not necessarily defined by European forms of abstraction. Most Latin American artists under discussion here were working in a figurative style, yet their commitment to mixing humanism and politics with a modernist-inflected style speaks to their unique outlook and the particular brand of modernism developed in the Americas in the 1930s. Furthermore, many artists in the Americas who worked with the form of figurative modernism known as Social Realism also were concerned with creating national identities that would distinguish them from Europe by focusing on local subject matter. Many of the artists at the New School worked within this style, contributing to the heterogeneity of modernism in New York in the 1930s and 1940s.

In their study of the New School, Peter Rutkoff and William Scott describe the institution as an "established feature of New York cultural life" that has earned a "place of unique significance to twentieth-century social thought."[3] Associated with modernism and liberalism, the New School was founded in 1918 by dissident academics from Columbia University seeking an alternative to the conventional university system. Ever since, the school and its faculty have been known for their interdisciplinary approach, leftist orientation, and theoretical bent. While diverse philosophies have been advocated by the faculty, an overriding faith in scientific rationalism, political democracy, and democratic humanism have reigned. In 1933, under the leadership of director Alvin Johnson, it became a haven for European intellectuals escaping the regimes of Hitler and Mussolini. These expatriates founded the University in Exile, which was renamed the Graduate Faculty in 1934, when it became the research division of the New School. Combining American intellectual thought with European philosophies, the Graduate Faculty developed a reputation for academic rigor and serious scholarly inquiry of the highest order, and it became the home of several of the greatest thinkers of the twentieth century.[4]

Another notable educational program at the New School was its adult education program, which continues to this day as the New School for General Studies. In the 1930s and early 1940s it was one of the two divisions that comprised and defined the New School. With no admissions requirements, modest course fees, and a slate of serious intellectuals and artists serving as freelance faculty, the adult education division fostered a sense of intellectual freedom, experimentation, and eclecticism that became hallmarks of the New School. Perhaps less known and less celebrated than its sister graduate division, the adult education program—specifically the art workshops—was nonetheless also home to some of the most influential artists of the period. In the 1920s and 1930s Johnson turned the New School into a modern cultural center by shifting the emphasis from the social science curriculum to the arts, and by commissioning Joseph Urban to create a new International Style building at 66 West Twelfth Street. Specialized art spaces were created, a series of murals were commissioned for the new building, and new studio art and art history curricula were devel-

oped, turning the New School into a lively site for the creation of heterogeneous modern styles.

While the New School's founding and history are associated with European and U.S. intellectuals, it is important to note that Latinos and Hispanics were at the heart of the institution, with regard to the arts, from this early period. The New School commissioned a well-known mural cycle by the Mexican muralist José Clemente Orozco for the new Urban building between 1930 and 1931, illustrating the themes of universal brotherhood and opposing systems of political thought. As the only surviving example of modern Mexican muralism in New York, Orozco's cycle is historically significant. Diane Miliotes recently shed new light on the works by placing them in the multiple contexts of the Delphic Circle (a literary group in New York committed

José Clemente Orozco (1883–1949). *Struggle of the Orient*, 1930–31. Mural. The New School Art Collection, New York. © 2010 Artists Rights Society (ARS), New York / SOMAAP, Mexico City.

Camilo Egas (1889–1962). *Ecuadorian Festival*, 1932. Mural. The New School Art Collection, New York.

to reviving Greek ideals, international peace, and brotherhood), the New School, and Orozco's own ambitions within the New York art world.[5]

Johnson's commission of Camilo Egas's mural *Ecuadorian Festival* is further testimony to the New School's status as a center for progressive modernism and the central role Latin American artists played in developing it. Egas began working on his mural a year after Orozco completed his cycle. (Thomas Hart Benton also created a mural at the New School, completed the same year.) Unlike Orozco's multipaneled fresco, *Ecuadorian Festival* is a single large (8 by 16 feet) oil on canvas that conforms to the scale of public mural painting. Created for the anteroom of the original dance studio, the work captures the movements of indigenous figures participating in a local ritual. Art historian Michele Greet, one of the only scholars to focus on Egas's mural, explains that the artist, rather than documenting a specific festival, chose to depict a generic celebration with native costumes, traditional instruments, and vendors from various regions. Instead of making a social point, Egas focuses here on cultural identity. This, Greet writes, aligns his work more with the "localized subject matter of 'American scene painting' than with the radical politics of social realism." Because of this emphasis, Egas's mode of production would have represented the "most progressive form of artistic expression for Johnson," in the context of the 1930s in the Americas.[6]

In addition to expressing the indigenism that was fashionable at the time, *Ecuadorian Festival* embodies the ways in which artists in the Americas combined

Camilo Egas (1889–1962). *Harvesting Food in Ecuador*, 1935. Mural. The New School Art Collection, New York.

European styles with American realities to forge a figurative modernism. Egas draws the viewer into the work through the figures in the foreground, many of which are life-size and gather at the bottom edge of the picture plane, appearing to swarm toward the viewer's space. Egas described the scene as "something that reflects the moments of happiness into which the natives of Ecuador immerse themselves, so colorful and simultaneously so solid; strong in body yet anxious to enjoy their festivals."[7] Yet rather than depicting a bucolic scene, Egas's image conveys instability, disruption, and anxiety, a tension that results from formal strategies that recall those of the historical avant-gardes. To begin with, the image is marked by its distinctive centrifugal composition; figures are pressed out to the margins, creating three oblong groups with expanses of empty space between them. The meandering processions of figures and dancers produce curvilinear lines throughout the pictorial space, which contrast with the sharp angles created by the figures' tall ceremonial hats. Distortion in the form of awkward, elongated figures—who have dour faces and heads lowered in a somber gesture—is complemented by a sharp disruption of scale between foreground and background, resulting from a dramatically tilted and stacked composition where the figures are pushed toward the picture plane. By combining such modernist spatial and compositional strategies with local subjects and figuration, Egas created a hybrid modernism.

Camilo Egas (1889–1962). *Harvesting Food in North America*, 1935. Mural. The New School Art Collection, New York.

In 1935, Egas completed two smaller murals for the New School, *Harvesting Food in Ecuador* and *Harvesting Food in North America*, which contrast agricultural practices in the two locations. As Greet has pointed out, these murals are distinguished by the way they "insert Indigenism into the larger body of proletarian imagery that was emerging throughout the Americas."[8] The murals became an integral component of the stark modernist design of the Twelfth Street building, and when they were unveiled in 1935, they were praised by a newspaper critic for meeting, "in an unusually satisfying way, the demands of modern decoration."[9] The murals were installed on the mezzanine floor in the Caroline Tilden Bacon Room, designed by Paul Lester Wiener, a German-born U.S. modernist architect and urban planner who had applied the theory of Raumlösung, or spatial solutions, to the project. Through the use of color, light, and modular space, Wiener broke down a long tunnel-like area into two smaller units and installed the paintings on the east and west walls.[10] Wiener's simple yet elegant design, with its sense of structure and use of pliable walls, respected and complemented Urban's building and continued the New School's association with international modernism. The surprising marriage of modernist interior design with pictorial indigenism was characteristic of the eclectic tenor of 1930s New York and Latin American modernism.

In the two later murals, Egas appropriated the language, style, and subject matter of Mexican muralism, but he also adapted to the specific spatial and ideological concerns of mural painting in America. By 1935, Egas had been in New York for eight years and must have been aware of the muralists' various large-scale projects in the United States; these works had garnered widespread attention and, in some cases, infamy, as in the destruction of Rivera's mural for Rockefeller Center [see Edward J. Sullivan's essay, page 202]. Egas's Ecuador panel borrows specific poses and figural types from Diego Rivera's murals, in particular *Sugar Cane*, a portable fresco that Rivera painted on site at the Museum of Modern Art and Egas would have seen, and its source panel, *Slavery in the Sugar Mill* (at the Palacio de Cortes, Cuernavaca, Mexico). However, unlike Rivera's murals, which U.S. audiences often considered politically radical, Egas's subject matter was appropriate to the room's function as a space for quiet social gatherings. While proletarian labor is a staple of Marxist and Social Realist iconography, Egas's images of rural laborers working in harmony on the land produced a calming effect rather than a provocative one. Egas may have been trying to avoid the lukewarm critical response to Orozco's New School murals, which focused on the cycle's failure to conform to the academic tradition of mural decoration. Indeed, critics praised Egas's *Harvesting* murals as exemplars of decorative design, focusing on their "closely knit design," "warm harmony of colors," "rhythmic lines," and "architectural harmony."[11]

Mural painting was not Egas's only major contribution to the New School. In 1929, he also was one of the first to teach studio art at the school. More significantly, in 1932 he helped found the art workshops, which he would direct for thirty years, until his death in 1962. Controlling the character of the program, he had a profound influence on generations of students who passed through the doors of the New School. "Interdisciplinary studio courses in the visual arts directed toward the professionally minded student,"[12] the art workshops were the studio art component of the adult education division. The "workshops" followed the pedagogical model of the Bauhaus, the famous and influential German modernist school of art and design. Egas began by teaching a workshop in modern art, which focused on developing individuality rather than imparting specific techniques. By 1938 and for almost twenty-five years afterward, he taught oil painting, drawing, murals, and frescoes. The mural component of the course stressed materials, composition, and the relationship to architecture, elements that critics had praised in his own mural practice. Although he made few changes to this fundamental painting/drawing course over the years, Egas also co-taught in 1947–48 and 1950–51 advanced painting and composition with U.S. painter Robert Gwathmey, whose work focused on depictions of the South, specifically African American life and the daily existence of farmers and workers. Although by the 1940s and 1950s Egas had shifted styles from indigenism to Surrealism,

Gwathmey painted within a socially engaged modernist idiom, as Egas had in the 1930s. Egas and Gwathmey restricted their courses to full-time students, who had to submit examples of work and be interviewed for admission. The course description emphasized that "two painters of widely divergent backgrounds" were combining their efforts. While Egas never joined the leftist ranks as Gwathmey did (he was a committed Communist), the two artists still had much in common, creating local American imagery with a modern vocabulary.

In addition to his own teaching, Egas's stewardship of the art workshops brought great talent to the school, turning it into a program that was recognized internationally as a locus of vanguard modernism. In 1957, Hans Simon, in the catalogue introduction for an exhibition of Egas's paintings at the New School, said that "this department is a testimonial to his efforts. He built it up and brought it to its present significance."[13] And in the catalogue commemorating Egas's death, Julian E. Levi, who succeeded him as director, said that his predecessor "was proud of the faculty he assembled over a period of thirty years. By glancing at the list of those who taught here, it is evident that his sense of quality was extraordinary."[14] The list of artists Egas hired as faculty at the New School is remarkable not only because of their later renown—Berenice Abbott, Lisette Model, Stuart Davis, and Yasuo Kuniyoshi are just a few of the best-known artists—but also because of the plurality of styles and approaches they represented. Antonio Frasconi, who taught at the New School in the 1950s, remembers that Egas's choice of teachers coincided with his belief that art was about being true to oneself, no matter what the current fashion, and that art functioned as a mirror of life. To Frasconi, Egas was "a personality close to the cultural *ambiente* of New York."[15]

Although a humanist perspective and a socially engaged modernism may have connected most of these artists, the New School faculty represented a pronounced heterogeneity of styles, from figurative modernism to Surrealism. And even those artists who practiced realism rejected the nationalistic tendencies of U.S. regionalism. Rutkoff and Scott describe the artists who taught at the New School as "outsiders" —Jews, immigrants, refugees, American provincials of modest means—who had come to New York to make a name for themselves.[16] While many faculty members went on to success or critical acclaim during or after their tenure at the New School, several influential artists set up shop during Egas's directorship, including the Swiss-born Surrealist artist Kurt Seligmann, who taught etching and printing in 1951–52, and the Abstract Expressionist Richard Pousette-Dart, who taught painting in 1958. Most significant in the advancement of the New School as a center for avant-garde activities, however, was the establishment of Alexey Brodovitch's Design Laboratory (1941–59) and Stanley William Hayter's Atelier 17 (1939–50), both extremely influential workshops that had a strong impact on the postwar generation of U.S. artists.

Diego Rivera (1886–1957). *Sugar Cane*, 1930.
Fresco, 57⅛ x 94⅛ in. (145.1 x 239.1 cm).
Philadelphia Museum of Art, Gift of Mr. and Mrs.
Herbert Cameron Morris, 1943. © 2010 Banco de
México Diego Rivera Frida Kahlo Museums Trust,
Mexico, D.F. / Artists Rights Society (ARS). The
Philadelphia Museum of Art / Art Resource, NY.

Diego Rivera (1886–1957). *Slavery in the Sugar Mill*,
1929–30. Mural, Palacio de Cortes, Cuernavaca,
Mexico. 171¼ x 111 in. (435 x 282 cm). © 2010
Banco de México Diego Rivera Frida Kahlo Museums
Trust, Mexico, D.F. / Artists Rights Society (ARS).
Schalkwijk / Art Resource, NY.

Robert Gwathmey (1903–1988). *Singing and
Mending*, 1948. Oil on canvas. 25³⁄₁₆ x 30⅛ in.
(64 x 76.5 cm). Philadelphia Museum of Art, Gift
of Edna S. Beron, 1984. Art © Estate of Robert
Gwathmey ∕ Licensed by VAGA, New York, NY. The
Philadelphia Museum of Art ∕ Art Resource, NY.

Furthermore, during Egas's tenure as director, a distinguished art history faculty included renowned scholars such as Rene d'Harnoncourt, who taught "The Arts of Mexico" in 1935–36, and Meyer Schapiro, whose lectures on modern painting were "one of the key points of entry into the life of art in New York," according to art critic Hilton Kramer. "Those lectures, always crowded with artists and writers, were dazzling performances that left one in no doubt that the great work of the modern painters stood at the very center of life."[17]

In the midst of this dynamic and vibrant art scene was a stable of Latin American (and Hispanic) artists who helped to make the New School an icon of modernity and progressive thinking. The Spaniard José de Creeft taught sculpture from 1933 to 1939 and then again from 1944 to 1970; the Mexican photographer and printmaker Emilio Amero taught lithography from 1936 to 1938 and then painting and drawing in the summer of 1963; the Cuban painter Mario Carreño taught painting from 1946 to 1951, taking a leave of absence in 1948 to Chile and Argentina; one of Carreño's students, the Puerto Rican painter Julio Rosado del Valle, taught painting in 1947 and 1948; the Argentinian-born Uruguayan printmaker Antonio Frasconi taught "Color, Black and White Woodcuts" from 1951 to 1958; and the Colombian sculptor Edgar Negret was at the New School in 1959 and 1960. It should be noted, however, that Egas did not choose artists based on nationality. Even though many of them dealt with native subject matter, they did not necessarily identify themselves as Latin American artists, but rather were part of the broader cosmopolitan cultural art scene of New York.

Some of these artists brought experimental techniques or media to the New School. Amero opened a new lithographic studio at the school and taught lithography, but as an experimental photographer and filmmaker who had worked with photograms and other avant-garde techniques beginning in 1930, he might have introduced montage, superimposition, and modernist fragmentation to his classes. Distinct from his colleagues in Mexico, many of whom took up indigenist themes and espoused a state-sponsored cultural nationalism in the wake of the Mexican Revolution, Amero instead turned to abstraction and a Machine Age aesthetic. In 1935, the year before he began teaching at the New School, he exhibited drawings, watercolors, oils, lithographs, photographs, and photograms at the Julien Levy gallery in New York, famous for its display and promotion of European Surrealism and avant-garde photography. Although Amero later took up Mexican themes, in New York his production focused on innovative photographic experimentation.

In the spring of 1951, Carreño revamped the standard oil painting course and introduced New School students to painting with lacquer. An experimental medium, lacquer was famously utilized by Siqueiros, who used it with New York artists in his experimental workshop on Fourteenth Street in 1936. Carreño had first worked

with the medium in 1937 and was reintroduced to it when he assisted Siqueiros
on a mural the Mexican painted for the foyer of Carreño's home in Cuba in 1943.
The description for his course, "Oil and Lacquer Painting, Drawing, and Composition" states:

> Lacquer, commonly known as "Duco," makes a very rich texture. Its quick
> drying properties permit finishing a picture in one session and layers of paint
> can be applied endlessly without damaging the picture. Moreover it allows the
> addition of foreign objects to the painted surface, which thus acquires relief. Its
> durability and permanence have been tested under rough outdoor conditions.
> It was first employed in the fine arts by the Mexican muralists.[18]

Carreño's use of the medium at this historical juncture is significant. Although he
was part of the second wave of the Cuban *vanguardia* who applied Cubist and
Surrealist approaches to local themes, by the 1950s Carreño was working primarily
in geometric abstraction. His class thus formed a bridge between the experimental
work with lacquer that Siqueiros introduced in the 1930s and the very different use
of the material in the 1960s by, for example, Minimalist artists.

Other artists who taught at the New School continued in the tradition of socially
aware modernism that had defined the institution from its early days. In the midst
of the Cold War, leftist artists such as Frasconi made woodcuts that conveyed social
commentary. Figurative yet abstracted, and concerned with the human condition,
Frasconi's prints updated a longstanding printmaking tradition in the Americas.
Starting out as a political caricaturist in the weekly publications *Marcha* and *La
Línea Maginot* in Montevideo, Frasconi arrived in New York having already been
influenced by sources as diverse as German Expressionism, the Mexican muralists, the
Taller de la Gráfica Popular, and Japanese woodcuts. Coming from an underdeveloped
country, Frasconi said that "painting was not an option" for him. But woodcut is an
inherently practical and democratic medium, and anyone can pick up a piece of wood
and print a woodcut by making a rubbing. And by continuing to make woodcuts even
within the cultural milieu of New York, Frasconi followed his artistic as well as his ideological imperatives. As the artist would tell his students, the woodcut was only a tool:
"If you're an artist you can do anything with any medium. . . . [I]t's about having something to say."[19]

Camilio Egas is not well known today, but he was very active in the artistic
milieu of 1930s New York and earned significant critical acclaim during his lifetime.[20]
He was a major figure in pictorial indigenism, and in New York his Surrealist compositions were often well received by critics.[21] But perhaps his most important contribution to international modernism came in the unique mix of artists he brought
together for the faculty of the New School's art workshops. As a whole, the artists

Emilio Amero (1901–1976). *Untitled* (Hands), 1932. Photogram, gelatin silver print. The Art Institute of Chicago, Julien Levy Collection, Gift of Jean Levy and the Estate of Julien Levy. Photograph by Greg Harris. Reproduction, The Art Institute of Chicago.

who taught at the New School embodied an intermingling of ideas and aesthetics from the United States, Europe, and Latin America; in so doing, they "enlarged the cultural horizons of the entire institution"—and of New York City in turn.[22] It is thanks to Egas and the diversity of American artists who taught at the New School that the university earned its reputation as an institution of progressive aesthetic modernism.

NOTES

I am grateful to Edward J. Sullivan for commissioning this essay and for his consistent support and inspiration. In addition, I have relied on the expertise and generosity of many individuals in compiling information for this essay, including Carmen Hendershott, Librarian, Fogelman Library, New School University; Jenny Swadosh, Assistant Archivist, Kellen Archives, Parsons The New School for Design; and Rafael Diazcasas, Marie Difilippantonio, Michele Greet, Miguel Frasconi, and Antonio Frasconi.

1. William B. Scott and Peter M. Rutkoff, *New York Modern: The Arts and The City* (Baltimore: Johns Hopkins University Press, 1999), xvii.

2. Ibid., xix.

3. Peter M. Rutkoff and William B. Scott, *New School: A History of The New School for Social Research* (New York: The Free Press/Macmillan, 1986), xi and xii; the following paragraph is indebted to Rutkoff and Scott's study.

4. Ibid., xii

5. Diane Miliotes, "The Murals at the New School for Social Research (1930–31)," in *José Clemente Orozco in the United States, 1927–1934*, ed. Renato González Mello and Diane Miliotes (Hanover, NH: Hood Museum of Art, 2002).

6. Michele Greet, *Beyond National Identity: Pictorial Indigenism as a Modernist Strategy in Andean Art, 1920–1960* (University Park: Penn State University Press, 2009), 93–95; the following paragraphs on Egas rely heavily on Greet's research.

7. Egas cited in Henry Laville, "Algo sobre arte," *El Comercio* (Lima) (January 1933), quoted in Greet, *Beyond National Identity*, 95.

8. Greet, *Beyond National Identity*, 99

9. Carlyle Burrows, "Native and Foreign Art—A Museum Show," *New York Herald Tribune*, June 10, 1935; clipping in New School Arts and Public Programs Collection, Anna-Maria and Stephen Kellen Archives, Parsons The New School for Design, New York.

10. M. U., "Egas's Murals at New School," *The New York Sun*, June 7, 1935, 14; clipping in New School Arts and Public Programs Collection, Anna-Maria and Stephen Kellen Archives, Parsons The New School for Design, New York.

11. Ibid. and "Space Theory Well Applied," *World Telegram*, June 8, 1935.

12. Julian E. Levi, "Correspondence," *Julian E. Levi Papers, 1846–1981* (Washington, DC: Smithsonian Institution, 1962), microfilm reels 483–86, cited in Greet, *Beyond National Identity*, 320, n. 18.

13. Hans Simon, "Introduction," *Egas: New Paintings*, exhibition catalogue (December 2–17, 1957), New School; Egas folder, Fogelman Library, New School University, courtesy of Carmen Hendershott.

14. *Camilo Egas: Commemorative Exhibition* (New York: New School for Social Research, 1963), unpaginated.

15. Antonio Frasconi, interview with the author, September 17, 2009.

16. Rutkoff and Scott, *New School*, 61–62.
Significant non-Latino faculty members during the period under discussion included the following (the years they taught at the school and the field or courses they taught are provided when known):
U.S. photographer Berenice Abbott (1935–1950s), photography
U.S. photographer Lisette Model (1950s), "Small Camera in Photography Today"; "Photographing
    New York and its People"
U.S. abstract painter Stuart Davis (1934–50), "Modern Color-Space Composition in Drawing and
    Painting," beginning and advanced (students and professionals)
Spanish sculptor José de Creeft, sculpture
Lithuanian-born U.S. sculptor William Zorach (1936–40)
German painter Kurt Roesch (1933–36), painting
U.S. painter Yasuo Kuniyoshi (1934–50)
U.S. sculptor Seymour Lipton (1939–65)

Swiss/U.S. painter and printmaker Kurt Seligmann (1951–52), etching and printing
U.S. printmaker Robert Blackburn (1951–52), lithography
U.S. painter Richard Pousette-Dart (1958), painting
Russian/U.S. photographer and designer Alexey Brodovitch (1941–59), "Art Applied to Graphic
  Journalism, War Propaganda, Advertising"
British painter and printmaker Stanley William Hayter (1944–50)
Belgian Charles Leirens, photography

17. Hilton Kramer, editor of *The New Criterion*, quoted in "Meyer Schapiro, Art Historian and Critic, Dies at 91," *New York Times*, March 4, 1996.

18. *New School Bulletin*, spring 1951, courtesy Carmen Hendershott, Fogelman Library, New School University.

19. Frasconi, interview with the author.

20. María Helena Barrera-Agarwa, "La Saga vital y crítica de Camilo Egas en Nueva York," *Ecuadorian Council of Culture Magazine* (January 2009). I am grateful to Michele Greet for making me aware of this source.

21. "The Art of Camilo Egas," *World Telegram*, November 23, 1946.

22. Rutkoff and Scott, *New School*, 63.

BEFORE MAMBO TIME:

New York Latin Music in the Early Decades (1925–45)

JUAN FLORES

In the summer of 1929, on the eve of the Great Depression, New York's Latino neighborhoods were filled with the sounds of "Lamento Borincano," a newly recorded song by the Puerto Rican composer Rafael Hernández. From record stores and tenement windows sounded the haunting melody and mournful lyrics of that classic "lament" to the fate of poor migrants in the face of economic crisis, and it immediately struck a chord not only with the "Borincanos" (Puerto Ricans), but with Latino working people throughout the hemisphere. Indeed, "Lamento Borincano" has been called the anthem of Latino migrants and "the first Latin American protest song."[1] There are by now literally hundreds of versions, in countless musical styles and from nearly all Latin American countries, often with an adjusted title: "Lamento Argentino" or "Lamento Cubano." And it was composed and recorded in Latino New York by a young Puerto Rican musician who went on to write more than two thousand songs and become one of the preeminent Latin American composers of all time.

The following year, 1930, saw the initial recording and immediate popularity of another historic song, "El Manisero" ("The Peanut Vendor"), as played by the famed Don Azpiazú band, the Havana Casino Orchestra, with lead vocalist Antonio Machín (and, of some historical note, with the young Mario Bauzá playing trumpet). This contagious tune, with its seductive swaying rhythm and playful double entendres, also captured audiences of the time, to the point that it even initiated a decade-long obsession, the so-called "rhumba craze" of the 1930s, as it took hold among audiences of all backgrounds in the United States and around the world. Like "Lamento Borincano," "The Peanut Vendor" generated countless versions in subsequent years, notably those by the Trio Matamoros, Louis Armstrong, and Duke Ellington, among many others. "El Manisero" was not actually a "rhumba" (the misspelling is indicative), but rather a *son pregón*, meaning a Cuban *son* based on the call of a street vendor (*pregón*). Such technicalities aside, the appeal of the song is never in question: It is sheer entertainment in tune with the bustling popular culture of the times; indeed, it was first introduced to American audiences at its premiere on Broadway earlier that year. Antonio Machín, whose irresistible voice surely had much to do with the song's feverish reception and who went on to spend many years in New York with his influential group Cuarteto Machín, was sometimes referred to as "el Rudy Valentino cubano."

Machito's Afro-Cubans, ca. 1945. Photographer unknown. Courtesy of Graciela Pérez.

Left to right: Machito, singer Graciela, and musical director Mario Bauzá.

Don Azpiazú's Havana Casino Orchestra, ca. 1930s.
Photographer unknown. Courtesy of Raul Azpiazú.

Once again, though it was already popular in Cuba as sung by the illustrious female vocalist Rita Muntaner, the song got its historic start in New York City.

Two songs, both longtime standards of the Latin American repertoire, and both recordings from the same time and place—Nueva York circa 1930—but with diametrically opposed relations to the New York Latino community and its cultural presence. Of course both attest to the growing size of that population, and to the powerful role of the nascent New York–based recording industry in defining popular musical taste, not only among Latinos but also about Latinos in the eyes (and ears) of the broader public. And both, interestingly, are about economic transactions, whether the produce brought by the solitary peasant to the desolate town market or the sale of paper cones of peanuts in the shell. But while "Lamento Borincano" is a narrative commentary on the crushing social conditions facing the Latino and Latin American masses and has remained popular mainly among Latinos, "El Manisero" was the first crossover hit, providing Latinos and non-Latinos with entertainment and diversion in the face of that decidedly unpleasant reality. Rafael Hernández's signature song evokes real-life suffering and struggle, disillusion, pride, and nostalgia for a distant homeland, while the peanut vendor's cry is a playful, passing serenade, an invitation to sensual delights that is dependent on an obliviousness toward the misery of the everyday world. One is grounded in Puerto Rican experience and musical sensibilities; the other is unmistakably of Cuban vintage.

Here is a striking duality of style and meaning, a contrast richly illustrative of the wide-ranging divergences in the musical, cultural, and social experiences of New York's Latino communities over the decades. The implicit class, ethnic, and ideological differences between these two early Latino megahits may perhaps be traced back to those evident in the earliest concentrations of Cubans and Puerto Ricans in New York in the later nineteenth century. It was a community that expressed strong solidarity in the face of lingering Spanish colonial rule, and comprised the professional and intellectual elite on the one hand and the far more numerous artisan workers on the other. Bernardo Vega, the foremost chronicler of a century of Latino experience in New York (1850–1950), offers a detailed account of these complex class interactions in his invaluable memoir, which includes numerous references to musical and other cultural events of those years.[2] During the late nineteenth and early twentieth centuries, in the decades prior to the advent of commercial recording, established genres like the *danzón*, the *danza*, the bolero, and the *guaracha* enjoyed broad appeal across class and ethnic lines. But it was the former two, generally associated with the middle-class and more elite sectors, and the periodic performances by touring operatic and orchestral troupes, that drew the most attention and accolades from the Spanish-language press of the time and were thus most generally identified with the tastes of the entire community. Vega makes no mention of more directly popular forms like *guajira* and *jíbaro* music (genres like *décima*, *punto*, *seis*, and *aguinaldo* stemming from the Cuban and Puerto Rican peasant or country repertoires), or of the Afro-Cuban and Afro-Puerto Rican forms of *rumba* and *son*, or *bomba* and *plena*, though there can be little doubt that those styles did carry appeal and were played among the artisans and working people who made up the majority of the exile populations. Songs with social themes were of course very widespread among these highly politicized communities, with the many patriotic, anticolonial compositions in a range of musical and poetic genres carrying appeal among both professional and working-class groups, though the abundant repertoire of proletarian hymns and calls-to-battle remained exclusive to the more impoverished and less formally educated among the militant activists of the period.

But even prior to the beginning of studio recordings in the mid-1920s, the tango rage of the 1910s introduced the attraction of commercial and exotic offerings among American audiences, and helped establish a gulf between supposedly "Latin" music and dance styles and the tastes of the Latino community itself. The tango did of course enjoy a long life of immense popularity among Latinos of all nationalities, especially as part of the repertoire (along with the bolero) of the traditional small groups featuring guitar, bongo, and voice, like Rafael Hernández's Trio Borinquen, the earliest of them, or, beginning in the 1930s, such revered groups as the Trio Matamoros, the Trio Mayarí, the Cuarteto Marcano, and the Cuarteto Flores. But the tango that landed in New York and the rest of the United States around 1914 was strictly an entertainment and commercial package, rich in exoticist allure but far removed from its humble and African-descended roots in the underworld of turn-of-the-century Buenos Aires. Instead, the tango notoriously came to New York by way of Paris and Broadway, and its earliest practitioners described it as a "descendant of the eighteenth-century minuet" and as "courtly and artistic." Gone was its derivation from the prodigiously influential *habanera* of Afro-Cuban roots, and its relation to ragtime and the beginnings of jazz. Again, though representative of "Latino" musical style for the broad listening and dancing public, the tango of that first Latin dance fad bore scant if any relation to New York's Latino community. It was an early example of what music journalist and historian John Storm Roberts called "the Latin tinge," in his pathbreaking 1979 book.[3]

Far more relevant to the community's musical realities, and still preceding the advent of recording, was the remarkable experience of Rafael Hernández and other Afro-Puerto Rican musicians during World War I. As recounted by Ruth Glasser in *My Music Is My Flag: Puerto Rican Musicians in Their New York Communities* (1997), Hernández and his fellow musicians from the island were recruited by celebrated African American bandleader James Reese Europe into the army's most prestigious marching band, the all-Black 369th Infantry's "Hellfighters" Band; they proceeded to tour with them in France to huge acclaim among European audiences.[4]

At war's end, Hernández and some of the most prominent and promising Puerto Rican musicians of the early century settled in New York, in part because of the swelling ranks of the Puerto Rican migrant community (especially after the decreeing of U.S. citizenship in that same year, 1917) and also because of the growing attraction of the budding recording industry based in New York. The composer of "Lamento Borincano," who went on to become the most famous of all Puerto Rican musicians, eventually lived in Mexico and Cuba before returning in his later years to his beloved Puerto Rico. But he composed many of his most celebrated songs in New York, and in 1927 his sister Victoria opened the city's first and best-known Latin music store on Madison Avenue and 114th Street in El Barrio. Through the efforts and accomplishments of his sister—his best-known musical group, Cuarteto Victoria, was named in her honor—and because of his active role in the musical life of the time, Rafael Hernández's name is identified in a direct way with the New York Latino community and its music. His repertoire included many tangos, but unlike the tango craze and later the "rhumba craze" of the 1930s, his music and that of the many other prominent musicians to settle in New York during those years stands as a direct expression of community life, including that of its less privileged but quite numerous inhabitants.

The first studio recordings of Cuban and Puerto Rican popular dance styles date from 1926–27. Of greatest historical importance were the *son* sextets from Havana, notably the Sexteto Habanero and the Sexteto Nacional led by the major composer of early *son*, Ignacio Piñero, and the groups organized by Puerto Rican vocalist and bandleader Manuel Jiménez, also known as Canario, best known for their *plenas*. Canario ranged widely, having been formed in the traditions of bolero and *música jíbara*, and served as the original vocalist of Trio Borinquen. Canario's most significant recording was none other than the June 14, 1929, session of "Lamento Borincano," an historic occasion that also was the debut recording by Pedro Ortíz Dávila, the young Puerto Rican commonly known as "Davilita" who had arrived but a year earlier and who went on to become the premier vocalist in New York Latin and Spanish Caribbean music through the 1930s and early 1940s.

Though the initial recordings of Puerto Rican and Cuban music were made at the same time, and though by 1930 the Puerto Rican population in New York had swelled to more than double that of the Cubans, the musical styles and presence of the latter group would eclipse those of the former, right down to the present day. *Son cubano* became the stylistic trunk of the main trends and eras to follow, from conga and mambo to cha-cha, Latin jazz, *pachanga*, boogaloo, and salsa, and even became the best-known and preferred style of many Puerto Rican musicians and audiences themselves. Native Puerto Rican styles, on the other hand, from *danza* to *bomba*, *plena*, and *música jíbara*, never really transcended their national and ethnic origins in a massive way, and were only in rare instances incorporated into those more widely diffused

Cuarteto Victoria, n.d. Photographer unknown. Salon Rafael Hernández, Interamerican University, Puerto Rico.

Left to right: Davilita, Rafael Rodríquez, Francisco "Paquito" López Cruz, and Rafael Hernández.

Canario and his group, 1931. Photographer unknown. Courtesy of Pedro Malavet Vega, Ponce, Puerto Rico.

Left to right, in white shirts: Peyín Serrano, Pedro Marcano, Francisco "Paquito" López Cruz, José Armengol Díaz, and Ramón Quirós. Manuel "Canario" Jiménez is in suit and tie.

and commercially viable genres of Latin music. Thus, in the 1930s and early 1940s it was the successes of Don Azpiazú's Havana Casino Orchestra and then of the highly influential bandleader and impresario Xavier Cugat, who came to New York around 1920 from Spain via Cuba, that brought Latin music in its watered-down Cuban form to mainstream American audiences on Broadway and in Hollywood, and for years at New York's Waldorf Astoria Hotel and other upscale ballrooms of the time.

The familiar narrative of Latin music history tells of this ascendancy of the tango-"Manisero" lineage of the "Latin tinge," Cuban-based dance music diluted for the entertainment of largely white, middle-class, and non-Latino audiences, in the ballroom, in films, on the radio, and in the most saleable recordings. The focus is on the so-called downtown scene, the strongly Cuban-influenced, tropicalized face of Latin culture, which was clearly where the money and the glamour were to be found in Latin music and entertainment of the day. It reached its peak in the late 1940s and 1950s with Desi Arnaz, the most visible of all the musically inclined sons of Cuba, playing Mr. Babalú in New York and Los Angeles clubs and Ricky Ricardo on the wildly popular television show *I Love Lucy*. Cuban American novelist Oscar Hijuelos attempted to capture this version of the New York Latin music scene in his 1990 Pulitzer Prize–winning novel *The Mambo Kings Play Songs of Love*.[5] It is indicative of the Latino racial and class experience that Desi Arnaz's well-known identity as Mr. Babalú was really a cover version, a white-face rendition of the signature act of the great Miguelito Valdéz, the towering Afro-Cuban vocalist. This outright appropriation was of course only the most glaring instance of the racial exclusions and white-skin privilege at work in the world of Latin music in that era. Countless are the stories of clubs restricting their bands and audiences to light-skinned musicians (flyers would actually include the words "para raza blanca"), and bandleaders went along with such segregationist policies. Mario Bauzá had many memories of prejudice against Black Latino musicians, and Bobby Capó recalled vividly how Xavier Cugat refused his services, saying, "What a pity you are so dark."

None of which is to say that the "downtown" clubs rejected music of quality and authenticity. A major venue was the Havana Madrid Night Club, which opened on 51st Street and Broadway in 1938. The opening act itself was of some historic note, in that it featured the renowned female *son* group, Grupo Anacaona, with famous lead vocalist Graciela, Machito's sister, and accompanied by the legendary vocalist for the Sexteto Nacional, Alfredito Valdéz. The Havana Madrid remained a key venue for the "rhumba craze," its combination of forceful Afro-Cuban dance music and the usual "tropical" and "Spanish" ephemera lending it a quality all its own in Latin New York history. The Chateau Madrid played a similar magnetic role beginning in the early 1950s, its house band led by the well-known conguero Cándido Camero and featuring musical luminaries, like the illustrious Mexican singer Toña la Negra, from all over

Xavier Cugat and Carmen Miranda, ca. 1940s.
Photographer unknown. BMI Archives.

Desi Arnaz, ca. 1939. Photographer unknown. BMI
Archives.

Flyer for Columbus Day dance organized by the
Club Azteca, 1932. Jesús Colón Papers, Archives
of the Puerto Rican Diaspora, Centro de Estudios
Puertorriqueños, Hunter College, CUNY. Benigo
Giboyeaux for the Estate of Jesús Colón and the
Communist Party of the United States of America.

The words "para raza blanca" appear at the bottom
of the flyer.

GRAN BAILE
ORGANIZADO POR EL
CLUB AZTECA
PARA CELEBRAR LA
FIESTA DE LÀ RAZA
a beneficio de los damnificados de
PUERTO RICO
EN EL BALL ROOM DEL HOTEL PENNSYLVANIA
CALLE 33 Y SEPTIMA AVENIDA
Sabado 15 de Octubre de 1932
A LAS 9 P. M.

2 - ORQUESTAS - 2

ADMISION:
Caballeros: adelantado $1.00 . . . . Damás $1.00
"   en la Taquilla . . . $1.50

Con autorizacion del Puerto Rico Hurricane Relief Committee.
No es requirito traje de etiqueta.   Para raza blanca.

Tickets de venta en: Librería Cervantes - 62 Lenox Avenue; Fotografía Torres - 224 West 116th Street;
Restaurant El Rancho - 57 Lenox Avenue; Constance Hand Laundry 104 W. 111th Street y en los princi-
pales establecimientos de Manhattan, Brooklyn, Queens, Bronx y Richmond.
Triangle Printing Company, 9 West 19th St., New York.

Latin America and the Caribbean. These two early venues, of course, anticipate the unparalleled fame of the Palladium Ballroom.

The "uptown" scene, on the other hand, comprised Puerto Rican, Cuban, and other Latino musicians and audiences more organically linked to the neighborhoods and communities that became increasingly Puerto Rican working class over the decades. Ironically, while the "rhumba craze" was in full swing, and New York Latin music was achieving commercial success and a level of public visibility not commensurate with its generally negligible musical significance, the more down-home music of the city's expanding Latino communities was actually experiencing a veritable renaissance of talent and production. Though the prolific Afro-Cuban community could certainly boast the unquestioned importance of such pre-1940s greats as flutist Alberto Socarrás, pioneering bandleader Mario Bauzá, and many others, the foremost Puerto Rican musicians of that period in all styles and genres came to live, compose, perform, and record in New York. Alongside Rafael Hernández, the major composers of Puerto Rican popular song, from Pedro Flores and Plácido Acevedo to Noro Morales and Bobby Capó, were all in New York between 1925 and 1945. Together they produced thousands of boleros, *sons*, and *guarachas*, many of which live on, their authorship often unknown, in the songbook of twentieth-century Puerto Rican and Latin American music.

In contrast to the show-business music of the downtown variety, and even to the generally light lyrics and ephemeral themes of the mambos and cha-chas of the subsequent generation, much of this voluminous, primarily Puerto Rican output of the

1930s consists of songs, generally progressive and anticolonial in tenor, about Puerto Rican and Latino politics, migration, and communities in New York City during the Depression years. In featuring themes of patriotism and nostalgia, making do in a hostile environment, and in some cases even an ironic appreciation for some of the benefits of modern urban life, this expansive repertoire makes it possible to appreciate the diverse "representation of New York City in Latin music," as ethnomusicologist Peter Manuel demonstrates in a helpful study of song lyrics.[6] Like Rafael Hernández, Pedro Flores and Plácido Acevedo wrote and performed scores of songs with strong social content, as well as infectious good humor in vernacular idiom, which have remained dear to the hearts of Latinos everywhere ever since. Pedro Flores's song "Despedida," for example, a moving response to the drafting of young Puerto Ricans to fight in World War II, was recorded in 1939 by the Cuarteto Flores with Daniel Santos in the lead vocal, and became the biggest hit of the period and another Latin American standard.

Hernández, Flores, Acevedo, and many other prominent musicians, like Davilita, Augusto Coen, and Pedro ("Piquito") Marcano, made up a rich and varied musical community with its own venues in East Harlem, the Bronx, and Brooklyn, most notably the magnetic Park Palace dance hall on Fifth Avenue and 110th Street in Manhattan. The "uptown" scene also had its own distinctive, locally based audience more savvy of the musical idioms at the center of Caribbean and Latin American traditions than the audiences of the flashier, more touristic downtown clubs. Its repertoire was not primarily made up of the indigenous Puerto Rican forms, such as *música jíbara*, *bomba*, or *plena*, nor the more experimental innovations of musicians like Socarrás or Bauzá or the Puerto Rican Juan Tizol in their seminal roles in premier African American jazz bands. Rather, their foremost though unheralded achievement was to bring more broadly pan-Latino genres like bolero and *guaracha* to their highest level of mastery, and to relate them to the lived social realities of their peoples and communities. In subsequent decades, and especially in the 1950s, the "uptown" repertoire expands to include a renaissance of *música jíbara* by some of its foremost practitioners, like the great Ramito, La Calandria, and Moralito, many of whom came to live in New York as part of the massive postwar migration; they had been preceded by Chuito el de Cayey, who already enjoyed immense popularity in New York in the later 1930s and 1940s. During the 1950s, the working-class Latino community delighted in universally popular trios like the Trio Los Panchos and Trio Vegabajeño, as well as in down-home, lively, and often jocular merengues as written, performed, and recorded by the most popular exponents of the Trujillo years, New York–based Dominican musicians of the stature of Dioris Valadares, Alberto Beltrán, and Angel Viloria.

But this story is getting ahead of itself in tracing forward this generally marginalized thread of the more familiar narrative of New York's Latin music. Despite its

headway into the mainstream of North American musical culture and the robust
volume and quality of musical production and consumption, the pre-1945 chapter of
Latin music history in New York is all but overshadowed in relative significance by
the transformative developments in the years to come. Indeed, it is not unreasonable
to regard 1945 as the propitious beginning of that cultural history, rather than as the
"end" of a war and a generation, and that earlier period, with the quaint but sometimes awkward fit between immigrant music and new social experiences, more as a
prelude to the main event. For when Mario Bauzá, percussionist Chano Pozo, and the
all-time greatest of Latin orchestras, Machito and his Afro-Cubans, link up with master jazz pioneers of the stature of Dizzy Gillespie and Charlie Parker, and together
mesmerize audiences in venues from the historic Palladium Ballroom to Carnegie
Hall, we come to witness a moment of artistic and cultural innovation perhaps unsur-
passed in popular music history.

This special postwar encounter, which coincided with the massive influx of
Puerto Ricans from the island, not only witnessed the emergence of the first major
Latin music styles, mambo and Cubop, that were actually created and popularized
in the United States. Beyond that, in those pivotal years the historical narrative
shifted, because some of the most seasoned and boldly creative musicians of the time
succeeded in solidifying an inextricable intersection, or "marriage of love" as Machito
called it, between Afro-Latin and African American music that would set the cross-
cultural paradigm for Latin music ever since. This "revolution" occurred, and perhaps
could only occur, in New York City; it is at the same time profoundly reflective of

Latino life in the city as the Latino presence approached a maturity approximating what it would become in our own time. When talk is of New York Latin music, the post-1945 mambo era appears to be when it all got going; then, with the *pachanga*, boogaloo, and salsa of the subsequent generation, Latino musical roots finally struck deep in the fertile soil of the New York diaspora.

From the present-day vantage point of the salsa and post-salsa generations, it thus takes a stretch of historical memory and imagination to hearken back to the days of Rafael Hernández and the first-ever recording of "The Peanut Vendor," and the richly atmospheric but old-fashioned sounds of the many trios, cuartetos, and big bands of the earlier decades. Happily, though, creative history is not about erasure and discarding but, rather, attests to continuities and reinvention. "Lamento Borincano" has enjoyed dozens of salsa versions, and has even made its appearance in hip hop, merengue, reggaeton, and scores of other more recent musical styles and formats. Songs by Pedro Flores continue to inspire modern-day dance and Latin jazz bands, even boldly experimental ones like the Fort Apache Band and Grupo Folklórico y Experimental Nuevayorquino. And perhaps most memorably of all, and resonating through the decades of Latin music history, there is the legendary Afro-Cuban singer Graciela, whose career extends back to 1930s Cuba, where she sang with the world famous Grupo Anacaona, and whose renown as the most distinguished Latina vocalist is rivaled only by that of her celebrated compatriot Celia Cruz. Until her recent passing in April 2010, Machito's sister and longtime vocalist in his historic orchestra was still singing and making honorary appearances, a vibrant Afro-Latina New Yorker well into her nineties. What better testament to the endurance and resilience of Latino culture in Nueva York through the decades and generations of constantly changing musical temperament.

NOTES

This text is dedicated to the memory of Graciela. The author would like to thank Harry Sepúlveda, René López, and Henry Medina for their helpful comments and suggestions.

1. José Luis González, "The 'Lamento Borincano': A Sociological Interpretation," in *Puerto Rico: The Four-Storeyed Country* (Princeton, NJ: Markus Wiener Publishers, 1993), 85–90.

2. Bernardo Vega, *Memoirs of Bernardo Vega*, ed. César Andreu Iglesias (New York: Monthly Review Press, 1984).

3. John Storm Roberts, *The Latin Tinge: The Impact of Latin American Music on the United States* (New York: Oxford University Press, 1979, 1999).

4. Ruth Glasser, *My Music Is My Flag: Puerto Rican Musicians and Their New York Communities, 1917–1940* (Berkeley: University of California Press, 1995).

5. Oscar Hijuelos, *The Mambo Kings Play Songs of Love* (New York: Farrar, Straus, and Giroux, 1989).

6. Peter Manuel, "Representations of New York City in Latin Music," in *Island Sounds in the Global City: Caribbean Popular Music and Identity in New York*, ed. Ray Allen and Lois Wilcken (New York: New York Folklore Society, 1998), 23–43.

CONTRIBUTOR BIOGRAPHIES

Carmen Boullosa has published fifteen novels, most recently *La virgen y el violín* and *El complot de los románticos*; three of her novels (*They're Cows, We're Pigs*; *Leaving Tabasco*; and *Cleopatra Dismounts*) are available in English. She is also a poet, playwright, and essayist. Boullosa received the Xavier Villaurrutia Prize of Mexico, the Anna Seghers and the Liberaturpreis of Germany, and the Café Gijón Prize of Spain. She has been a Guggenheim Fellow and a Cullman Center Fellow, and has held the Andrés Bello Chair at New York University and the Alfonso Reyes Chair at La Sorbonne. She is currently Distinguished Lecturer at City College, CUNY, and host of the Emmy Award–winning television program *Nueva York*.

James D. Fernández has been Associate Professor in the Department of Spanish and Portuguese at New York University since 1995. From 1988 to 1995, he was Assistant Professor in Yale University's Department of Spanish and Portuguese. He served as the founding director of NYU's King Juan Carlos I of Spain Center from 1995 to 2007. Many of his most recent scholarly publications focus on the historical and cultural links between Spain, Latin America, and the U.S. in the nineteenth and twentieth centuries. He is co-editor, with Peter N. Carroll, of the collection of essays *Facing Fascism: New York and the Spanish Civil War* (2007).

Juan Flores is Professor of Latino Studies in the Department of Social and Cultural Analysis at New York University. His publications include *Divided Borders: Essays on Puerto Rican Identity* (1993), *From Bomba to Hip-Hop: Puerto Rican Culture and Latino Identity* (2000), and *The Diaspora Strikes Back: Caribeño Tales of Learning and Turning* (2009). He is the co-editor of *A Companion to Latina/o Studies* (2007) and *The Afro-Latino Reader* (2010) and translator of *Memoirs of Bernardo Vega* (1984) and *Cortjio's Wake* (2004). He was recently awarded the Casa de las Americas Extraordinary Prize for studies on Latinos in the United States for his book *Bugalu y otros guisos: ensayos sobre culturas latinas en Estados Unidos*, as well as the Latino Legacy Award of the Smithsonian Institution.

Anna Indych-López is Associate Professor of Art History at the City College of New York and at the Graduate Center of the City University of New York, where she teaches courses on twentieth-century Latin American art and Euro-American modernism. She has contributed numerous essays on modern Mexican and Latin American art to international journals and exhibition catalogues. Her book *Muralism without Walls: Rivera, Orozco, and Siqueiros in the United States, 1927–1940* (2009) was the recipient of a College Art Association Wyeth Foundation for American Art publication grant and was published as part of the University of Pittsburgh Press's interdisciplinary series Illuminations: Cultural Formations of the Americas.

Richard L. Kagan is Arthur O. Lovejoy Professor of History at the Johns Hopkins University, where he has been a member of the faculty since 1972. He is the author and/or editor of eleven books as well as numerous articles, essays, and reviews. Recent publications include *Urban Images of the Hispanic World, 1493–1793* (2000); *Spain and America: The Origins of Hispanism in the United States* (2002), written with Abigail Dyer; *Inquisitorial Inquiries: The Brief Lives of Secret Jews and other Heretics* (2004); *El Rey Recatado: Felipe II, la Historia y los Cronistas del Rey* (2004); *Atlantic Diasporas: Jews in the Age of Mercantilism* (2008), co-edited with Philip Morgan; and *Clio and the Crown: The Politics of History in Medieval and Early Modern Spain* (2009). He was awarded the title of Comendador in the Order of Isabela la Católica by King Juan Carlos I for his contributions to promote understanding of the history and culture of Spain.

Katherine E. Manthorne has helped to foster a hemispheric dimension of American art, identifying artistic dialogues across the Americas. This began with her doctoral dissertation, the exhibition *Creation and Renewal: Views of Cotopaxi by Frederic Edwin Church* (National Museum of American Art, Washington, D.C., 1985), and her first book, *Tropical Renaissance. North American Artists Exploring Latin America, 1839–1879* (1989). She has also contributed to *Nexus New York: Latin/ American Artists in the Modern Metropolis* at El Museo del Barrio (2009) and *Fern Hunting Among These Picturesque Mountains: Frederic Edwin Church in Jamaica* at Olana (2010). She is Professor of Art History at the Graduate Center, City University of New York.

Cathy Matson is Professor of History at the University of Delaware and Director of the Program in Early American Economy and Society at the Library Company of Philadelphia. Her work specializes in the economic culture and ideology of the Atlantic world from 1500 to 1800. Matson's publications include *A Union of Interests: Political and Economic Thought in Revolutionary America* (1990; 2000; 2005), *Merchants and Empire: Trading in Colonial New York* (1998; 2003; 2006), *The Economy of Early America: Historical Perspectives and New Directions* (2006; 2007), and *The American Experiment: A History of the United States* (2002; 2005; 2008). She is working on her fourth book, *A Gamblers' Ocean: The Economic Culture of Commerce in Philadelphia, 1750 to 1811.*

Lisandro Pérez is Professor and Chair of the Department of Latin American and Latina/o Studies at John Jay College of Criminal Justice, City University of New York. Until the summer of 2010 Pérez served for twenty-five years on the faculty of Florida International University in Miami, where he founded and directed its Cuban Research Institute. He also served as the editor of the journal *Cuban Studies* from 1999 to 2004 and is the co-author of the book *The Legacy of Exile: Cubans in the United States* (2003). He authored the chapter on Cubans for *The New Americans: A Guide to*

Immigration Since 1965 (2007). In 2004–05, Pérez was a fellow at the Center for Scholars and Writers of the New York Public Library, where he carried out research for a book on the Cuban community in New York City during the nineteenth century.

Virginia Sánchez Korrol is Professor Emerita, Brooklyn College, City University of New York. She researches and writes about Puerto Rican and Latino history in New York City, highlighting the role of women. She is author of *From Colonia to Community: The History of Puerto Ricans in New York City* (1994); co-author of *Women in Latin America and the Caribbean* (1999); and co-editor of *Latina Legacies: Identity, Biography and Community* (2005) and the award-winning *Latinas in the United States: A Historical Encyclopedia* (2006). Her most recent publication is *Pioneros II: Puerto Ricans in New York City, 1948–1998* (2010).

Marci Reaven is a public historian and managing director of City Lore, where she directs Place Matters, City Lore's joint project with the Municipal Art Society to promote and protect places of history and tradition throughout New York City. She is the co-author of Place Matters' guidebook to New York City, *Hidden New York: A Guide to Places that Matter* (2006). Reaven curated the exhibit *Missing: Streetscape of a City in Mourning* with Steve Zeitlin (New-York Historical Society, 2002), and is the author and producer of many films, exhibits, and public programs. She holds a Ph.D. in U.S. history from New York University.

Edward J. Sullivan is the Helen Gould Sheppard Professor of the History of Art at the Institute of Fine Arts and the Department of Art History, New York University. He is the author of over thirty books and exhibition catalogues on Iberian and modern Latin American art and has served as guest curator for numerous exhibitions on these topics in museums in Latin America, North America, and Europe. His most recent publications include *The Language of Objects in the Art of the Americas* (2007) and *Juan Soriano in Mexico 1935–50* (2008).

Mike Wallace is co-author of the Pulitzer Prize-winning *Gotham: A History of New York City to 1898* (1998) and author of *A New Deal for New York* (2002), which examines the future of post–September 11 Gotham in light of its past. His series of essays exploring the ways history is used and abused in American popular culture have been collected in *Mickey Mouse History and Other Essays on American Memory* (1996). He is Distinguished Professor of History at John Jay College of Criminal Justice and founder of the Gotham Center for New York City History at the CUNY Graduate School, devoted to the study and popular promotion of the history of New York City. He served as a senior historical consultant and talking head for Ric Burns's PBS special *New York: A Documentary Film*. Wallace is now working on the second volume of *Gotham: A History of New York City*.

SELECTED BIBLIOGRAPHY

Acosta-Belén, Edna, and Carlos E. Santiago. *Puerto Ricans in the United States: A Contemporary Portrait*. Boulder, CO: Lynne Reinner Publishers, 2006.

Adelman, Jeremy. *Sovereignty and Revolution in the Iberian Atlantic*. Princeton, NJ: Princeton University Press, 2007.

Adorno, Rolena. "Washington Irving's Romantic Hispanism and Its Columbia Legacies." In *Spain in America: The Origins of Hispanism in the United States*, edited by Richard L. Kagan. Urbana: University of Illinois Press, 2002.

Albion, Robert Greenhalgh. *The Rise of New York Port, 1815–1860*. New York: Scribner, 1970.

All America Cables, Inc., and Alfred K. Fricke. *A Half Century of Cable Service to the Three Americas*. New York: All America Cables, Inc., 1928.

Ameringer, Charles D. "The Panama Canal Lobby of Philippe Bunau-Varilla and William Nelson Cromwell." *The American Historical Review* 68, no. 2 (1963): 346–63.

Anreus, Alejandro. *Orozco in Gringoland: The Years in New York*. Albuquerque: University of New Mexico Press, 2001.

Antón, Alex, and Roger E. Hernández. *Cubans in America: A Vibrant History of a People in Exile*. New York: Kensington Books, 2002.

Ayala, César J. "Social and Economic Aspects of Sugar Production in Cuba, 1880–1930." *Latin American Research Review* 30, no. 1 (1995): 95–124.

———, and Laird W. Bergad. "Rural Puerto Rico in the Early Twentieth Century Reconsidered: Land and Society, 1899–1915." *Latin American Research Review* 37, no. 2 (2002): 65–97.

———, and Rafael Bernabe. *Puerto Rico in the American Century: A History Since 1898*. Chapel Hill: University of North Carolina Press, 2007.

Baker, George W. Jr. "The Wilson Administration and Nicaragua, 1913–1921." *The Americas* 22, no. 4 (1966): 339–76.

Barbier, Jacques A., and Allan J. Kuethe, eds. *The North American Role in the Spanish Imperial Economy, 1760–1819*. Manchester, UK: Manchester University Press, 1984.

Barnitz, Jacqueline. *Latin American Artists in New York Before 1950*. New York: Godwin-Ternbach Museum, Queens College, 1981.

———. *Latin American Artists in the United States 1950–1970*. Queens, NY: Godwin-Ternbach Museum, Queens College, 1983.

———. *Latin American Artists in New York since 1970*. Austin, TX: Archer M. Huntington Gallery, 1987.

Basilio, Miriam, et al., eds. *Latin American and Caribbean Art: MoMA at El Museo*. New York: El Museo del Barrio and the Museum of Modern Art, 2004.

Beer, Amy Barnes. "From the Bronx to Brooklyn: Spanish-Language Movie Theaters and Their Audiences in New York City, 1930–1999." PhD diss., Northwestern University, 2001.

Bender, Thomas. *New York Intellect: A History of Intellectual Life in New York City, from 1750 to the Beginnings of Our Own Time*. New York: Knopf; distributed by Random House, 1987.

Bercovici, Konrad. *Around the World in New York*. New York: The Century Company, 1924.

Berlin, Ira, and Leslie M. Harris. *Slavery in New York*. New York: New Press; distributed by W. W. Norton, 2005.

Bernardini, Paolo, and Norman Fiering. *The Jews and the Expansion of Europe to the West, 1450 to 1800*. European Expansion and Global Interaction, vol. 2. New York: Berghahn Books, 2001.

Bigelow, John. *William Cullen Bryant*. New York: Chelsea House, 1980.

Boone, M. Elizabeth. *Vistas de España: American Views of Art and Life in Spain, 1860–1914*. New Haven, CT: Yale University Press, 2007.

Brickhouse, Anna. "'A Story of the Island of Cuba': William Cullen Bryant and the Hispanophone Americas." *Nineteenth-Century Literature* 56, no. 1 (2001): 1–22.

Brown, Jonathan. "The Image of Spain in the United States." In *Spain in America: The Origins of Hispanism in the United States*, edited by Richard L. Kagan. Urbana: University of Illinois Press, 2002.

Brown, Jonathan C., and Alan Knight. *The Mexican Petroleum Industry in the Twentieth Century*. Austin: University of Texas Press, 1992.

Brown, Matthew. *Adventuring Through Spanish Colonies: Simón Bolívar, Foreign Mercenaries and the Birth of New Nations*. Liverpool: Liverpool University Press, 2006.

Bryant, William Cullen. *The Letters of William Cullen Bryant*, edited by William Cullen Bryant II and Thomas G. Voss. 6 vols. New York: Fordham University Press, 1975–92.

Bunau-Varilla, Philippe. *Panama: The Creation, Destruction, and Resurrection*. London: Constable, 1913.

Burgos, Adrián. "The Latins From Manhattan: Confronting Race and Building Community in Jim Crow Baseball, 1906–1950." In *Mambo Montage: The Latinization of New York*, edited by Agustín Laó-Montes and Arlene M Dávila. New York: Columbia University Press, 2001.

Burnett, Christina Duffy, and Burke Marshall. *Foreign in a Domestic Sense: Puerto Rico, American Expansion, and the Constitution*. Durham, NC: Duke University Press, 2001.

Burrows, Edwin G., and Mike Wallace. *Gotham: A History of New York City to 1898*. New York: Oxford University Press, 1999.

Burstein, Andrew. *The Original Knickerbocker: The Life of Washington Irving*. New York: Basic Books, 2007.

Butler, Smedley D. *War Is a Racket*. New York: Revisionist Press, 1974.

Cabranes, José A. "Citizenship and the American Empire: Notes on the Legislative History of the United States Citizenship of Puerto Ricans." *University of Pennsylvania Law Review* 127, no. 2 (1978): 391–492.

Calder, Bruce J. *The Impact of Intervention: The Dominican Republic During the U.S. Occupation of 1916–1924*. Princeton, NJ: Markus Wiener Publishers, 2006.

Calvo Sotelo, Joaquín. *Nueva York en retales*. Madrid: Editorial Dossat, 1947.

Camba, Julio. *La ciudad automática*. Madrid: Espasa Calpe, 2003.

Cañas, Dionisio. *El poeta y la ciudad: Nueva York y los escritores hispanos*. Madrid: Cátedra, 1994.

———. "New York City: Center and Transit Point for Hispanic Cultural Nomadism." In *Literary Cultures of Latin America: A Comparative History*, edited by Mario J Valdés and Djelal Kadir. New York: Oxford University Press, 2004.

Cancel, Luis R., ed. *The Latin American Spirit: Art and Artists in the United States, 1920–1970*. New York: Bronx Museum of the Arts and Harry N. Abrams, 1988.

Carroll, Peter N., and James D. Fernández. *Facing Fascism: New York and the Spanish Civil War*. New York: Museum of the City of New York and NYU Press, 2007.

Casanovas, Joan. *Bread or Bullets!: Urban Labor and Spanish Colonialism in Cuba, 1850–1898*. Pittsburgh: University of Pittsburgh Press, 1998.

Castonguay, James. "The Spanish-American War in US Media Culture." *American Quarterly* 51, no. 2 (1999).

Castro-Klaren, Sara. "Framing Pan-Americanism: Simon Bolivar's Findings." *CR: The New Centennial Review* 3, no. 1 (2003): 25–53.

Castro Leal, Antonio. *La novela del México Colonial, Xicoténcatl*. Mexico: Editorial Aguilar, 1964.

Centro de Estudios Puertorriqueños. *Divided Arrivals: Narratives of the Puerto Rican Migration, 1920–1950*. New York: Centro de Estudios Puertorriqueños, 1998.

———. *Sources for the Study of Puerto Rican Migration, 1879–1930*. New York: Centro de Estudios Puertorriqueños, 1982.

Chaffin, Tom. *Fatal Glory: Narciso López and the First Clandestine U.S. War Against Cuba*. Baton Rouge: Louisiana State University Press, 2003.

Chamberlin, Vernon A., and Iván A. Schulman. *La Revista Ilustrada de Nueva York: History, Anthology, and Index of Literary Selections*. Columbia: University of Missouri Press, 1976.

Chase, Allan. *Falange: The Axis Secret Army in the Americas*. New York: G. P. Putnam's Sons, 1943.

Chavez, Thomas E. *Spain and the Independence of the United States: An Intrinsic Gift*. Albuquerque: University of New Mexico Press, 2002.

Chenault, Lawrence R. *The Puerto Rican Migrant in New York City*. New York: Russell & Russell, 1970.

Chernow, Ron. *Alexander Hamilton*. New York: Penguin Press, 2004.

———. *The House of Morgan: An American Banking Dynasty and the Rise of Modern Finance*. New York: Atlantic Monthly Press, 1990.

Cleveland, Richard J. *A Narrative of Voyages and Commercial Enterprises*. Boston: C. H. Peirce, 1850.

Coatsworth, John H. "American Trade With European Colonies in the Caribbean and South America, 1790–1812." *William and Mary Quarterly* 24, no. 2 (1967).

Colby, Gerard, and Charlotte Dennett. *Thy Will Be Done: The Conquest of the Amazon: Nelson Rockefeller and Evangelism in the Age of Oil*. New York: HarperCollins, 1995.

Collier, Simon. *The Life, Music, and Times of Carlos Gardel*. Pittsburgh: University of Pittsburgh Press, 1986.

Colón, Jesus. *Lo que el pueblo me dice . . .* Houston: Arte Público Press, 2001.

———. *A Puerto Rican in New York, and Other Sketches*. New York: Arno Press, 1975.

———. *The Way It Was and Other Writings*. Houston: Arte Público Press, 1993.

Colón López, Joaquín. *Pioneros Puertorriqueños en Nueva York: 1917–1947*. Houston: Arte Público Press, 2002.

Corn, Wanda M. *The Great American Thing: Modern Art and National Identity, 1915–1935*. Berkeley, Los Angeles, and London: University of California Press, 1999.

Cuenca Esteban, Javier. "The United States Balance of Payments With Spanish America and the Philippine Islands, 1790–1819." In *The North American Role in the Spanish Imperial Economy, 1760–1819*, edited by Jacques A. Barbier and Allan J. Kuethe. Manchester, UK: Manchester University Press, 1984.

Cullen, Deborah, ed. *Nexus New York: Latin/American Artists in the Modern Metropolis*. New York: El Museo del Barrio and New Haven, CT: Yale University Press, 2009.

Dallett, Francis James. "Paez in Philadelphia." *The Hispanic American Historical Review* 40, no. 1 (1960): 98–106.

Davis, Melvin Duane. "Collecting Hispania: Archer Huntington's Quest to Develop Hispanic Collections in the United States." PhD diss., University of Alabama, 2005.

de Burgos, Julia. *Obra poética*. San Juan: Editorial del Instituto de Cultura Puertorriqueña, 2004.

de Onís, José. "The Alleged Acquaintance of William Cullen Bryant and José María Heredia." *Hispanic Review* 25, no. 3 (1957): 217-20.

de Secada, Alexander G. "Arms, Guano, and Shipping: The W. R. Grace Interests in Peru, 1865-1885." *The Business History Review* 59, no. 4 (1985): 597-621.

DeGuzmán, María. *Spain's Long Shadow: The Black Legend, Off-Whiteness, and Anglo-American Empire*. Minneapolis: University of Minnesota Press, 2005.

Delgado, Linda C. "Jesus Colon and the Making of the New York City Community, 1917 to 1974." In *The Puerto Rican Diaspora: Historical Perspectives*, edited by Carmen Teresa Whalen and Víctor Vázquez-Hernández. Philadelphia: Temple University Press, 2005.

Delpar, Helen. *The Enormous Vogue of Things Mexican: Cultural Relations Between the United States and Mexico, 1920-1935*. Tuscaloosa: University of Alabama Press, 1992.

Diaz Espino, Ovidio. *How Wall Street Created a Nation: J. P. Morgan, Teddy Roosevelt, and the Panama Canal*. New York: Four Walls Eight Windows, 2001.

Díaz Guerra, Alirio. *Lucas Guevara*. Houston: Arte Público Press. 2001.

Doolen, Andy. "Reading and Writing Terror: The New York Conspiracy Trials of 1741." *American Literary History* 16 (2004): 377-406.

Duncan, Jason K. *Citizens or Papists?: The Politics of Anti-Catholicism in New York, 1685-1821*. New York: Fordham University Press, 2005.

Dushkin, Alexander Mordecai. *Jewish Education in New York City*. New York: The Bureau of Jewish Education, 1918.

Eichner, Alfred S. *The Emergence of Oligopoly: Sugar Refining as a Case Study*. Baltimore: Johns Hopkins University Press, 1969.

Elliott, John Huxtable. *Empires of the Atlantic World: Britain and Spain in America, 1492-1830*. New Haven, CT: Yale University Press, 2006.

Ely, Roland T. "The Old Cuba Trade: Highlights and Case Studies of Cuban-American Inter-dependence During the Nineteenth Century." *Business History Review* 38, no. 4 (1964): 456-78.

Erb, Claude Curtis. "Nelson Rockefeller and United States-Latin American Relations, 1940-1945." PhD diss., Clark University, 1982.

Espina, Concha. *Singladuras; viaje Americano*. Madrid: Compañía Iberoamericana de Publicaciones, 1932.

Evans, R. Tripp. *Romancing the Maya: Mexican Antiquity in the American Imagination, 1820-1915*. Austin: University of Texas Press, 2004.

Faber, Eli. *Jews, Slaves, and the Slave Trade: Setting the Record Straight*. New York: New York University Press, 1998.

Fay, Eliot G. "Ruben Dario in New York." *Modern Language Notes* 57, no. 8 (1942): 641-48.

Federal Writers' Project. *New York Panorama: A Companion to the WPA Guide to New York City*. New York: Pantheon Books, 1984.

Fernández, James D. "'Longfellow's Law': The Place of Latin America and Spain in U.S. Hispanism, circa 1915." In *Spain in America: The Origins of Hispanism in the United States*, edited by Richard L. Kagan. Urbana: University of Illinois Press, 2002.

Ferrer, Ada. "Cuba, 1898: Rethinking Race, Nation, and Empire." *Radical History Review* 73 (1999): 22-46.

———. "The Silence of Patriots: Racial Discourse and Cuban Nationalism, 1868-1898." In *Jose Martí's "Our America": From National to Hemispheric Cultural Studies*, edited by Jeffrey Grant Belnap and Raul A. Fernandez. Durham, NC: Duke University Press, 1998.

Figueroa, Frank M. "Miguelito Valdes: Mr Babalu: Act I, Cuban Roots." *Latin Beat Magazine* (2007).

———. "Miguelito Valdes: Mr Babalu: Act II, New York Transplant." *Latin Beat Magazine* (2007).

Flores, Juan. *From Bomba to Hip-Hop: Puerto Rican Culture and Latino Identity*. New York: Columbia University Press, 2000.

Foner, Philip Sheldon. *A History of Cuba and Its Relations With the United States*. New York: International Publishers, 1962.

Foy, Charles R. "Ports of Slavery, Ports of Freedom: How Slaves Used Northern Seaports' Maritime Industry to Escape and Create Trans-Atlantic Identities, 1713-1783." PhD diss, Rutgers, The State University of New Jersey, 2008.

Frasconi, Antonio, and Nat Henthoff. *Against the Grain: The Woodcuts of Antonio Frasconi*. New York: Macmillan, 1975.

Friedman, Max Paul. *Nazis and Good Neighbors: The United States Campaign Against the Germans of Latin America in World War II*. New York: Cambridge University Press, 2003.

Galasso, Regina. "Latin From Manhattan: Transatlantic and Interamerican Cultural Production in New York (1913-1963)." PhD diss., Johns Hopkins University, 2008.

García Lorca, Federico. *Poeta en Nueva York, Conferencias, Notas varias*. Buenos Aires: Losada, 1942.

———. *A Poet in New York*. New York: Grove Press, 2008.

García-Muniz, Humberto. "The South Porto Rico Sugar Company: The History of a U.S. Multinational Corporation in Puerto Rico and the Dominican Republic, 1920-1921." PhD diss., Columbia University, 1997.

Gaulin, Kenneth. "The Flying Boats: Pioneering Days to South America." *The Journal of Decorative and Propaganda Arts* 15 (1990): 78-95.

Gehring, Charles T., Jacob Adriaan Schiltkamp, and Peter Stuyvesant. *Curacao Papers, 1640-1665*. Interlaken, NY: Heart of the Lakes, 1987.

Gelfand, Noah L. "Jews in New Netherland: An Atlantic Perspective." In *Explorers, Fortunes, and Love Letters: A Window on New Netherland*, edited by Martha Dickinson Shattuck. Albany, NY: New Netherland Institute and Mount Ida Press, 2009.

Glasser, Ruth. *My Music Is My Flag: Puerto Rican Musicians and Their New York Communities, 1917-1940*. Berkeley: University of California Press, 1995.

Goldman, Shifra M. *Dimensions of the Americas: Art and Social Change in Latin America and the United States*. Chicago and London: University of Chicago Press, 1994.

González, Evelyn Diaz. *The Bronx*. New York: Columbia University Press, 2004.

González, José Luis. "The 'Lamento Borincano': A Sociological Interpretation." In *Puerto Rico: The Four-Storeyed Country*, 85-90. Princeton, NJ: Markus Wiener Publishers, 1993.

González, Juan. *Harvest of Empire: A History of Latinos in America*. New York: Viking, 2000.

González, Manuel Pedro. "Two Great Pioneers of Inter-American Cultural Relations." *Hispania* 42, no. 2 (1959): 175–85.

Goodfriend, Joyce D. *Before the Melting Pot: Society and Culture in Colonial New York City, 1664–1730*. Princeton, NJ: Princeton University Press, 1996.

———, ed. *Revisiting New Netherland: Perspectives on Early Dutch America*. Leiden and Boston: Brill, 2005.

Grandin, Greg. *Empire's Workshop: Latin America, the United States, and the Rise of the New Imperialism*. New York: Metropolitan Books, 2006.

Greet, Michele. *Beyond National Identity: Pictorial Indigenism as a Modernist Strategy in Andean Art, 1920–1960*. University Park: Penn State University Press, 2009.

Gutman, Margarita. *Buenos Aires, 1910: Memoria del Porvenir*. Buenos Aires: Gobierno de la Ciudad de Buenos Aires, 1999.

Haggerty, Sheryllynne. *The British Atlantic Trading Community, 1760–1810: Men, Women, and the Distribution of Goods*. Leiden and Boston: Brill, 2006.

Haslip-Viera, Gabriel. "The Evolution of the Latino Community in New York City: Early Nineteenth Century to the Present." In *Latinos in New York: Communities in Transition*, edited by Gabriel Haslip-Viera and Sherrie L. Baver. Notre Dame, IN: University of Notre Dame Press, 1996.

———, and Sherrie L. Baver, eds. *Latinos in New York: Communities in Transition*. Notre Dame, IN: University of Notre Dame Press, 1996.

———, et al., eds. *Boricuas in Gotham: Puerto Ricans in the Making of New York City*. Princeton, NJ: Markus Wiener Publishers, 2004.

Hemingway, Andrew. *Artists on the Left: American Artists and the Communist Movement, 1926–1956*. New Haven, CT: Yale University Press, 2002.

Herbermann, Charles George, Edward A. Pace, et al. *The Catholic Encyclopedia*. New York: The Encyclopedia Press, Inc., 1913.

Hodges, Graham Russell. *Root and Branch: African Americans in New York and East Jersey, 1613–1863*. Chapel Hill: University of North Carolina Press, 1999.

Hoffnung-Garskof, Jesse. "The Migrations of Arturo Schomburg: On Being Antillano, Negro, and Puerto Rican in New York. 1891–1917." *Journal of American Ethnic History* 21, no. 1 (2001): 3–49.

Horsmanden, Daniel, and Serena R. Zabin. *The New York Conspiracy Trials of 1741*. Boston: Bedford/St. Martin's, 2004.

Hurlburt, Laurance P. *The Mexican Muralists in the United States*. Albuquerque: University of New Mexico Press, 1989.

———. "The Siqueiros Experimental Workshop: New York, 1936." *Art Journal* 35, no. 3 (1976): 237–46.

Indych-López, Anna. *Muralism without Walls: Rivera, Orozco, and Siqueiros in the United States, 1927–1940*. Pittsburgh: University of Pittsburgh Press, 2009.

Irwin, Robert McKee. "The American Renaissance and the Mexican Renacimiento." *The New Centennial Review* 8, no. 1 (2008): 235–51.

Jacobs, Jaap. *New Netherland: A Dutch Colony in Seventeenth-Century America*. Leiden and Boston: Brill, 2005.

Jaksic, Ivan. *The Hispanic World and American Intellectual Life, 1820–1880*. New York: Palgrave Macmillan, 2007.

Jiménez, Juan Ramón. *Diario de un poeta reciencasado*. Madrid: Visor, 1997.

Johnson, Alvin. *Notes on the New School Murals*. New York: New School for Social Research, 1943.

Johnson, Sherry. *The Social Transformation of Eighteenth-Century Cuba*. Gainesville: University Presses of Florida, 2001.

Joseph, Gilbert, Catherine LeGrand, et al., eds. *Close Encounters of Empire: Writing the Cultural History of U.S-Latin American Relations*. Durham, NC: Duke University Press, 1998.

Kagan, Richard L. "From Noah to Moses: The Genesis of Historical Scholarship on Spain in the United States." In *Spain in America: The Origins of Hispanism in the United States*, edited by Richard L. Kagan. Urbana: University of Illinois Press, 2002.

———, ed. *Spain in America: The Origins of Hispanism in the United States*. Urbana: University of Illinois Press, 2002.

Kamen, Henry. *The Disinherited: The Exiles Who Created Spanish Culture*. London and New York: Allen Lane, 2007.

———. *Empire: How Spain Became a World Power, 1492–1763*. New York: HarperCollins, 2003.

Kanellos, Nicolás. *Hispanic Firsts: 500 Years of Extraordinary Achievement*. Detroit: Gale, 1997.

———. "José Alvarez de Toledo y Dubois and the Origins of Hispanic Publishing in the Early American Republic." *Early American Literature* 43, no. 1 (2008).

———. *En otra voz: Antología de literature hispana de los Estados Unidos*. Houston: Arte Público Press, 2002.

———, Kenya Dworkin, et al., eds. *Herencia: The Anthology of Hispanic Literature of the United States*. New York: Oxford University Press, 2002.

———, and Helvetia Martell. *Hispanic Periodicals in the United States, Origins to 1960: A Brief History and Comprehensive Bibliography*. Houston: Arte Público Press, 2000.

Kinsbruner, Jay. *Independence in Spanish America: Civil Wars, Revolution, and Underdevelopment*. Albuquerque: University of New Mexico Press: 1994).

Kirk, John M. "Jose Martí and the United States: A Further Interpretation." *Journal of Latin American Studies* 9, no. 2 (1977): 275–90.

Klein, Richard B. "The American Association of Teachers of Spanish and Portuguese: The First 75 Years." *Hispania* 75, no. 4 (1992): 1036–79.

Kramer, Paul. "Nelson Rockefeller and British Security Coordination." *Journal of Contemporary History* 16, no. 1 (1981): 73–88.

LaFeber, Walter. *The Panama Canal: The Crisis in Historical Perspective*. New York: Oxford University Press, 1989.

Langa, Helen. *Radical Art: Printmaking and the Left in the 1930s*. New York and Los Angeles: University of California Press, 2004.

Laó-Montes, Agustín, and Arlene M. Dávila. *Mambo Montage: The Latinization of New York*. New York: Columbia University Press, 2001.

Lazo, Rodrigo. *Writing to Cuba: Filibustering and Cuban Exiles in the United States.* Chapel Hill: University of North Carolina Press, 2005.

Lepore, Jill. *New York Burning: Liberty, Slavery, and Conspiracy in Eighteenth-Century Manhattan.* New York: Alfred A. Knopf, 2005.

Lewis, James A. "Anglo-American Entrepreneurs in Havana: Background and Significance of the Expulsion of 1784–1785." In *The North American Role in the Spanish Imperial Economy, 1760–1819,* edited by Jacques A. Barbier and Allan J. Kuethe. Manchester, UK: Manchester University Press, 1984.

Linderman, Gerald F. *The Mirror of War: American Society and the Spanish-American War.* Ann Arbor: University of Michigan Press, 1974.

Liss, Peggy. *Atlantic Empires: The Network of Trade and Revolution, 1783–1826.* Baltimore: Johns Hopkins University Press, 1983.

López Mesa, Enrique. *La Comunidad Cubana de New York: Siglo XIX.* Havana: Centro de Estudios Marianos, 2002.

Lynch, John. *The Spanish American Revolutions, 1808–1826.* 2nd ed. New York: W. W. Norton, 1986.

Manuel, Peter. "Representations of New York City in Latin Music." In *Island Sounds in the Global City: Caribbean Popular Music and Identity in New York,* edited by Ray Allen and Lois Wilcken, 23–43. New York: New York Folklore Society, 1998.

Marichal, Caros. *La Bancarrota del Virreinato: Nueva Espana y Las Finanzas del Imperio Espanol, 1780–1810.* San Diego, CA: Fondo de Cultura Económica, 1999.

Martí, José. *Ensayos y crónicas.* Madrid: Cátedra, 2004.

———. *Poesía completa.* Madrid: Alianza Editorial, 2001.

———, and Philip Sheldon Foner. *Inside the Monster: Writings on the United States and American Imperialism.* New York: Monthly Review Press, 1975.

Mátos-Rodriguez, Felix V., and Pedro Juan Hernandez. *Pioneros: Puerto Ricans in New York City, 1892–1948.* Charleston, SC: Arcadia Publishing, 2001.

Matson, Cathy. *Merchants and Empire: Trading in Colonial New York.* Baltimore: Johns Hopkins University Press, 1998.

McAvoy, Muriel. *Sugar Baron: Manuel Rionda and the Fortunes of Pre-Castro Cuba.* Gainesville: University Presses of Florida, 2003.

McCadden, Joseph, and Helen M. McCadden. *Félix Varela: Torch Bearer From Cuba.* San Juan: Félix Varela Foundation, 1984.

McCadden, Joseph J. "The New York-to-Cuba Axis of Father Varela." *The Americas* 20, no. 4 (1964): 376–92.

Mewburn, Charity. "Oil, Art, and Politics: The Feminization of Mexico." *Anales del Instituto de Investigaciones Estéticas* 72 (1998): 73–133.

Meyer, Donald C. "Toscanini and the Good Neighbor Policy: The NBC Symphony Orchestra's 1940 South American Tour." *American Music* 18, no. 3 (fall 2000): 233–56.

Meyer, Doris, and Victoria Ocampo. *Victoria Ocampo: Against the Wind and the Tide.* Austin: University of Texas Press, 1990.

Meyer, Gerald. "Marcantonio and El Barrio." *Centro* 4, no. 2 (1992): 66–87.

Miliotes, Diane. "The Murals at the New School for Social Research (1930–31)." In *José Clemente Orozco in the United States, 1927–1934,* edited by Renato González Mello and Diane Miliotes. Hanover, NH: Hood Museum of Art, 2002.

Mirabal, Nancy Raquel. "De Aquí, De Allá: Race, Empire, and Nation in the Making of Cuban Migrant Communities in New York and Tampa, 1823–1924." PhD diss., University of Michigan, 2000.

———. "'No Country but the One We Must Fight For': The Emergence of an Antillean Nation and Community in New York City, 1860–1901." In *Mambo Montage: The Latinization of New York,* edited by Agustín Laó-Montes and Arlene M. Dávila. New York: Columbia University Press, 2001.

Molloy, Sylvia. "His America, Our America: José Martí Reads Whitman." In *Breaking Bounds: Whitman and American Cultural Studies,* edited by Betsy Erkkila and Jay Grossman. New York: Oxford University Press, 1996.

Montes Huidobro, Matías, ed. *El Laúd del Desterrado.* Houston: Arte Público Press, 1995.

Moore, E. R. "José María Heredia in the United States and Mexico." *Modern Language Notes* 65, no. 1 (1950): 41–46.

Morales, Ed. *The Latin Beat: The Rhythms and Roots of Latin Music from Bossa Nova to Salsa and Beyond.* Cambridge, MA: Da Capo Press, 2003.

Moreno Fraginals, Manuel. *The Sugarmill: The Socioeconomic Complex of Sugar in Cuba, 1760–1860.* New York: Monthly Review Press, 1976.

Moreno Villa, José. *Pruebas de Nueva York.* Valencia: Pre-Textos, 1989.

———. *Vida en claro.* Mexico City: Fondo de Cultura Económica, 1976.

Moya Pons, Frank. *History of the Caribbean: Plantations, Trade, and War in the Atlantic World.* Princeton, NJ: Markus Wiener Publishers, 2007.

Muller, Gilbert H. *William Cullen Bryant: Author of America.* Albany, NY: State University of New York Press, 2008.

National Portrait Gallery (Smithsonian Institution) and Sociedad Estatal para la Acción Cultural Exterior (Spain). *Legacy: Spain and the United States in the Age of Independence, 1763–1848 / Legado: España y Los Estados Unidos en la Era de la Independencia, 1763–1848.* Washington, DC: Smithsonian Institution; Spain: Sociedad Estatal para la Acción Cultural Exterior, 2007.

Neale-Silva, Eduardo. *Horizonte humano: Vida de José Eustasio Rivera.* Mexico and Buenos Aires: Fondo de Cultura Económica, 1960.

Neumann, William L. "United States Aid to the Chilean Wars of Independence." *The Hispanic American Historical Review* 27, no. 2 (1947): 204–19.

O'Brien, Thomas F. *The Century of U.S. Capitalism in Latin America.* Diálogos. Albuquerque: University of New Mexico Press, 1999.

———. *Making the Americas: The United States and Latin America From the Age of Revolutions to the Era of Globalization.* Albuquerque: University of New Mexico Press, 2007.

———. *The Revolutionary Mission: American Enterprise in Latin America, 1900–1945.* Cambridge Latin American Studies 81. New York: Cambridge University Press, 1996.

———. "'Rich Beyond the Dreams of Avarice': The Guggenheims in Chile." *Business History Review* 63 (1989): 129–31.

O'Callaghan, E. B., and Berthold Fernow, eds. *Documents Relative to the Colonial History of the State of New York.* 15 vols. New York, 1856–87.

O'Connor, Francis V. "The Influence of Diego Rivera on the Art of the United States During the 1930s and After." In *Diego Rivera: A Retrospective*, edited by Cynthia Newman Helms. Detroit: Founders Society, Detroit Institute of Arts, in association with W. W. Norton, 1986.

O'Flanagan, Patrick. *Port Cities of Atlantic Iberia, 1500–1900.* Aldershot, UK: Ashgate Publishing, 2008.

Ogorzaly, Michael A. *Waldo Frank, Prophet of Hispanic Regeneration.* Cranbury, NJ: Associated University Presses, 1994.

Ojeda Reyes, Félix, and Vito Marcantonio. *Vito Marcantonio y Puerto Rico: Por los Trabajadores y por la Nacíon.* Río Piedras, PR: Ediciones Huracán, 1978.

Oles, James. "Orozco at War: Context and Fragment in *Dive Bomber and Tank* (1940)." In *José Clemente Orozco in the United States, 1927–1934*, edited by Renato González Mello and Diane Miliotes. Hanover, NH: Hood Museum of Art, 2002.

———, Marta Ferragut, et al. *South of the Border: Mexico in the American Imagination, 1917–1947.* Washington, DC: Smithsonian Institution Press, 1993.

Ortiz, Altagracia. "Puerto Ricans in the Garment Industry of New York City, 1920–1960." In *Labor Divided: Race and Ethnicity in United States Labor Struggles, 1835–1960*, edited by Robert Asher and Charles Stephenson. Albany: State University of New York Press, 1990.

Pantoja, Antonia. *Memoir of a Visionary.* Houston: Arte Público Press, 2002.

Pérez, Lisandro. *Cubans in Gotham: Immigrants, Exiles, and Revolution in Nineteenth-Century New York.* New York University Press, [forthcoming 2010].

Pérez, Louis A. *On Becoming Cuban: Identity, Nationality, and Culture.* Chapel Hill: University of North Carolina Press, 2008.

———. *The War of 1898: The United States and Cuba in History and Historiography.* Chapel Hill: University of North Carolina Press, 1998.

Pérez y González, María. *Puerto Ricans in the United States.* Westport, CT: Greenwood Press, 2000.

Peterson, Roy M. "Bryant as a Hispanophile." *Hispania* 16, no. 4 (1933): 401–12 .

Piña-Rosales, Gerardo. *Escritores Españoles en Estados Unidos (Spanish Writers in the U.S.).* New York: Academia Nortamericana de la Lengua Española, 2007.

Polcari, Stephen. "Orozco and Pollock: Epic Transfigurations." *American Art* 6, no. 3 (1992): 36–57.

Porter, Kenneth Wiggins. *John Jacob Astor, Business Man.* New York: Russell & Russell, 1966.

Powell, Philip Wayne. *Tree of Hate: Propaganda and Prejudices Affecting United States Relations With the Hispanic World.* New York: Basic Books, 1971.

Poyo, Gerald Eugene. *With All, and for the Good of All: The Emergence of Popular Nationalism in the Cuban Communities of the United States, 1848–1898.* Durham, NC: Duke University Press, 1989.

Price, Jacob. "Economic Function and the Growth of American Port Towns in the Eighteenth Century." *Perspectives in American History*, 8 (1974): 121–86.

Quirarte, Vicente. "Benito Juárez and New York City." *The Brooklyn Rail* (December 2006–January 2007), http://www.brooklynrail.org/2006/12/express/benito-jua.

Rachum, Ilan. "Origins and Historical Significance of Día de la Raza." *Revista Europea de Estudios Latinoamericanos y Del Caribe* 76 (2004).

Racine, Karen. *Francisco de Miranda: A Transatlantic Life in the Age of Revolution.* Wilmington, DE: Scholarly Resources, 2003.

Ramos, Julio. *Divergent Modernities: Culture and Politics in 19th Century Latin America.* Durham, NC: Duke University Press, 2001.

Rasmussen, Waldo, ed. *Latin American Artists of the Twentieth Century.* New York: The Museum of Modern Art, 1993.

Reich, Cary. *The Life of Nelson A. Rockefeller: Worlds to Conquer, 1908–1958.* New York: Doubleday, 1996.

Remeseira, Claudio Iván. "A Splendid Outsider: Archer Milton Huntington and the Hispanic Heritage in the United States." Unpublished manuscript, 2002.

Rivas, Darlene. *Missionary Capitalist: Nelson Rockefeller in Venezuela.* Chapel Hill: University of North Carolina Press, 2002.

Rivera Ramos, Efrén. *American Colonialism in Puerto Rico: The Judicial and Social Legacy.* Princeton, NJ: Markus Wiener Publishers, 2007.

Roberts, John Storm. *The Latin Tinge: The Impact of Latin American Music on the United States.* 2nd ed. New York: Oxford University Press, 1999.

Robertson, William Spence. *The Life of Miranda.* Chapel Hill: University of North Carolina Press, 1929.

Rodríguez, Clara E. *Puerto Ricans: Born in the U.S.A.* Boulder, CO: Westview Press, 1991.

Rondón, César Miguel. *The Book of Salsa: A Chronicle of Urban Music from the Caribbean to New York City.* Chapel Hill: University of North Carolina Press, 2008.

Roorda, Eric. *The Dictator Next Door: The Good Neighbor Policy and the Trujillo Regime in the Dominican Republic, 1930–1945.* Durham, NC: Duke University Press, 1998.

Rosenberg, Emily S. *Financial Missionaries to the World: The Politics and Culture of Dollar Diplomacy, 1900–1930.* Durham, NC: Duke University Press, 2003.

———. *Spreading the American Dream: American Economic and Cultural Expansion, 1890–1945.* New York: Hill and Wang, 1982.

Rostagno, Irene. "Waldo Frank's Crusade for Latin American Literature." *The Americas* 46, no. 1 (1989): 41–69.

Rotker, Susana. *The American Chronicles of José Martí: Journalism and Modernity in Spanish America.* Hanover, NH: University Press of New England, 2000.

Ruiz, Vicki L., and Virginia Sánchez Korrol, eds. *Latina Legacies: Identity, Biography and Community.* New York: Oxford University Press, 2005.

———. *Latinas in the United States: A Historical Encyclopedia.* Bloomington: Indiana University Press, 2006.

Rutkoff, Peter M., and William B. Scott. *New School: A History of The New School for Social Research.* New York: The Free Press/Macmillan, 1986.

Ryan, Leo Raymond. *Old St. Peter's, the Mother Church of Catholic New York (1785-1935).* New York: United States Catholic Historical Society, 1935.

Salazar, Boris. *La otra selva.* Bogotá: Tercer Mundo, 1991.

Salazar, Max. *Mambo Kingdom: Latin Music in New York.* New York: Schirmer Trade Books, 2002.

Salvucci, Linda. "Anglo American Merchants and Stratagems for Success in Spanish American Markets, 1783-1807." In *The North American Role in the Spanish Imperial Economy, 1760-1819,* edited by Jacques A. Barbier and Allan J. Kuethe. Manchester, UK: Manchester University Press, 1984.

———. "Atlantic Intersections: Early American Commerce and the Rise of the Spanish West Indies (Cuba)." *Business History Review* 79, no. 4 (2005): 781-809.

———. "Merchants and Diplomats: Philadelphia's Early Trade with Cuba." *Pennsylvania Legacies* 3 (2003): 6-10.

Sampson, Robert. *John L. O'Sullivan and His Times.* Kent, OH: Kent State University Press, 2003.

Sánchez Korrol, Virginia. *From Colonia to Community: The History of Puerto Ricans in New York City.* Berkeley: University of California Press, 1994.

Sawin, Martica. *Surrealism in Exile and the Beginnings of the New York School.* Cambridge, MA: MIT Press, 1995.

Schama, Simon. *The Embarrassment of Riches: An Interpretation of Dutch Culture in the Golden Age.* New York: Knopf; distributed by Random House, 1987.

Schell, William. *Integral Outsiders: The American Colony in Mexico City, 1876-1911.* Wilmington, DE: SR Books, 2001.

Schmidt, Benjamin. *Innocence Abroad: The Dutch Imagination and the New World, 1570-1670.* New York: Cambridge University Press, 2001.

Schmidt, Hans. *Maverick Marine: General Smedley D. Butler and the Contradictions of American Military History.* Lexington: University Press of Kentucky, 1987.

Schmitz, Christopher. "The Rise of Big Business in the World Copper Industry 1870-1930." *The Economic History Review* 39, no. 3 (1986): 392-410.

Schoonover, Thomas David. *Uncle Sam's War of 1898 and the Origins of Globalization.* Lexington: University Press of Kentucky, 2003.

Schwartz, Rosalie. *Flying Down to Rio: Hollywood, Tourists, and Yankee Clippers.* College Station: Texas A & M University Press, 2004.

Scott, William B., and Peter M. Rutkoff. *New York Modern: The Arts and the City.* Baltimore: Johns Hopkins University Press, 1999.

Scroggs, William O. *Filibusters and Financiers: The Story of William Walker and His Associates.* New York: Macmillan, 1916.

Scrymser, James Alexander. *Personal Reminiscences of James A. Scrymser in Times of Peace and War.* Easton, PA: Eschenbach Printing Company, 1915.

Selva, Salomón de la. *Antología mayor.* Managua: Fundación UNO, 2007.

———. *Narrativa.* Managua: Fundación UNO, 2008.

Shattuck, Martha Dickinson. *Explorers, Fortunes, and Love Letters: A Window on New Netherland.* Albany, NY: New Netherland Institute and Mount Ida Press, 2009.

Shea, John Gilmary. *History of the Catholic Church Within the Limits of the United States.* New York: Arno Press, 1978.

Sheinin, David. *Beyond the Ideal: Pan Americanism in Inter-American Affairs.* Westport, CT: Greenwood Press, 2000.

Shelley, Thomas J. *Greenwich Village Catholics: St. Joseph's Church and the Evolution of an Urban Faith Community, 1829-2002.* Washington, DC: Catholic University of America Press, 2003.

Shorto, Russell. *The Island at the Center of the World: The Epic Story of Dutch Manhattan and the Forgotten Colony That Shaped America.* New York: Doubleday, 2004.

Singleton, Esther. *Dutch New York.* New York: Dodd, Mead, 1909.

Statham, E. Robert. *Colonial Constitutionalism: The Tyranny of United States' Offshore Territorial Policy and Relations.* Lanham, MD: Lexington Books, 2002.

Stein, Louise K. "Before the Latin Tinge: Spanish Music and the "Spanish Idiom" in the United States, 1778-1940." In *Spain in America: The Origins of Hispanism in the United States,* edited by Richard L. Kagan. Urbana: University of Illinois Press, 2002.

Stein, Stanley J., and Barbara H. Stein. *Silver, Trade, and War: Spain and America in the Making of Early Modern Europe.* Baltimore: Johns Hopkins University Press, 2000.

Stellweg, Carla. "'Magnet-New York': Conceptual, Performance, Environmental and Installation Art by Latin American Artists in New York." In *The Latin American Spirit: Art and Artists in the United States, 1920-1970,* edited by Luis R. Cancel. New York: Bronx Museum of the Arts and Harry N. Abrams, 1988.

Stratton, Suzanne L., ed. *Spain, Espagne, Spanien: Foreign Artists Discover Spain, 1800-1900.* New York: Spanish Institute, 1993.

Sturman, Janet Lynn. *Zarzuela: Spanish Operetta, American Stage.* Urbana: University of Illinois Press, 2000.

Sublette, Ned. *Cuba and Its Music: From the First Drums to the Mambo.* Chicago: Chicago Review Press, 2004.

Sullivan, Edward J. *Latin American Art in the Twentieth Century.* London: Phaidon Press, 1996.

Swierenga, Robert P. *The Forerunners: Dutch Jewry in the North American Diaspora.* Detroit: Wayne State University Press, 1994.

Tablada, José Juan. *La Babilonia de hierro: Crónicas neoyorkinas.* Mexico City: UNAM, 2000.

———. *Obras IV: Diario (1900-1944),* edited by Guillermo Sheridan. Mexico City: Nueva Biblioteca Mexicana, UNAM, 1992.

Taylor, Wayne Chatfield, and John Lindeman. *The Creole Petroleum Corporation in Venezuela.* New York: Arno Press, 1976.

Teitelboim, Volodia. *Gabriela Mistral, pública y secreta.* Mexico City: Editorial Hermes, 1993.

———. *Huidobro, La marcha infinita.* Mexico City: Editorial Hermes, 1996.

Thomas, Hugh. *The Slave Trade: The History of the Atlantic Slave Trade, 1440–1870*. New ed. London: Phoenix, 2006.

Thomas, Lorrin Reed. "Citizens on the Margins: Puerto Rican Migrants in New York City, 1917–1960." PhD diss., University of Pennsylvania, 2002.

Toledo, Josefina. *Sotero Figueroa, Editor de Patria. Apuntes para una biografía.* Havana: Editorial Letras Cubanas, 1985.

Totoricaguena, Gloria P. *Basque Diaspora: Migration and Transnational Identity.* Reno: Center for Basque Studies, University of Nevada, 2005.

———, Emilia Sarriugarte Doyaga, et al. *The Basques of New York: a Cosmopolitan Experience.* Vitoria-Gasteiz: Eusko Jaurlaritzaren Argitalpen Zerbitzu Nagusia / Servicio Central de Publicaciones del Gobierno Vasco, 2003.

Tucker, Norman Paul, and Boston Athenaeum. *Americans in Spain: Patriots, Expatriates, and the Early American Hispanists, 1780–1850.* Boston: The Athenaeum, 1980.

Uggen, John F. "Archer Harman y la Construcción del Ferrocarril del Sur." *Procesos: Revista Ecuatoriana De Historia* 20 (2003): 37–54.

———. "The Emergence of Multinational Enterprise in Ecuador: The Case of the Ecuadorian Corporation." *Business and Economic History On-Line* 6 (2008).

Unger, Irwin, and Debi Unger. *The Guggenheims: A Family History.* New York: HarperCollins, 2005.

United States Office of Inter-American Affairs. *History of the Office of the Coordinator of Inter-American Affairs.* Washington, DC: U.S. Government Printing Office, 1947.

Van Hensbergen, Gijs, and Pablo Picasso. *Guernica: The Biography of a Twentieth-Century Icon.* New York: Bloomsbury, 2004.

Van Vechten, Carl. *The Music of Spain.* New York: A. A. Knopf, 1918.

Varela, Félix. *Xicoténcatl*, translated by Guillermo I. Castillo-Feliu. Austin: University of Texas Press, 1999.

Varela-Lago, Ana María. "Conquerors, Immigrants, Exiles: The Spanish Diaspora in the United States (1848–1948)." PhD diss., University of California, San Diego, 2008.

Vargas Vila, José María. *Diario Secreto.* Bogotá: Arango Editores, Áncora Editores, 1989.

Vázquez Pérez, Marlene. "The Strong Connection Between New York and Cuban Literature." CUBANOW.NET (2008), http://www.cubanow.net/pages/loader.php?sec=7&t=2&item=4138.

Veeser, Cyrus. *A World Safe for Capitalism: Dollar Diplomacy and America's Rise to Global Power.* New York: Columbia University Press, 2002.

Vega, Bernardo. *Memoirs of Bernardo Vega: A Contribution to the History of the Puerto Rican Community in New York*, edited by César Andreu Iglesias. New York: Monthly Review Press, 1984.

Villaverde, Cirilo. *Apuntes Biográficos de Emilia Casanova de Villaverde. Escrito por un contemporaneo.* New York, 1874.

———. *Cecilia Valdés.* Caracas: Biblioteca Ayacucho, 1981.

Watts, John. *The Letter Book of John Watts, Merchant and Councillor of New York.* Collections of The New-York Historical Society. New York: The New-York Historical Society, 1928.

Whalen, Carmen Teresa, and Victor Vazquez, eds. *The Puerto Rican Diaspora.* Philadelphia: Temple University Press, 2005.

Whitaker, Arthur Preston. "In Defense of Neutral Rights: The United States Navy and the Wars of Independence in Chile and Peru." *The American Historical Review* 73, no. 4 (1968): 1267–68.

———. *The United States and the Independence of Latin America, 1800–1830.* New York: Russell & Russell, 1962.

White, Trumbull. *Puerto Rico and its People.* New York: Arno Press, 1975 [© 1938].

Wilder, Craig Steven. *A Covenant with Color: Race and Social Power in Brooklyn.* New York: Columbia University Press, 2000.

Williams, James Homer. "An Atlantic Perspective on the Jewish Struggle for Rights and Opportunities in Brazil, New Netherland, and New York." In *The Jews and the Expansion of Europe to the West, 1450 to 1800*, edited by Paolo Bernardini and Norman Fiering. New York: Berghahn Books, 2001.

Williams, Stanley Thomas. *The Spanish Background of American Literature.* Hamden, CT: Archon Books, 1968.

Young, Cynthia. "Havana Up in Harlem: Leroi Jones, Harold Cruse and the Making of a Cultural Revolution." *Science & Society* 65, no. 1 (2001): 12–38.

Zentella, Ana Celia. *Growing Up Bilingual: Puerto Rican Children in New York.* Malden, MA: Blackwell, 1997.

Zimmermann, Warren. *First Great Triumph: How Five Americans Made Their Country a World Power.* New York: Farrar, Straus and Giroux, 2002.

INDEX

This volume has been published in conjunction with the exhibition *Nueva York: 1613–1945*, organized by the New-York Historical Society and El Museo del Barrio, New York, New York, and held at El Museo from September 17, 2010, through January 9, 2011.

Nueva York: 1613–1945 has been generously supported by Cablevision's Optimum family of products; by a grant from The Rockefeller Foundation New York City Cultural Innovation Fund; by the New York City Department of Cultural Affairs; by American Express; by the Ford Foundation; by Goldman Sachs; by Con Edison; by the Fanjul family in memory of their ancestor, Manuel Rionda; and by Furthermore: a program of the J. M. Kaplan Fund.

Published in 2010 by the New-York Historical Society, 170 Central Park West, New York, NY, 10024, USA, in association with Scala Publishers Ltd., Northburgh House, 10 Northburgh Street, London EC1V 0AT, United Kingdom.

Distributed outside the participating venues in the book trade by Antique Collectors' Club Limited, 6 West 18th Street, Suite 4B, New York, NY 10011, USA.

Printed and bound in China
10 9 8 7 6 5 4 3 2 1

ISBN 978-0-916141-23-3 (paperback)
ISBN 978-1-85759-639-7 (hardcover)

For the New-York Historical Society:
Volume Editor: Edward J. Sullivan
Project Editor: Valerie Paley

For Scala Publishers:
Design: Katy Homans
Project Manager: Kate Norment